D0209127

Finding Our Fathers

Finding Our Fathers
The Unfinished Business of Manhood

Samuel Osherson

THE FREE PRESS
A Division of Macmillan, Inc.
NEW YORK

Collier Macmillan Publishers
LONDON

The Free Press
A Division of Macmillan, Inc.
866 Third Avenue, New York, N.Y. 10022

Collier Macmillan Canada, Inc.

Printed in the United States of America

printing number

1 2 3 4 5 6 7 8 9 10

Library of Congress Cataloging-in-Publication Data

Osherson, Samuel
   Finding our fathers.

   Includes index.
   1. Men—Psychology. 2. Fathers and sons.
I. Title.
HQ1090.085 1986   305.3′1   85–28035
ISBN 0–02–923690–8

Credits

Our thanks are extended to the authors, publishers, and copyright holders who have granted permission to reproduce the following selections in this volume.

CREDITS

To my father and mother,
Louis and Adele,
with love and respect

I am that father whom your boyhood lacked
and suffered pain for lack of. I am he.

This is not princely, to be swept away
by wonder at your father's presence.
No other Odysseus will ever come,
for he and I are one, the same.

—Homer's *Odyssey,* Book XVI,
Translated by Robert Fitzgerald

Contents

Preface

Mark Twain once observed that at the age of twelve a boy starts imitating a man, and he just goes on doing that for the rest of his life. I suspect there comes a moment in most men's lives when they confront the question of how much imitating they are doing, as opposed to feeling a rich, confident sense of their own manhood.

For me that moment came during a period of particular personal crisis, in what now seem like the old days, about five years ago. I felt blocked in my work. My wife and I were experiencing one miscarriage after another while trying to start our family. In addition I shared some of my mentor's grief as his wife struggled with a life-threatening cancer. These experiences were my first direct encounters as an adult with the reality of loss and my human helplessness in the face of it. At first I could hardly articulate my sense of vulnerability when confronting the knowledge that those I love, within and outside my family, could be cut down. Writing has always been the way I've tried to sort things out. The strength of books has all my life given me strength; and so it's not surprising that I started keeping a journal when I felt in the grip of experiences I found so difficult to understand.

This book really began with that journal. To free time for this personal sorting out, I cut back on my work commitments, and for a year spent part of every day writing. At first I wrote mainly about the present and the frustrations I felt with work and love, but then came memories and feelings about the past, about my childhood and adolescence, my mother and father. When my difficult and conflicted relationship with my father came into focus, I realized that I had found the man I had been searching for, the father who, more by his absence than his presence, was the key to the sense of emptiness and vulnerability in my life. The journal helped me to gradually expand and enliven my relationship with my father, and to appreciate the loving and caring sides of him that had been there all along.

During this time I had the opportunity to hear about the lives of many other men. I was directing a longitudinal study of a large number of Harvard men who were about age forty. My research gave me the opportunity to talk in a relaxed, unhurried manner with successful men from around the country about many aspects of their lives.

From these talks I began to see how profound and painful were the consequences of the predictable dislocation between fathers and sons, a separation we take for granted in our society. Many of the male–female skirmishes of our times are rooted in the hidden, ongoing struggles sons have with their fathers, and the varying ways grown sons try to complete this relationship in their careers and marriages. Yet despite their importance, fathers remain wrapped in mystery for many men, as we idealize or degrade or ignore them. And in doing so we wind up imitating them, even as we try to be different.

The frustrations and yearnings of the men I talked with echoed my own and moved me deeply, possibly because we came of age at the same time, and are at similar points in the life cycle.

So I set out to write a book about men's unfinished business with their fathers. I wanted to bring together my two ways of understanding men, the personal sorting out of the journal and the broad knowledge based on what many men had told me. I wanted the book to have a reasoned professional perspective and a personal voice as well. I hope the rendering of men's lives in this book will convey both empathy and honesty about the plight of being male today.

Acknowledgments

In the long process of writing this book a number of people have provided me with the honest reactions and critical support that a writer needs to finish his project. I wish to thank in particular Jane Barnes, Tracy Barnes, Larry Weinstein, Bill Novak, George Goethals, Stanley King, Shepherd Bliss, Barbara Schwartz, Betty Freidan, Carol Gilligan, Lael Wertenbaker, Anne Alonso, Donald Bell, Joan and Ethan Bolker, Tracy MacNab, Zick Rubin, Elliot Mishler, Olivia and Rob Wilson, Diana Dill, Maureen Mahoney, Patricia Reinstein, Benson Snyder, George Vaillant, Douglas Heath, and Nick Kaufman.

Gerta Kennedy Proesser provided invaluable help in organizing rambling journal entries into coherent and interesting material for a book. Most of all, she provided confidence and insight at a time when I wasn't sure whether to keep going or not.

Kitty Moore, a senior editor then at The Free Press, saw the value in the book I wanted to write and helped me give it initial shape. Laura Wolff of The Free Press provided very helpful editorial feedback and patient encouragement as successive drafts were transformed into the final version.

ACKNOWLEDGMENTS

Joseph Pleck, of the Wellesley Center for Research on Women, gave freely of his time and ideas through many long discussions. Among those interested in the field of men's studies many think Joe ought to be declared a national treasure.

This book could not have been written without the contributions of the men and women who have openly and honestly talked with me about their lives: the participants in my research, students in courses on adult development at Harvard and elsewhere, and clients in therapy. Their names and lives have been disguised within the text for the sake of confidentiality, but this does not detract from the debt I feel I owe them for allowing me to learn from their experiences. I hope they will accept my thanks.

Since this book went through several drafts over several summers, I depended on friends in New Hampshire to provide perhaps the single most important thing to a writer: a quiet room in which to work. Many thanks to Barry and Karen Tolman, Mike French and Beth Williams, and Pat and Prentice Colby. Invariably the rooms they provided looked out on rolling meadows, weathered stone walls, and sturdy forests. This is a better book for the views they provided.

My greatest debt in writing this book is to my wife, Julie Snow Osherson, for the love and support and excellent critical advice at numerous points, without which I doubt this book would have been born.

Finally, I would like to thank my parents, Adele and Louis Osherson, for their enthusiasm for this project.

Finding Our Fathers

Introduction:
Men's Unfinished Business

The forty-two-year-old doctor sits forward in his chair, talking about a recent visit with his father. His parents are divorced, as is he, but the whole family was recently brought together in St. Louis by a younger brother's wedding.

"I spent a lot of time talking to my mother, hearing about family news from her, but my father was so quiet and isolated. He seemed to stay so much in the background." The doctor turned slightly in his chair. Suddenly his tone reveals great yearning: "My father gave me a ride back to the airport yesterday; we were alone together. The whole way there I wanted to talk to him, make some connection with him, hear how he felt about me, talk to him about all that's happened between us. But he hardly said anything to me. We just drove out there in silence."

Tears well up in his eyes as he admits: "Actually, I was scared of what he thought about me, of how much time I spent with my mother rather than him at the wedding. . . . Just like growing up." He cries, then anger masks his sadness and yearning when he concludes, "But what difference does it make? It does no good to try to talk to my father."

*   *   *

In this book I shall explore and explain how men's early and on-going relationships with their fathers shape the intimacy and work dilemmas men coming of age today face. My focus is on the emo-tional vulnerabilities of normal adult men as we struggle with the demands of work and family in our lives. What I hope to show is that to understand men's feelings about love and work we need to understand our unfinished business with our fathers.

I had the good fortune to meet the doctor quoted above and to learn about his life because he was part of the Adult Development Project, which I directed at Harvard. The project is a longitudinal study of 370 men who graduated from Harvard in the mid-1960s, supported with generous funding from the National Institute of Education.[1]

I also draw on other research, including detailed interviews with twenty men who made dramatic changes in their careers at midlife, plus my clinical experience in counseling men of differing ages and circumstances.[2] The portrait that emerges is based on what I heard from men in both research and therapy settings* and is rooted too in my gradual understanding of my own conflicts as a man. Our work cannot be successfully divorced from our personal lives; listening to other men talk about their insecurities about love, their difficult interactions with women, and their ambivalences about work prompted me to examine my own more carefully. Some of what I've learned appears in the chapters that follow. By weaving together vignettes from my own life with case vignettes and discussion of research and theory, I mean to deepen the tex-ture of each chapter and penetrate the shroud of silence and shame that often surrounds men's discussion of their common struggles with identity and intimacy.

My conversations with men were eye-opening to me and often very disturbing, despite the comfortable offices and lavish homes I visited, and despite the self-assured tones of the men's talk. Com-mon themes kept cropping up. The 1960s generation is now ap-

---

*To protect confidentiality, some biographical details about individuals have at times been changed in case discussions. In certain instances, composite cases have been created by combining information from several individuals.

proaching midlife. We are moving into positions of power, and our coming of age has been strongly influenced by the women's movement. Many men showed confusion about the intimacy issues in their lives, particularly with wives, children, and their own parents. Many men seemed prepared for the demands of a career—even if unsuccessful or conflicted about work, that part of life made some intuitive sense to them, and they were relatively at ease talking about it. It was in the arena of love that most of their pain seemed to reside. Our conversations would sooner or later get around to what it was like to have a working wife or a wife who stopped working to have children, or how to get more fully into the family rather than just being "the provider," or how to manage a reconciliation with father. Here men's talk became intense and their voices raw, less confident. It is difficult to quantify such matters, but in the vast majority of my interviews men seemed perplexed about the dilemmas and contradictions of modern family life and wanted to talk about them.

The Role of Our Fathers

To understand these dilemmas we need to start with the special importance of fathers to men, in both childhood and adulthood. Fathers have been overlooked for too long, by their own sons as well as by psychologists and others analyzing the family.

We know that the boy is searching deeply throughout his childhood, beginning around age three, for a masculine model on which to build his sense of self. Research evidence shows that between the ages of three and five boys begin to withdraw from mothers and femininity, becoming quite stereotyped and dichotomized in their thinking about what it means to be "like Daddy" and "like Mommy."[3] Little boys begin to segregate by sex, to focus on rules rather than relationships, and to emphasize games of power, strength, and achievement. Eventually they repress their wishes to be held, taken care of, and cuddled, the wish "to burrow among women."[4]

The press to identify with father creates the crucial dilemma for boys. Boys have to give up mother for father, but who *is* father? Often a shadowy figure at best, difficult to understand. Boys rarely experience fathers as sources of warm, soft nurturance. The most salient adult object available for the boy is his mother, or other female caretakers such as relatives and childcare providers. What does it mean to be male? If father is not there to provide a confident, rich model of manhood, then the boy is left in a vulnerable position: having to distance himself from mother without a clear and understandable model of male gender upon which to base his emerging identity.

This situation places great pressure on the growing son, as well as the father. We often misidentify with our fathers, crippling our identities as men. Distortions and myths shape normal men's pictures of their fathers, based on the uneasy peripheral place fathers occupied in their own homes. Boys grow into men with a *wounded father* within, a conflicted inner sense of masculinity rooted in men's experience of their fathers as rejecting, incompetent, or absent.

The interviews I have had with men in their thirties and forties convince me that the psychological or physical absence of fathers from their families is one of the great underestimated tragedies of our times.[5] I believe there is considerable sense of loss hidden within men, having to do with their fathers. Shere Hite's survey of 7,239 men revealed that "almost no men said they had been or were close to their fathers."[6] Judith Arcana writes that in interviews for her book on mothers and sons only "about 1 percent of the sons described only good relations with their fathers."[7]

The psychologist Jack Sternbach examined the father–son relationship in seventy-one of his male clients. He found fathers were physically absent for 23 percent of the men; 29 percent had psychologically absent fathers who were too busy with work, uninterested in their sons, or passive at home; 18 percent had psychologically absent fathers who were austere, moralistic, and emotionally uninvolved; and 15 percent had fathers who were dangerous, frightening to their sons, and seemingly out of control. Only 15 percent of Sternbach's cases showed evidence of fathers appropriately involved with their sons, with a history of nurturance and trustworthy warmth and connection.[8]

In their excellent recent compendium on our understanding of the father–child relationship, *Father and Child: Clinical and Developmental Considerations*, the psychiatrists Stanley Cath and Alan Gurwitz, the psychologist John Ross, and other contributors emphasize the importance of filling in the gaps in understanding "the forgotten parent," the father, who for years has remained "a twilight figure" in the minds of men. Phrases like "the father hunger" in men and "paternal deprivation" run throughout this provocative book.[9] Its appearance coincides with the coming of age of the 1960s generations, their entrance into the parenting phase of their lives, when they move from being sons only to becoming themselves fathers.

Fathers appear as crucial, if puzzling and stolid, figures in much of the recent "confessional" writings of men, who often want to sort out their work and family choices and difficulties.[10] In the wry words of the Wellesley College psychologist Joseph Pleck, "In the *New York Times'* 'About Men' column, sandwiched between the articles filled with nostalgic longing for the good old days when sexism went unchallenged, and those with upbeat advice on upscale male grooming, poignant recollections of men's bittersweet relationships with their fathers appear regularly."[11]

The sense of loss extends into adulthood, as many sons try to resolve their guilt, shame, and anger at their fathers in silent, hidden, ambivalant ways. Some men unconsciously seek better fathers at work who will forgive them and leave them feeling like a "good son." And, too, many sons' relationships with their fathers shape in subtle ways how they respond to their wives and children. At home some men become determined to avoid the passivity or dependency they saw in their fathers. Others feel unable as husbands or fathers themselves to live up to the heroic standards their fathers seemed to set.

For those of us who have come of age during and after the 1960s, the process of identifying with father has become even more complex, given our changing societal expectations about gender. We grew up amidst traditional sex roles in which fathers were the financial providers, while mothers were the emotional providers in the family. Many sons identified with fathers who presented a traditional image of masculinity, yet they are now asked to play a different role in their own adult families. Many of us strive to be different from our fathers while also unconsciously trying to live up to their image.

The Normal Male Struggle with Separation and Loss

We have begun to understand much more about the way in which early family life shapes the psyches and gender identities of boys and girls. The earliest experiences of attachment to mother and father have a profound impact on the psychological lives of children, and there are differences in the experiences of boys and girls. Both parts of the separation-individuation process in childhood are problematic for boys:

1. Psychological separation from mother

2. Identification and bonding with father

Every child begins life in full union with mother. Erikson characterized the first stage of life in terms of the struggle between trust and mistrust. Trust refers to the infant's sense that the world is secure, stable, and trustworthy. That sense of the trustworthiness of the world is communicated to the infant by the mother, a message negotiated at her breast. In our infancy we experience the world as mother: soft, warm, responsive.[12]

In the earliest weeks and months of life there is very little differentiation of self from mother. Yet for boys, proper sex-role identification means we must separate and renounce mother *and* we must identify with father. For psychoanalysts that is the way the powerful Oedipal drama is resolved: The son accepts that he cannot hold onto mother and begins to turn toward father.

Letting go of mother is problematic for boys in several ways. First, the organization of the family and the structure of parenting in our society make most early caretaking a feminine activity; we usually experience caretakers as women.[13] Mothering is a close, tactile holding and caregiving, while fathering is more amorphous. We know our fathers from a distance; they may be warm but are usually more remote.

The young boy may feel a great sense of loss, terror, and fear of abandonment in the recognition that as a male he is different from women. Often there is a struggle with attachment: Can I exist without mother, or as different from her? In early childhood there is a mutual process of separation and withdrawal between mother and son; mothers expect their sons to be more independent and less clinging, while the young boy wants fiercely to emphasize his rudimentary conception of being a man.

For many boys the only way to let go of what seems feminine is to devalue or ridicule it (from which springs the masculine tendency to denigrate women or such "womanly" sides of themselves as their "dependency"). We need to repress and hide (even from ourselves) our wishes to be taken care of longer, to remain close to mother.

Yet the boy also struggles with the problem of how to hold onto the parts of himself that seem like his mother or that depend on her. Those parts include the wish to be held, to be comforted and taken care of, as well, often, as the more playful, imaginative sides of self. Many men I've counseled remember mothers as emotive and playful or associate creativity, self-expression, and imagination with a friendly female relative, such as an artistic aunt who showed them how to paint.

What I am suggesting is that men don't have a true opportunity as little boys to grieve over the loss of mother, to master their wishes to be female, to continue to be taken care of by mother and women, and to complete the process of separation and individuation from women. Early on we experience women as the ones who fill us up, who comfort and take care of us, without having an opportunity in growing up to learn how to fill ourselves and to feel full while truly separate from women. We do not learn to be cared for, to get nurturance and intimacy from, men—beginning with the first men in our lives, our fathers, and ending with ourselves.

The end result of the boy's separation-individuation struggle is that men carry around as adults a burden of vulnerability, dependency, or emptiness within themselves, still grieving, reliving a time when going to mother for help as they wanted to was inappropriate, and they wouldn't or couldn't go to father with the confusion, anger, or sadness they felt. When men are put in touch with this pain today, they will respond ambivalently: with rage or shame, attempting to prove their independence, as well as with curiosity and a desire to heal the wound they feel.

That is not to say that childhood determines everything about the adult behavior of men. Grown men are not little children and don't behave exactly as they did at age three or five or thirteen. However, our childhood experiences do shape what we expect from both women and other men, in ways that influence how we respond to the work and family pressures of modern times.

Men come to expect women to take care of them; we see women as the caretakers and don't feel really able to take care of ourselves. As with any loss that occurs too quickly or sharply, we idealize what we lose as a way of holding onto it and rigidly stamp out any signs of our own neediness. As boys look to mothers in childhood, so too do men subtly look to their wives to take care of them in ways that they cannot ask for directly and often are not themselves aware of.

When men do ask directly for help they often feel angry or sad. I am struck by how often in a marriage with changing roles, or during times of work–family stress, a man will not talk it over with his wife or ask her for help, saying that he feels like a little kid or it seems "unmanly." What men are saying is that they feel infantilized when needy around women, because women are supposed to give help only to little boys, and they are reexperiencing a point in development where they got stuck: turning to mother for help and feeling embarrassed, inappropriate, as if doing something wrong that had to be hidden. We don't learn to negotiate with women or to feel comfortable about our own vulnerability—it must be hidden and repressed—so when we ask, we do so in manipulative or subtle ways, seeking to have the woman give us what we need without our taking responsibility for asking or receiving. So, many men truly remain little boys.

Family Life Today

Current family situations are rekindling issues of separation and loss that men have not had a chance to work out in growing up. The issues center on our own vulnerability and dependency as men; uncertainties about our identities and about what it means to be a man; and the needs for support and reassurance many of our own fathers masked beneath the surface of traditional family arrangements and passed along—unmet—to their sons. The normal demands of family life today are powerfully shaped by men's early experiences with father and mother, and by the lessons learned from those experiences about what it means to be male.

Often men's reactions to their wives' involvement with work or with their children reflect childlike feelings of abandoment and the hunger for parental attention and nurturance.

When a wife goes off to work, we may feel without realizing it some of the vulnerability and anger we experienced as a child wanting to hold on to Mother and trying to let go of her. The fact that many of our fathers went off to work every day, leaving us alone with our mothers, increased their importance to us and weakened our fathers' roles as the transitional figures necessary to complete the normal process of separation-individuation from mother. And, too, having rarely observed his father taking a secondary place to his mother, a man may not know how confidently to support a wife who works.

One day a successful thirty-eight-year-old lawyer in a luxurious Manhattan office was telling me about his marriage. That confident, engaging man's tone suddenly became plaintive: "Without wanting to sound patronizing, I always assumed any wife of mine would have a career of her own. I just never anticipated it would be like *this*." The *this* referred to the mix of loss, feelings of abandonment, and unmet dependency needs he felt on evenings and weekends when his wife devoted her time and energy to her career rather than to him.

The plaintive lawyer was not alone in his feelings of abandonment. A successful university professor also talked about the darker side of a dual-career marriage. Thoughtful and gentle, he was clearly proud of his wife's achievements in becoming established in a counseling center now that the children were older. Yet he stopped at one point in our talk and reflected that "confidence is an illusion, you know, and I need my wife to bolster my belief that I *can* be successful, get the writing done I need every week, publish those articles in the tenure race. Since my wife's been working she has much less time to pay attention to me, and I know maintaining confidence in myself is a continuing struggle for me."

Similarly the arrival of children may rekindle some of our wishes to be taken care of in that blissful way, as well as our desperate desire to prove that we have given up such wishes and are independent. Becoming a father may also spark an identity struggle for the man who, lacking role models in his past, is not at all sure how to be a father who *is* present for his children.

A business executive told me with pride how involved he had been in the birth of his daughter. Yet he spoke sheepishly about how betrayed he felt by his wife's continuing commitment to her demanding career as a lawyer now that their first child was born. For ten years they had shared most of their spare time. Now with his wife juggling her law practice and the care of a one-year-old, it seemed to this man as if "she has time for everything but me."

Spreading his hands in front of him in a shy gesture of embarrassed neediness, he exclaimed, "The new baby is doing fine, but how about the old baby? Me!"

There are numerous circumstances in adult life that leave us feeling childlike—needy, helpless, powerless to change things. In growing up men have great difficulty coming to terms with dependency and vulnerability, often because our fathers showed us that such feelings were unacceptable, that to be successful men, to win our fathers' approval, achievement was what counted. Our vulnerability and dependency became papered over by an instrumental, competent pose as adults or by focusing on what we do well: our ability to achieve in the work world.

Yet, despite our self-assurance about work, uncertainties abound there as well. Much of the uncertainty concerns how much of a commitment to make to career success; there is discomfort with the sense of self that the competitive workplace fosters. One puzzled Washington official, the Associate Director of a powerful government agency, said to me in dismay, after an interview filled with heroic stories of his success: "One major concern does bother me. . . . I feel more and more like a well-honed tool for my boss." Then the clue: "He's like a father to me." Many men today wonder, how much like my boss or my mentor do I have to live my life?

Clearly the capacity for autonomy, independence, and a separate identity is essential for healthy adult life. But our emphasis on those qualities in boys obscures the struggle they experience in separating from mother and father. Because we have not been more able to nurture the needy, vulnerable parts of ourselves, we carry around within an angry, sad, childlike residue, which often shapes our adult relationships with wife, children, boss, and our own parents.

Men used to be protected from their unfinished business with mothers and fathers by the traditional division of labor. But those of us who have grown up during the decades in which the women's movement became a powerful force are experiencing social changes of epic proportions: the clear and direct movement of women into positions of greater power and equality in the workplace and the movement of men into family life. Regardless of whether men truly are taking greater part in family life (and the evidence suggests there is indeed some small movement in that direction), men are not being sheltered from parts of life they had to repress or devalue in order to grow up.[14] Today, when a wife goes to work, when a baby arrives, or when the family reorganizes upon the departure of children to college, the man is less able to turn to traditional sex roles and expectations. He is often put back in touch with feelings of helplessness and powerlessness that he did not entirely master as a child and is caught by surprise, often feeling a pain he can't really understand.

The volatile nature of this situation is exacerbated by the mutual distrust between the sexes. In this time of changing sex roles men and women often look at each other with suspicion. Many women feel impatient with men's resistance to change, feeling that men are just trying to hold onto their power in relationships or are hopelessly deficient in their capacity for intimacy. Men in turn often become defensive around women, feeling accused and criticized by the women's movement. Some men then try to hide the powerlessness or incompetence they feel behind an emotionally armored posture. In many marriages today neither spouse has much sympathy or patience for the husband's childlike fears and anxieties as both try to develop new work–family arrangements in their life together.

Both sexes today seem to share a stereotype: that men are distant and unconnected, while relationships are the female speciality. Many people believe that women care more than men about love. Yet the division of the sexes into men as rational and women as feelers is simply untrue, a harmful and dangerous myth. For all that feminism has contributed to our culture, it has also brought with it a subtle idealization of women and a less subtle denigration or misunderstanding of men. My work with men convinces me that there is a male vulnerability in relationships that can be traced back to our early childhood experiences of separation and loss. The key to the unfinished business of manhood is unraveling and letting go of our distorted and painful misidentifications with our fathers.

In order to understand men's adult conflicts with work and intimacy in today's world we have to understand the ways the boy comes to experience himself, women, and men, as well as his ongoing relationships as a grown man with the mother and father of his childhood. Each chapter of this book identifies the different vulnerabilities and pressure points that men experience in adult life at work and at home, shaped by the conflictful relationships we experience with father and mother.

The next several chapters of this book explore the ongoing separation-individuation struggle between men and their fathers not only in terms of their joint difficulties growing up but also in terms of the ways men often symbolically act out their unfinished business with father in their careers and with mentors. A "lifelong" father–son dance is traced in these chapters; the partners seem separate yet are joined, moving apart then coming closer as the dance evolves, their seemingly independent actions actually united by deeper rhythms. Later chapters will turn to men's adult families, examining the way in which the wounded father within men is provoked—and often healed—by wives who work, by the experience of both failed and successful pregnancy, and by becoming more fully involved themselves as fathers.

It is possible to heal the wounded father within. Men are not passive victims; much of our wish to be more involved with our children or to become mentors at work, much of the hunger for intimacy that many men reveal, is actually an attempt to heal the wound within ourselves, so that we can become more confident and nurturing as men. As we learn more about the adult life cycle, we are discovering that people reexperience issues of separation and individuation from parents throughout adulthood. Dr. George Vaillant, the director of the Grant Study, a longitudinal study of Harvard men, concludes: "Over and over throughout the study, the lesson was repeated: childhood does not end at 21. Even these men, selected in college for psychologic health, continued for the next two decades to wean themselves from their parents."[15]

I have talked to enough men to know that both work and family can be a healing experience for men; particularly in our experiences as nurturing husbands and fathers, we can heal our relationship with our own fathers and mothers, letting go of oppressive fantasies about what happened to us growing up male. Yet too there are many men who continue to act out with bosses and wives unfinished business with their fathers and mothers.

Healing the wounded father within is a psychological and social process that unfolds over time and involves exploring one's own history, testing out and exploring a new sense of self, and understanding the complex crosscurrents within our families which affected us as we grew up. Later chapters explore what is involved as an adult in that healing process at work and at home. Certainly it means tolerating the angry and needy feelings that our work and family life provoke today, and not trying to discard too quickly those uncomfortable, childlike feelings of powerlessness beneath the pose of male competence and identity.

The Wounded Father Within

I saw this little boy within myself one summer day at our cabin in New Hampshire several years ago. It happened during a period when I felt stuck and frustrated in my work. Despite the sunshine outside I was hard at work inside on a book whose point had completely escaped me. A sinking feeling came over me. I was walking through snowdrifts of words, knee-high, bored by what I was saying, angry and frustrated underneath.

My wife was watching my daily melodrama of frustration. One morning, to cheer me up, she suggested we take a hike on one of our favorite trails.

"No, I can't. I want to finish this chapter, Julie. I can't take time off," I replied through gritted teeth.

"Well, how's it going?"

"Terrible. I hate this writing. Why am I doing this? Does it have to be so hard?"

I saw an expression of sorrow, irritation, and boredom cross Julie's face, the sort of look people get when they see those they love hurting themselves again. And in the same way. For the nth time. This time she unloaded:

"You've said this a million times, Sam. When are you going to listen to yourself? Why don't you take time off and think things through? You're not sure what you want to say in that book, or even if you're going about it in the right way.

"You're like a kid walking down the street pulling this red wagon full of rocks behind you, crying and asking for help." As boys look to mother so too men look to their wives to provide us comfort and nurture without our having to take our pain seriously. As a little boy I would go to my mother with my pain (feeling embarrassed and inappropriate) but I never was able satisfactorily to go to my father with it.

I appreciated Julie's concern and ultimately did take her advice to put the book aside. Yet in identifying my expectations and the game I was playing she was also calling off the game. I felt shamed and angry. An angry inner voice shouted back:

"You owe me!"

Here was the traditional bargain men make with women: I work hard and suffer, and she will be sympathetic and comforting and reassuring. Often men's inability to let go of mother seems like a consolation prize for the absence of a reassuring sense of father.

There I was in this beautiful New Hampshire countryside, suffering—and she was supposed to comfort me, not challenge me to grow up! She wasn't living up to her part in my passion play.

If my anger then had more voice, I might have said, "You're a woman, you wouldn't understand—you can't possibly know what it feels like to be a man."

An image of my father watching TV sullenly after a hard day's work comes to mind. My mother seemingly more cheerful, energetic, my father looking beaten down in a way that couldn't really be talked about. He was, after all, a big success at work, but the sense of entrapment he felt was not an appropriate topic for family talk, or so it seemed to me at the time.

To my shock, sitting in that summer cabin several years ago, I saw that angry as I was at my father's sad, powerless face in our house, that part of him was in me as well. And my wife had pointed to an angry, trapped part of myself that I was afraid to confront.

In some remote recess where we see ourselves clearly, I bumped into a frightening truth: I felt powerless to take control of my life. I was making Julie into my mother while I'd become my father in this passion play, or at least my image of my father. John Updike's lesson came to mind, explored in Rabbit Angstrom's journey through adulthood: The fate of American men is to remain little boys, never gaining their freedom from mother or father.

For men to feel empowered, to come to terms with our identities and deal honestly with our wives, our children, and the demands of careers, means healing the wounded father within, an angry-sad version of ourselves that feels unloved and unlovable. That means coming to terms with that distorted person we never knew well enough: father. The next chapter explores the vulnerabilities and pressure points of the father–son relationship and their consequences for men's adult lives.

1

Unspoken Debts:
Men's Struggle to Separate
from Father

On a bleak February day a forty-year-old investment analyst for a prestigious Wall Street firm was telling me about his childhood and how rejected he felt by his father. Both Harvard graduates, we sat in the living room of his bachelor apartment on the East Side of New York. He spoke in a calm, matter-of-fact way about painful disappointments.

As we talked of his father, tears suddenly came to his eyes, and he stood up from his chair. Without a word he walked out of the room to a bathroom across the hall. In a few moments he came back red-eyed, blowing his nose. He didn't mention the interruption; he might just as well have left the room to take a phone call.

"You feel sad about the way things went with your father," I ventured in a sympathetic tone.

"Well," he replied, blowing his nose as if to scare away his longing, "it's all over now, my father died five years ago."

His father may have died, but the sense of longing and bitterness had not. Like many men, the financier obviously feels conflict about his father. He is trying to act as if his father is unimportant even as his yearning for the man is expressed through his tears.

Not all men remember their fathers as rejecting. Some have very heroic memories of their fathers. One doctor lovingly described his father dressed up as George Washington in his town's annual Fourth of July picnic; he kept a framed photograph from one of those events on his office desk.

What does stand out in men's talk of their fathers is a mysterious, remote quality. Whether describing heroes, villains, or someone in between, most men know little of their father's inner lives, what they thought and felt as men. The first man in our life was a puzzling, forbidding creature.

There is compelling evidence that fathers remain, psychologically, very significant figures for men in adulthood. The thirties and forties are a crucial time. In young adulthood a man may be able to drive through life assuming that things are "worked out" with father or that "my father is who he is, it doesn't matter to me," but as we age into our thirties and forties the need for reconnecting becomes more pressing. The reworking of our image of our father, a deepening of its texture, is part of that great shift in motives and value that mark the midlife years—what has been called "the second journey" of adulthood. "Naming your father"—coming to terms with who he really is, stripped of the distortions of childhood—is a key to every man's ability to allow a richer identity to emerge as he ages.

In his article "Fathers and Sons: The Search for Reunion," the psychologist Zick Rubin identifies an inportant theme for men at midlife and their fathers: the search for a closer connection after the distance that developed during adolescence and young adulthood. What is striking about Rubin's data is how few fathers and sons achieve that connection, how many men experience "father-hunger."[1]

Part of what gets in the way of reconciliation between fathers and sons is our conflict around separating from our fathers. Like the red-eyed financier, men often seem on the one hand to want their fathers' love but also not to want it, to prove that they can get along without it. I think this points to the difficulties sons have as children in coming to terms with their fathers, the way in which things seem hopeless or too highly charged between them. As in most areas of our lives, we often separate from significant figures by getting distance from them without working through our intense, mixed feelings.

A reviewer of a recent anthology of male poetry found himself "most moved by the father and son poetry," yet felt constrained to refer to Yeats's comment to describe the volume "not the poetry of insight and knowledge, but of longing and complaint."[2] *Longing and complaint* toward our fathers. One son pens a "Letter to a Dead Father," five years gone, but the poet is "still waiting for you to say *my son, my beloved son.*" And in the silence he hurls a cruel accusation at his father: "Do you see now that fathers/who cannot love their sons/have sons who cannot love?" And he ends the poem with a bitter renunciation: "It was not your fault/and it was not mine/I needed/your love but I recovered without it/Now I no longer need anything."[3]

What is it like to live as a grown-up trying to prove that you "no longer need anything," as an angry lesson to a father who seemed also not able to love? The poet's unfinished sadness and hurt are apparent even as he denies it.

To speak of "fault" really misses the point. Fathers and sons are caught in a special trap. Given the traditional arrangement of families, identifiable, "normal" misunderstandings and disconnections can haunt the adult lives of both fathers and sons.

The Kosher Rebellion

For years my father felt like a heavy weight to me, an immovable force I could neither approach nor avoid, pressing on me with his remote sadness and distant judgmental quality. Our relationship felt as if it had frozen in some point in time, probably adolescence. As I grew into my thirties, married, he continued to seem unapproachable. Men often describe their fathers in terms of natural attributes, like mountains or rocks or other mute objects of nature, or else in terms of distance, often up, higher, imputing a judgmental quality to the old man, as in Dylan Thomas's plea: "And you my father, there on the sad height,/Curse, bless, me now with your fierce tears, I pray."[4]

I grew up in the 1950s in a household that reflected its own version of the silent, unacknowledged struggle around sex roles, which later was to find its voice in the women's movement. I remember that struggle as erupting the night my mother threw out the kosher dishes and brought shrimp into the house. The kosher rebellion, first hers and then mine, which followed, took place when I was a teenager.

My family started out as fairly traditional with respect to religion. We were a conservative Jewish family, more by my father's definition than my mother's. Keeping kosher means you can't eat milk and meat together, nor shrimp, scallop, lobster, or any shellfish, all forbidden. No pigs, either, or any meat not slaughtered in the kosher manner. Jewish families adhered to those complex rules in different ways. In my family the uneasy rules were that nonkosher meat could be eaten in restaurants, except for shellfish or pork products, which we were never to eat, and milk and meat could *never* be combined in the same meal at home or out of it. That moral calculus rules out cheeseburgers, ham and eggs, and, most important, veal parmigiana, a dish that was destined to occupy a rather large place in my psychic menu.

Some time in the mid-1950s my mother started to work outside the home. She had written short stories with some commercial success but then decided she wanted to get more steady work. She became skilled at editing and dubbing foreign film scripts in New York City, developed a reputation, and began to bring some significant income into the house. Then a funny thing happened. About that time she decided that the kosher stuff was too much, and she wasn't going to do it any more. All her life before marriage she had been used to eating shrimp and lobster, and she decided to do it again. At first she began eating shrimp on the sly in restaurants, taking it slow, not wanting to disturb my father. Then she started bringing in shrimp and hiding it in the freezer to eat when she was working on a job at home. It was a secret. Nobody talked about what was in those bags in the freezer. My brother and I were not going to say anything; my father must have known, but he never mentioned it. Finally, though, the revolution came out into the open. My mother flatly declared she was going to start eating shellfish at home if she wanted, and she wasn't going to keep kosher any more.

So how did my father deal with that? He dealt with it as many men do when confronted with an existential crisis of beliefs and values. He tried the two basic male strategies: He grew angry and threatening, and when that didn't work, he withdrew into silence and sulked. At least that's how I saw it at the time.

As a teenager, the whole thing scared the hell out of me. You have to understand that this didn't happen all at once. It was a prolonged struggle in our family. It took my mother years to get up her nerve. I've always felt that it was earning money that led her to feel she could assert herself in the relationship. Once she started bringing home the bacon, she felt she could certainly bring home the shrimp. When the kosher rebellion finally broke out, my younger brother and I had the disturbing choice of siding with one or the other of our parents.

Was it tempting to side with my mother! Especially when you're in an Italian restaurant with your parents for dinner and are dying to order veal parimigiana. There I was salivating, I could taste the juicy bubbling cheese on top of the soft meat. The forbidden fruit. What should a poor teenager do? At the age of fourteen, barely bar-mitzvahed, I ordered veal parmigiana right in front of my father.

I was terrified. My palms still sweat thinking about it. An elegant New York restaurant, the Vesuvio. All four Oshersons engrossed in their menus. Father is sitting on my right, my mother across the table, my brother on my left. Father finally orders chicken marsala, and Mom orders shrimp scampi. I stare at the menu. Shall I follow her in her rebellion? Old, boring eggplant or succulent veal parmigiana? Whose side of the family drama am I on?

The waiter waits impatiently with his pad, oblivious to the agony, the enormity of the choice I must make. My father turns his head and looks at me once, then glances down at his menu. Ah, that look of his. Did he mean to always look like a smoldering volcano?

"Veal parmigiana," I manage to choke out of my throat, certain that my father will lean over and throttle me with his bare hands. Would the waiter save me, pulling my father's strong arms off my neck? What an embarrassing scene that would be.

And how did my father react to his son's betrayal? He said and did nothing. The waiter wrote down the order, I ate the dinner. To his credit, my father ultimately accepted the change, accepted the whole revolution, and never said a word about the veal and cheese—that night or ever.

I thought I got off easy. For years I looked back on my mother as the strong one in the family, who helped liberate my father. After all, his kosherness was a way of holding onto *his* father and mother; he felt it as an obligation. My mother was saying, "I want a say in how we live," and she was telling him too that not everything had to be tied to the past. She was giving him a way out of his imprisonment, a window to greater freedom and choice in his life. She expanded his narrow, overly responsible, overly orderly view of things. So she freed him in other ways—his career, for example. My father felt trapped and frustrated by the family business, which he kept up partly as an obligation to his long-dead immigrant parents. My mother's revolt helped him examine the length of his own chains. He ultimately did leave the family business and did make some freeing decisions. Would he have been able to if the family had played along forever in the kosher domestic slavery? He had a wife who went out and took some chances, who got work for herself, which she enjoyed, and I think that example helped him along.

I still believe that, and I respect my parents very much for the loving and responsible way they have worked out differences and kept their marriage vibrant. Yet that dinner at the Vesuvio haunted me for years.

My mother semed like a much more attractive model of adulthood. She seemed optimistic, vital, energetic, and not locked into the past in a mournful way. Great—it seemed as if women had what I wanted, and what did Dad offer? Rules, rules, and more rules. Mom at least offered veal parmigiana.

For a long time, I suppose, I thought I had no father really and tried to fill in the void in the traditionally appropriate way, with surrogate fathers: my profession, Harvard, my employer, my boss. That's the way a person acts when he feels that the *real* person he needs to work things out with is unapproachable and too forbidding. Find a substitute.

Putting distance between my father and myself really didn't work, though. Eventually I recognized that my image of him was inside me. I was carrying along a sad, mournful, judgmental version of my father. At times, too many times, I acted that same way: rigid, judgmental, remote. I found myself searching psychology texts for a good definition of the idea of *introjection*, a psychological process whereby we take in conflictual figures, swallowing them whole in a distorted way, rather than *identifying* with parts of them in a more personally satisfying way.

In our silent male dance I learned little of my father's inner life. How could I have? He and I were locked into the family pattern of *protective denial*, whereby children and mother collude with father to "protect" him from emotionally challenging family subjects, denying too that the family has isolated and infantilized Dad. Instead you turn to mother for information and explanation, confirming the "feminine" work of being the emotional switchboard in the family. Father's vulnerability becomes a taboo, fearsome topic in this system.

Only years later did I see the guilt he struggled with, the silent passion: He felt he was letting his parents down. He was failing to keep his family in line around beliefs and values essential in his eyes as well as in theirs—to be a good, Orthodox, faithful Jew. And he probably felt betrayed by all of us, especially his wife. He had thought it was clear when they married: She'd keep a clean kosher household, he'd earn a good living. Now she was changing the rules about something he considered an article of faith.

When I think back to the kosher rebellion it pains me to realize how ridiculous, unapproachable, and massive my father seemed. Why did he insist on those rules, which made little sense? He couldn't explain why we needed to keep kosher except that Moses had apparently decreed it important two thousand years ago that I not eat shrimp and veal parmigiana. My father couldn't say it had to do with love, with keeping alive a set of family traditions that wrapped him in the love of *his* father and mother. For him, perhaps, a wife with ideas of her own meant the death of the father he was trying to keep alive.

His dilemma is understandable if we consider that men show their love symbolically, through their behavior, not their words. "Don't tell me you love me, show me you do" was a favorite directive of that generation. Such an imperative strips men of the opportunity to express their love verbally and emotionally more fully. Instead it is our behavior that must send the message; we become trapped in having to perform as signs of our love deeds and accomplishments that we might otherwise foreswear. Many men then become angry captives of choices that are not satisfying to them but remain the only way they can show their love for their parents and families.

So my father couldn't explain to us and couldn't separate from his parents. And I, in the full-blooded grip of adolescence, wasn't going to ask him what *his* father problem was. Instead he became identified with a dusty overlay of rules, pomposity, phoniness, and a vulnerability that couldn't be talked about. He was a pain in the neck, ridiculous and heroic and demanding at the same time. That became the substratum of my relationship with men and with authority figures for quite some time.

The Wounded Father

The wounded father is the internal sense of masculinity that men carry around within them. It is an inner image of father that we experience as judgmental and angry or, depending on our relationship with father, as needy and vulnerable. When a man says he can't love his children because he wasn't loved well enough, it is the wounded father he is struggling with.

There are three aspects to our image of the wounded father, all linked but separable. The son may remember father as wounded, with father's deep sadness, incompetence or anger dominating his image of the man. He may also remember father as wounding, evoking the loss and needy feelings the son experienced in having been rejected by or disappointing to the father. And thirdly, the son may introject and internalize distorted and idealized images and memories of father as he struggles to synthesize his identity as a man.

Consider this example. A middle-aged biologist told with some frustration of his attempt to become closer to his father after he married and had children. He described inviting his father to dinner at his home and watching his father sit silently and awkwardly between his daughter-in-law and grandchildren. The scene reminded the biologist of how peripheral his father had seemed during his childhood. "He was not a man who was easy to talk to—I made several attempts and was rejected." Reflecting on his father's death, he presents a wounded image of father:

"It was pretty tough, in fact, when my father died, at age seventy. I felt really bereft, because I didn't really know the man at all. He never, never would let go of his control, to speak openly. I had to get inklings of what he felt, listen in between the lines. And I felt so sorry for him. But the main feeling was of terrible loss, because I had never come to know him. I doubt if anybody had."

This man is first describing his father as having been wounded, silent, and remote and excluded within the family. "I felt so sorry for him." Yet too, the father wounds the son, as the biologist tells us that "the main feeling was of terrible loss." That is the neediness and yearning for his father that the son experiences. And finally, the wounded father lies in the sense of manhood this scientist internalized, based on his father's distant, controlled image in the home. He struggled throughout his life with a belief that the proper role for an adult man stops with being a distant provider and authority figure: "the whole parent-is-god syndrome, as if the father is put on earth just to be the disciplinarian."

The Wounded Father as a Misidentification

The internalized, wounded father is rooted in the son's experience of the father, a composite of fantasy and reality, not always corresponding to the reality of what father was really like or exactly what went on within the family. We are not talking of literal reality.

To understand this we must examine the psychological impact on the son of the father's absence from his family.

Everyone faces a dual separation struggle: from mother and from father. It isn't helpful to claim that separation problems lie generally more with one parent than the other. Clearly we all struggle to come to terms with the reality of both parents, and the family climate within which we grow up is the creation of all participants, not just one parent. Yet there are special problems attendant on coming to terms with each parent. And absence, either physical or more commonly psychological, complicates the son's relationship with the father.

When a person is absent, either physically or psychologically, you need to explain why that person is not there. Father absence provides fertile ground for a son's mistaken imaginings about his father. The son's understanding of his father's absence is crucial. That is where sons start to idealize or degrade their fathers, misidentifying with them, and struggling with shame and guilt themselves.

The fundamental male vulnerability rooted in the experience of father lies in our fantasies and myths to explain why father isn't there. Those are misunderstandings, usually unconscious and often very frightening to the son, that cripple our sense of our own manhood. The son may experience his father's preoccupation with work or emotional unavailability at home as *his own* fault. It's because of something the son has done that father doesn't pay attention to him. The son may feel not good enough as a man in the face of this powerful, successful father, who hasn't enough time for him. Or the son may perceive a secret weakness in his father—feeling he is less than a man—and become determined to avoid the same fate. Many men I have interviewed carry around a feeling of both having betrayed their father and having been betrayed by him.

Because of the emotional disconnection between fathers and sons, the father and son cannot easily untangle those misunderstandings. Numerous studies indicate that fathers spend relatively little time in close, leisurely interaction with their children. The family researchers Rebelsky and Hanks have suggested that fathers spend an average of thirty-seven seconds a day interacting with infants in the first three months of their life. Pedersen and Robson found an average of about an hour a day of direct play between fathers and nine-month-old infants, including time spent together on weekends.[5] The pattern continues as children age.

Our fathers worked hard. It's not that they didn't love their children. Yet their love was expressed from a distance. As the author James Carroll notes in a reivew of a new father's journal of his child's first year, "the curse of fatherhood is distance, and good fathers spend their lives trying to overcome it."[6]

The love of our fathers was clearly summarized by the puzzled father interviewed by Professor Zick Rubin, who couldn't understand his son's resentment at the lack of affection between them, explaining "if affection can be interpreted by what I *do*, than I think I'm an affectionate person."[7]

Our fathers did love us; they worked hard, they provided, they were in many ways on the outside of the family, and in their silent doing was the expression of their love. That is traditionally how men express love: by performing, being instrumental and *taking care of*, by protecting and providing. Yet that creates problems for the son in coming to know his father, and thereby men, as real peo-

ple. How does Dad deal with failure, with success, with the conflicts of choice and ambivalent wishes and dreams in his life? How
does Dad deal with mother and women? The son has to construct
an answer to those questions, depending on subtle cues and glim-
merings about what his father is feeling and thinking.

That is not in itself news; there is a considerable literature on
the problem of father absence. But what are the consequences for
the grown son today of a childhood relationship of distance with
his father?

First, we find that many men carry within them a childhood image of father and of their relationship to him. There is a cartoon
quality to father images, suggesting a view of father built up by
watching this person from a distance. What is striking is that often
the fathers in these cartoons are angry or disappointed with us.
They are often the images that a young boy might construct
around a large, intimidating, puzzling older figure. There often
seems a key time when the relationship got stuck or frozen—
puberty, adolescence, and early childhood are key stress points.

One therapist who works with fathers and adult sons laughingly described how often men will describe their fathers in larger-
than-life terms.

"Big Al? Do you want Big Al to come in?" a man might ask me
after going over the struggles he's had with his father. There's
often fear and awe in his voice.

"Then Big Al arrives for our appointment and turns out to be a
tiny, eighty-five-year-old man, short and gentle. But the father of
childhood lives on in these men's minds."

That is a problem with both parents. Children aren't privy to
the inner life of either parent in a very full way, nor should they
necessarily be. There are many misunderstandings between sons
and mothers, to be sure, many pressures and tensions that distort
the relationship. Yet on the whole I've been impressed by the
numbers of men who report being able to talk as children to their
mothers but not to their fathers. That continues throughout their
lives. In numerous studies men and women report a closer relationship with their mothers. In Komarovsky's studies of Ivy League
college students in the 1970s, she found that male undergraduates
talked about themselves more with their mothers than with their
fathers and were more satisfied with their relations with their
mothers. The undergraduates complained most that their fathers

were cold and uninvolved, giving too little of themselves.[8] As we'll see, men report being able to test limits and reality with mothers in ways they seem unable to with their fathers. Exaggerated emotions become associated with father: angry, sad, needy, or judgmental looks and stares become the bricks of which our experience of father is built.

Here are some variations of the wounded father that men carry within them, and their consequences for the adult life of the sons.

The All-Suffering Father

The current Governor of New York, Mario Cuomo, provides a striking description of a suffering father, which is one way he may look to a child. Cuomo thought often of his father during his bitter and trying election campaign. At one point he reminisces:

> "I knew him only as a person who worked twenty-four hours a day. We never sat down to dinner, or very rarely—on the holidays, in the later years. He never took me for a walk. He never had a man-to-man talk with me. I never saw him relaxed until, in later years, the store had to be closed on Sunday mornings after ten o'clock. . . . I think of him as being very affectionate, but I don't remember him putting his arm around me. You always had the sense that he had great feeling for you. You saw him providing for you, at enormous pain to himself. You saw him doing nothing for himself—never bought himself anything, never enjoyed himself. . . . *So the overwhelming impression we got was that this man was offering us his life: he didn't have to put his arm around you."*[9]

Cuomo presents here an "idealized" father, one in which self-sacrifice and hard work in the real world are the main components of masculine identity. Such an image of father is idealized in that it is built up largely out of the son's fantasy about him. The wounded father for some sons will lie in the expectation of having to live up to father's sacrifice: Father gave up so much for me, now I must repay it by being like father, or by justifying his sadness, his burden. Not to do so means to let father down, to see again before me his sad, all-suffering look. Some men may try to flee from the demands of that wounded, demanding father, feeling unable to meet the expectations; other men try to live up to them and become the all-sacrificing father of their childhood experience.

'From the growing son's point of view, a father who offers you his life presents a gift that can hardly be refused. The magnitude of that gift makes it difficult to bring up other matters, such as, "Dad, what are you feeling? Why do you work so hard? What do you expect of me? Why do I feel so angry and overburdened by you?"—all the existential questions that adolescent and even younger children normally have to answer as they grow. To fill the vacuum, many sons resort to fantasy, unconsciously developing explanations for why father is the way he is and why the relationship is the way it is. A man may feel unconsciously as if he drove his father out of the house, perhaps winning the oedipal battle—just Mom and I occupying the house while Dad is out busy working. Such "victories" are terrifying and lead some men to work hard to live up to father's image and avoid his imagined or real anger.

For a son who grows up with the experience of the all-suffering father, suffering and entrapment may seem the male fate. Father never escaped; he worked hard, and that becomes our task as well. To be a loving son means to work hard and suffer the manly pains that Dad did. Not to do so means to leave your father. It can be difficult to let go and partake of happiness as an adult when father is unhappy and suffering. We may identify with a deeply unhappy father too "good" to be selfishly happy in life. Loving and suffering in the world of work become confused. That is the male version of what is often thought of as a characteristic female dynamic: To love means to suffer within relationships.

The Saintly or Heroic Father

The father's coming and going may seem especially exciting to a young boy; the world of his mother, the family, may seem mundane and entrapping compared with the stories he hears about and from his father about the busy, intriguing world of work and "men's business." Traditional family roles in some families may encourage the idealization of Dad and devaluation of Mom, for in some families Dad, by virtue of his career outside the home, provides novelty and excitement to his family with his return at the end of the day. The grown son may feel that he can never live up to this heroic father unless he is also idealized—seen as the hero—within his own family. He may wish to appear to his wife and children as "the Knight in Shining Armor" who has the apparent freedom of his father to come and go as he pleases, off on busy world affairs and important errands.[10] His excessive expectations of adoration from his family may leave him feeling quite vulnerable when he tries to assume a realistic and involved fathering role in which his children can both admire him and criticize him for being human. One such man who had taken over considerable childcare responsibilities in his home told me how angry and embarrassed he felt when remembering his father's success as an army officer who would come home brimming with stories of "missions" and successes; not living up to such a vision of masculinity left him feeling at times like a weak little boy.

You can hear in men's talk how sons traditionally learn little about their fathers' inner lives—their feelings and thoughts, especially how empty or uncomfortable a man will feel struggling with his uncertainties as an adult. Cuomo's constant wondering how his father dealt with the "existential questions" he himself now faced during a difficult election campaign he might lose—failure, the sacrifices that come with a demanding career, the limits of paternal responsibility—lend a poignant note to his campaign diaries. Some men have little idea of the true expectations and feelings of their fathers, or of how their fathers themselves dealt with life dilemmas we all face: women, aging, the vicissitudes of power, disappointments of achievement. Confronting such common questions as an adult can leave some men feeling empty or like orphaned children. No wonder many of us turn harder to work or prefer to keep our minds "elsewhere."

The Secretly Vulnerable Father

It's true that many men have very positive, often heroic images of their fathers. Yet when men report worldly, successful fathers they often strike a compensatory note, as if aware of some secret weakness in father that was intolerable for the son to see or imagine. That too comes out of the traditional family structure and the father's place in it. While the traditional family often seems to glorify father, it also secretly degrades and undercuts the son's sense of masculinity.

One bank executive figured the best way to tell me about his father was to compare him to Paul Bunyan, the American folk hero. He reverently described his father reminiscing on the porch of their Maine summer home late at night during a recent visit about his dramatic intelligence exploits in the Office of Strategic Services during World War II. The breadth of knowledge, the strength of character awed the executive, as he told me of this father he idealized. A father he himself felt he never could live up to, who haunted him with the question "Can I ever be as successful as this father?" The wounded father for the executive lay in the image of father as secretly vulnerable. The executive provided the clue later, when he got to mother: "She was always on his case, constantly bitching at him, and I'll never forgive her for that." The great man could not hold his own in the family, and his son, now himself married, carries around a rage at women as dangerous and "hero"-breaking. He tries to avoid the same fate as his father by reassuring me, and thereby himself, that "I make the decisions in our family."

The traditional role of father in the family secretly communicated a sense of weakness to sons, which underlies the wounded father within men today. The traditional bargain that our parents entered into was that the woman takes care of the expressive, affective tasks in the family while the husband is the instrumental financial and material provider. He is the real-world caretaker, she the emotional caretaker. That arrangement gives mothers tremendous power in the family. They become the "affective switchboards" in the family, the center of the communication pattern; the kids turn to mother to deal with their dad, while father comes to depend on mother to tell him about what happened at home while he was gone during the day and how to deal with the more foreign world of the family.

As the children get older, father can be pushed even farther to the periphery of the family. Here is where the family pattern of "protective denial" becomes particularly destructive to sons, as their view of father comes to be largely shaped by mother. Professors Michael Farrell and Stanley Rosenberg of Dartmouth write of this pattern in their book *Men at Midlife*:

Mother and children often form secret alliances—deceiving, laughing about, and simultaneously protecting the husband. The wife recognizes the husband's efforts at maintaining an image of himself as patriarch. She seeks to avoid confrontation that might undermine his belief of being in control of the family and having their support and respect. Consequently, the relationship becomes entangled in a web of deception.[11]

Some men may develop openly degraded, frightening ideas about their fathers. A chemist, angry and scared of women, uncertain of his own abilities as a father and husband, told me this about his parents:

"I had grown up with a dislike for my father, a hatred at times. With dislike, suspicion, wondering what kind of person he was, and I realized later this was the result of what my mother had told me about him. Not exactly told me, but implied. She broke up several friendships he had, from early days when he was a boy, with other men, and the implication I got there was somehow they had homosexual overtones or something like that. Perhaps she didn't mean to put that in my head, but that's what I got—that it was wrong for a man to put his friends in an important position. His family was what needed it. And I thought so too as a child."

It sounded to me as if he was more worried about sexual identity than friendship. How terrible to have questions about your father's sexuality. I wondered aloud if he ever felt angry because his father wasn't there for him.

"No! It was my mother who was angry, and she was very vocal with me."

I persisted, wondering aloud, "I thought you agreed with her." Then his rage was tapped:

"Well, yes, my mother told me, what does a child believe! I felt that she was indeed being put upon and abused. Okay?"

So, dependent on his mother to understand his father, he was enraged and ashamed of his involvement with her. That rage was to haunt him through his twenties, thirties, and forties. At home and work, he carried around a "wounded" picture of his father. Like many men, he had to "read between the lines" to get this picture. This man's internal "wounded father" lay in his personally threatening experience of his father as somehow "less than a man" (Did that mean that he too was less than one?) and the angry, judgmental picture of a father who felt excluded by the close bond between his son and his wife. Out of his fear of a weak vulnerable father, this man constructed a sense of father as punitive and threatening. For this man such fears led to overcompensatory attempts to live up, to fulfill his manly responsibilities to his family, all the while angry and scared that maybe something was "wrong" with him. What his mother actually said about his father is as unclear to him as to us; he was responding to innuendo, tone of voice, what was unsaid about his father as much as what was said. His mother may have expressed some hidden sexual frustration or the envy and resentment of a wife who felt her husband was putting his friends above his marriage. Yet the outcome is illustrative of what happens to many sons in traditional marriages: They learn about their fathers through their mothers, absorbing a distorted image of their fathers and of masculinity.

Children often become ideal or surrogate partners for their parents. Many sons have become more perfect "husbands" for mothers frustrated by their husbands particularly once their frustrations were given voice by the reemerging women's movement of the 1950s. Sons become uncomfortable allies of their mothers in the parental struggle with family roles and marital power. Yet we must always attend to the son's misinterpretation and fantasy about what happened, rather than place "fault" at one person's doorstep.

The undercurrent of male vulnerability—the sense that something was wrong with the father that could never be discussed—which the son absorbs in his childhood family, can make male vulnerability a taboo topic for adult sons. Our fathers, according to the myth, were successful and powerful in the real world. But to us at home they seemed needy and vulnerable in a way that could not be talked about. That wounded father in our own history makes the entire topic of male vulnerability seem dangerous. We carry around a secret sense of our father as having been weak and needy, and perhaps we are the cause—do we perhaps suffer from the same disease? We aren't comfortable with other men's emotional neediness and vulnerability, because it reminds us of the father we could never help or of our own neediness, to which we were abandoned by our father.

As they grow older, many men have uncomfortable memories of their fathers' aging. Seeing their fathers never come to terms with getting older, with the loss of power and potency, many men are terrified that the same fate will befall them—the strange midlife and later adulthood behavior of men who try to deny their aging, who try desperately to hold onto a brittle sense of power, can often be traced to feelings they have about how their fathers dealt with their own aging.

Or becoming a parent may tap this. One man told me about the difficulty he had in coming home and just playing with his kids, what psychologists refer to as "adaptively regressing," by referring scornfully to his father as being "just like the fourth baby in our house." He was determined to avoid that fate, even if it meant giving up the capacity to enter freely into his children's world. One wonders about the wounded father awaiting his children. As the poet Wallace Stevens said, "it may be that one life is a punishment/ For another, as the son's life for the father's."[12]

Because of the secret weakness of our fathers, the family may become too uncomfortable a place for many grown sons, an arena in which our father never really mastered things. He went from seeming heroic outside to seeming sad and vulnerable in the home. Not only do grown sons struggle with a sense of not knowing how to behave as full men in the family, but also there is an emotional shadow over the family—it is a place where men become weak, needy little boys.

It is easy to underestimate the magical powers that men attribute to women. They are the masters of the interpersonal, feeling world in men's unconscious, as our experience of women is rooted in early experiencing of mother. If women have the power to reduce men to weakness, a determination to avoid being vulnerable to one's wife can form. As the family becomes more complex, with marriage and the arrival of children, a man may feel uncomfortably caught among nameless fears. One thirty-five year-old psychiatrist talked openly of "coming home after work, walking in the front door, and being actually scared of the back part of the house, the kitchen where I could hear my wife cooking and kids playing; it felt like it would rise up and swallow me, like an engulfing mother." The traditional family pattern may result in wounded images of mother and women, just as of father and masculinity. As the little boy may come to dread father's apparent secret weakness, he may too fear mother's secret power.

As the bank executive with the mother he perceived as unmerciful reminds us, men who grew up with weak fathers and strong mothers may interpret the mother–father dynamic to mean that women are dangerous, castrating, and destructive. Mother may not be seen as life-giving in comparison to father's aloofness, and the son may not be drawn to feminine qualities. Rather, the son may come to fear what he sees as the feminine wish to destroy men, to make them weak, needy, and helpless. The son may then blame the mother for the sense of loss he feels at his father's absence or may see his father as a helpless victim, too "good" or "moral" to fight back against what the son may interpret as the woman's pushy, unfair wish to dominate her husband. As adults such men may need to dominate their wives, to tame them, to disarm them before they can wreak their power in the home. In such marriages the husband will often treat the wife almost as a little girl, emphasizing her vulnerabilities and need to be taken care of, in contrast to his real-world competence, forcefulness, and independence.

The Angry Father

Many men carry around within themselves an angry or judgmental father. We feel our fathers to be disappointed in us. We imagine male authorities as easily provoked to wrath, and male authority itself may seem basically wrathful or violent. The angry father theme reflects the tension between fathers and sons growing up, the way that they are rivals to each other, with little opportunity to heal their connection.

For some men the sense of father as angry and hostile may reflect the son's fantasy of being responsible for having hurt or wounded the father. The angry chemist quoted above, for example, told me he felt sometimes that "I had married my mother, I was her husband." He felt, in other words, as if he had replaced his father. The brooding presence of the father he experienced reflected the anger he feared from his father for that act of betrayal.

Others feel they were rejected by or had themselves rejected their fathers. A painter, about forty-five years old and now divorced (as his parents were), offers an extreme version of the fearsome sense of betrayal men may carry into adult life:

"When I was about seven I was very close to my mother. It was my birthday and I had come home expecting my father, and he wasn't there. He was supposed to bring presents, so we were all disappointed. We lived in an isolated place. It was winter. The heat, the oil ran out, and my father hadn't paid the bill. His absence was very pronounced.

"I felt a lot of hatred toward him, a lot of disappointment. And I wished that day that he would never come back. He didn't turn up that night; he wasn't there the next morning either. My mother tried to make the most of it. In a way she was secretly pleased, which I colluded with. And later in the afternoon we heard over the radio that my father had had an automobile accident during an ice storm. He broke a hip and was in traction for several months. It was quite a scene seeing him totally immobilized in the hospital. For me it was as if I had magically done this. Such guilt, and my fear of my father later on as I was growing up."

We unconsciously imagine that father will get even with us for our betrayal of him. The painter feared his father and began making up fairy tales to explain his father's increasing absence from the disharmonious marriage: The great man (a banker) was off on long business trips, accomplishing great deeds. And here is a son's typical defense: For father home may be a disaster, but work provides a redeeming sense of greatness. And like father, like son.[13] Yet the unhappy painter provides a clue to father–son dynamics: He says he fears his father's power, yet gets closer to his truth when he reveals it is his *own* power that is most frightening. Speaking of the accident he says, "I felt I had done that to him and that also made me very frightened of myself. My powers, you know, guilty in terms of my collusion with mother."

That unfinished business with parents haunted this man in his own marriage, as he struggled with the power of his wife to deceive and seduce him away from his "manly" struggle and felt like a little boy himself, judged harshly by the father he carried around in his own mind. Trying as a father and husband to please the father, the manly lineage he hardly knew, afraid of "colluding" too much with his wife-mother, he did not know how to deal strongly and honestly with his wife, who seemed to have all the power.

Here is a man who was left alone with mother, who won

mother over from father. In a way he felt too strong for father, he had the power over his father, even though he experienced fear of the opposite: that his father would get even. Many men idealize their fathers, make them bigger than life, because they once felt too strong for their own good and now imagine a father who will punish them for their sins.

The Fierce Tears of Our Fathers

Yet it isn't just their own aggression that sons are experiencing; often a son may intuit his father's own real, hidden anger. Many of our fathers were not very happy men. Many of them were secretly angry and depressed, feeling considerable rage and depression at the traditional bargain they had made with their wives, exiled from their families, consigned to the public world of work. Having struck this bargain, which seemed entirely natural and which they were powerless to change, many men's fathers felt entrapped, like the bitter man who told me he could be either a lover or a provider, but not both:

"A person's a responsible husband, he goes to work. . . . He keeps his nose to the grindstone, he works and works so that his children can have clothing and food and shelter and all that. And that's one choice. If he is a person—married or not—who feels that the tremendous love that he had for the woman before he married her should go on and on . . . then he can't take time off from that. In other words, there's a division of energy and labor, so that either you cultivate the role of lover or cultivate the role of provider, but it has to be one or the other. In my case I never knew I had a choice. I was brought up to be responsible, to be the provider."

His anger and sense of loss erupt when he bitterly relates that he never knew his children except as objects: "I'd look at my kids not as somebody to be loved and cuddled and played with. I'd look at a kid as somebody to be examined to make sure the kid's not sick. You make sure the kid's not doing anything dangerous. . . . The kids always tell me there was an insurmountable wall. I felt that they were first of all a responsibility."

A sixty-year-old writer, a successful father of four, admitted: "Of course I was depressed, I really was furious at the deal I had made with my wife, that she provided comfort and security while I worked hard in the outside world. But how could I get angry at her—that was the deal all men make, you work hard, give up your life for your family. When you're angry with no place to go with it, you get depressed."

Clearly many men today who are trying to spend more time at home are responding to a sense that their fathers missed out on a valuable experience of intimacy and nurturing. Yet what of that anger and depression our fathers felt? That is inside many of us as well, and it becomes the stuff of which we imagine masculinity is made. We introject that version of fathers, so that when we become fathers it creates conflict, particularly when we want to involve ourselves in the family. Many new fathers' conflicts around parenthood lie in the fear of becoming the angry father they carry around in their heads, like the father who said that whenever he disciplined his kids he heard the angry voice of authority screaming "No!" at them.

There may be a kind of intergenerational revenge here, with some men acting out their fathers' hidden rage at their wives and children, even as these grown men are trying to be more nurturant husbands and fathers.

The lack of a fuller emotional repertoire between father and son is often taken to mean that as sons get older they lack male models of emotional accessibility. Thus men will speak of having to "invent" themselves as participating fathers or husbands. Yet that misses the more important point: The lack of a fuller, richer emotional repertoire also means that we can't work things out with our fathers and therefore carry around within us as adults a conflicted image of father.

Our fathers perhaps secretly feared us too. The ambivalent love between fathers and son is underestimated. It is the dark side of the high value boys are given in our society. Since so much of male identity is based on performance, sons will someday outdistance Dad. We become ambivalent objects, loved and feared by our fathers. Indeed, as we are learning more about fathers and children, researchers have proposed the phrase "Laius complex" to refer to the father's feeling of threat from the son and need to put him down. King Laius in the Oedipus drama haughtily refused to move aside on the road for his son, precipitating the fateful slaying.[14]

A son may represent a father's mortality in very uncomfortable ways. As the son becomes a man, the father must recognize his own aging, a thought captured powerfully in Donald Hall's poem "My Son, My Executioner."[15]

Fathers and sons may find it much easier to display anger and hostility to each other than caring and affection, given the son's conflicting pull to mother, the father's sense of being displaced and jealousy of his son, and the limited opportunities for men in the family to express a range of feeling to each other.

A thirty-three-year-old male graduate student remembered "feeling I could scare my father away but I couldn't make him come closer." From the father's point of view, a patient bitterly told of the time his father said to him, almost as an admission: "I didn't know I could be both your friend and your father when you were growing up." Some men may have fears of hurting their fathers with their aggression, like the painter quoted above, and may feel as if they are carrying around inside of them a rebellion that could destroy their fathers. From that may come a sense of being personally destructive, of having to make up as an adult for unnamed sins committed while growing up.

The son may feel a terror of his father's rage as well. The same man who said he could scare father away revealed a few moments later that he was himself scared away: "I could test the limits with my mother, push too far with her, but not with my father—going too far made him look like he'd kill me. I have lots of memories as a kid of father losing his control, looking enraged, all red in the face, even a few times chasing me around the house." So adolescent rebellion and the normal separation struggles of growing up can become mixed in with violence and aggression.

And indeed, many men denied a true language of intimacy have to keep in tight emotional control, for when their feeling life breaks through it is overwhelming. So father is indeed either too strong or too weak. Two personas are combined in the same person: powerful and vulnerable. Our fear is of hurting him or being hurt by him. Those two themes are acted out over and over again in the adult life of men: the search for and rejection of our fathers. We want redemption and want to destroy them; as one man joked, "We want our fathers and to eat them too."

The Mother's Role

Let's return to mother's role in the family, since we cannot under-stand the broken connection between fathers and sons without also considering mother. Since mother is often at the center of the family communication pattern sons and fathers often have to act out their struggles indirectly or symbolically, rather than con-fronting or connecting with each other directly.

A savvy older woman defended to me her role as the talker, the emotional switchboard in her family. "Dinner would get very quiet if I didn't say anything. All there was was talk of the activity of the day around the dinner table. Not a feeling between anyone in the room was mentioned until I opened my mouth."

It's easy to blame mother. I felt rage when I realized how much my mother got between my father and myself. But we all operate under conflicting pressures and divided loyalties. Many mothers may have been trying in all goodwill to "protect" husbands who they feared would drop dead of a coronary at the pace they were going or who revealed to them in the privacy of the bedroom or acted out at the dinner table their inability to deal with their own kids.

The result of the more open communication between son and mother is that the son may have a better, earlier chance to work out separation issues with her than with his father. Studies of high school youth by Wright and Keple, for example, found that boys often view their fathers as "helpful in a utilitarian sense" but "lack-ing significant personal and emotional involvement."[16] In sharp contrast to their views of fathers, Wright and Keple found that the teens viewed their relationship with their mothers as more sup-portive, unique, and irreplaceable.

One wonders what would happen if fathers played a more salient affective-expressive role during their sons' early develop-mental years, particularly before age five. Perhaps by adolescence fathers cannot play such a role, the tension between the genera-tions being too strong. In the past within many cultures there have been social rituals that initiate the teen into the group of men, giv-ing him the blessing of the elders. Within Orthodox Judaism the Bar Mitzvah served this function. Such rituals and rites defuse the intensity of the individual father–son relationship, providing both parties with what they so desperately need: a blessing from the male community, a welcome from fathers to their sons, and a thank-you from the sons to the fathers; a ritual purging of the tension and betrayals of growing up male.

The Impossible Wish to Be a Good Son

I have the impression that today the wish for forgiveness and reconciliation with father often goes unmet. Within the family fathers cannot communicate a sense of benevolent masculinity to their sons, and culturally we have distorted social rituals and initiation ceremonies. The rites of passage common to men in adolescence and young adulthood today involve joining such institutions as the army, football teams, medical schools, and large corporations. Those institutions play upon the young man's wish for an idealized father to love him, offering an exaggeratedly masculine way to live up and be a good son.

An embittered Vietnam vet, reflecting back years later on his difficult combat stint in the Marines, felt he owed the Corps one thing: It earned him the recognition and love of his father. He recalled: "My father and I never had any relationship. He wasn't a bad man. He just didn't show his emotions. He was at work the day I came home from boot camp. I wore my uniform and went to where he was. It was the first time I ever saw my father smile at something I did in my entire life. He actually turned around and said, 'you're a man.' I was 21 years old."[17]

Within the family, perhaps, the kind of fighting that leads to reconciliation between fathers and sons doesn't happen; it may have been short-circuited for my generation, projected onto the social screen of antiwar protest rather than entered into with our individual fathers. The image of father as too weak/too strong inhibits real struggle and fighting between father and son, the kind of separating that may happen between mother and son precisely because, by adolescence, distance and aggression between them are less frightening. As the graduate student said, "I could always test the limits with my mother, but not my father." He went on to describe feeling his father's hate in ways that he never experienced with mother. "My father would really withdraw his love. I felt that he could do it in such a rigid way, a way that my mother couldn't. When my father withdrew it felt like he might never come back."

Father may be seen as secretly furious and full of rage at a son who defies him, ready to explode at any minute, or he may seem wounded and hurt, too good to get angry but secretly terribly disappointed. In that way fathers become our superego, critically judging us for letting them down. If mothers become life-giving earth in the unconscious of men, then fathers become wrathful, judgmental gods.

Given the seeming impossibility of resolving the broken connection with their fathers, many men will go in search of father-surrogates to reassure them. As we'll see in Chapter 2, we try to work things out or to continue the dialogue with fathers with mentors. For men the family becomes the arena where things cannot be worked out. We must move on to work, and at work we unconsciously seek to resolve unfinished business with father. Since rebellions can't be worked out at their source, they are taken elsewhere.

What do not go away are the sons' wishes to obtain their fathers' love and to be good sons at last. In the past men could strive for a silent homage to their fathers, reassured by a life that looked like his—*paterfamilias*, success at work. That is no longer possible for many men, given the women's movement and other social changes. The distance and longing in men's feelings for their fathers lead us to try surreptitiously to live up, to pay back an unspoken debt, in a word to be a good son, finally, at the very same time as we confront social demands that we be truly different from our fathers.

We are missing a fundamental dilemma of the times if we don't pay attention to the fact that the women's movement intensifies men's sadness and terror at the loss of their fathers. Many men I've talked with who grew up in the 1950s and 1960s were drawn to their mothers. The women's movement had begun to take off, and there was a general sense of optimism about women, a sense of strength and vitality that contrasted with the stolidity of our fathers.

As a result many men have grown up with a guilty sense of collusion with mother and rejection of father, which lends an emotional undercurrent to adult male–female skirmishes: To collaborate and work with wife means to leave Dad. Perhaps the women's movement, in asking men to take a larger part in the family, touches on men's worst fantasies, that they will ally themselves with mother after all and abandon father entirely—that they will have no fathers.

Still on the subject of social-historical context, I'd like to offer a speculation about a deeper historical twist to the lives of men of the 1960s generation. Listening to men talk about coming of age during the 1960s it often seems to me that our fathers' degradation in our eyes became mixed in with the Vietnam struggle, confirming for many men an undercurrent of masculine evil. Many sons were drawn to the women's movement in one form or another because it seemed to express concerns about justice, caring, and morality that our fathers just stonewalled.[18]

The Wish for Odysseus

My purpose in this chapter is not to lament all the complications in the father–son relationship but rather to emphasize men's need to heal the wounded father within. As in so many aspects of men's bonds with those they love, we have overemphasized the role of separation and paid not enough attention to connectedness.

There is a note of Greek tragedy in men's relationship with their fathers. The great recognition scene in the Odyssey captures the wishes of both men better than the more familiar Oedipal drama. When the great warrior King Odysseus returns from more than a decade of wandering, he and the princely Telemachus hardly know each other. In a stunning moment the unconquerable warrior reveals himself to his teenage son:

> "I am that father whom your boyhood lacked and suffered pain for lack of. I am he. . . . This is not princely to be swept away by wonder at your father's presence. No other Odysseus will ever come, for he and I are one, the same. . . ."
>
> Throwing his arms around this marvel of a father, Telemachus began to weep. Salt tears rose from the wells of longing in both men, and cries burst from both as keen and fluttering as those of the great taloned hawk, whose nestlings farmers take before they fly. So helplessly they cried pouring out tears, and might have gone on weeping till sundown.[19]

_____ *41*

The wells of longing in both men. The Odysseus myth points to a deep yearning for each other in both father and son, and it contains a lesson for our times.

Like many men Telemachus spent his childhood among women. He was like many of us—his father was off fighting distant wars; the great man was a legend and a rumor to his son's ears. In the saga Telemachus faces a great problem. Having left to fight in the Trojan wars Odysseus' ship disappears on the return voyage; most of his kingdom assumes he is dead. So a large band of vile suitors have gathered in the city intent on marrying his Queen Penelope and usurping the kingdom. On the edge of manhood, young Telemachus hardly knows how to defend his mother from the threat. It is the miraculous return of his father that propels Telemachus into a confident and strong sense of manhood.

Is the task not the same for men today? The message is that for a man to grow up he must find the good and the strong in his own father—he must find the heroic in the figure he hardly knew. The alternative is to be dominated by vile, degraded images of manhood, represented by the suitors who threaten the kingdom.

The ending of the Odyssey may be misinterpeted: Odysseus and Telemachus together go out and slay the suitors in a bloody battle. One's first reaction is, "Oh, great! It's the same old story, father teaches son to be brutal. Football coaches can do as good a job!" But the real truth is metaphoric. Odysseus shows his son how to be a man and gives him confidence in his own strength. Today the task for men may seem different, but it's really the same. We need the father who helps us define masculine strength in a changing world, what Robert Bly has called "the moist father," strong and caring.[20] Our struggles lie in the family, with our wives, children, friends, and co-workers. Yet the task is the same: how to be a strong and present man in new, unfamiliar situations.

We have grown up thinking of Oedipal rivalry between father and son, the guilty wish to surpass the father, but we need also attend to the Odysseus theme, the wish to be like father, to find a father, a sturdy man we can rely on.

Consider a modern-day recognition scene. At the end of *Death of a Salesman* Biff, the eldest son of Willy Loman, searches for a common ground of feeling with his father late at night in the family kitchen. Biff, taller than his father, leans down and hugs Willy, who is seated kinglike against all sense of failure, in his chair. Crying and lamenting, Biff poignantly reaches out to Willy, and his father sits there stolidly, perplexed, shrugging his shoulders at his wife (who will later try to "explain" things to Biff), and *he doesn't hug back.*

Here there is no healing, no reconciliation between father and son. Willy, unable to tolerate his own sense of failure, will soon die in a car accident suicide while Biff remains fated to spin out a life that is its own payment for his father's.

It seems to me that we cannot really develop a new, satisfying sense of masculinity until we have also accepted and come to terms with how we learned what it meant to be male and female—in large part from our fathers and mothers. Until a man "names his father," sees him clearly, and accepts him for who he is and was, it is that much more difficult for him to grow up himself and become a father to his children, a husband to a wife, or a mentor to the younger generation at work. That is every man's task of healing the wounded father within.

Dealing with Authority:
Mentors and Fathers

"I'm always looking for father figures—they're very reassuring," the film director says to me confidingly, with a wry smile. He is forty-two years old and in the middle stages of what has become a promising career.

Who have been the father figures in his life?

He mentions his wife's father. "My father-in-law for sure—I often wished he was my own father. But you know, you find them at work too." He tells me of a prominent director, a man he worked for for many years. "He encouraged me, taught me a lot of what I know. He had faith in me." The man's voice trails off, as if remembering something painful. "Of course, I couldn't go back to work for him now, which is odd, because I could use some work at this point. But things have never been the same since I left, five years ago. Just the same, though, he was my mentor."

A mentor is a more senior, usually older, person in the world of work who serves a transitional function for the young person, helping him to become established in the adult world of work yet also nurturing his own special values and beliefs. More people *think* they have mentors than actually do in the true sense of the term: a close *nurturing* relationship between old and young in the work world. Given the nature of the workplace, the mentor is usually a male, particularly for men.

The mentor serves very important, healthy functions in helping the younger person mature into adulthood. Dr. George Vaillant has examined in detail the lives of successful men from college through later adulthood in what has come to be called the Grant Study. He found the presence of mentors central to men's career success and to their maturation as people. "The new role model of the late twenties and early thirties seemed associated with the acquisition of solid career identification."[1] Men with relatively unsuccessful careers either had not discovered mentors until their early forties or had mentors only in adolescence.

The mentee, too, serves an essential function for the mentor: By nurturing the younger person, the mentor keeps alive his own values and hopes, which helps him deal with his mortality and allows him to develop more "generative" parts of himself. Indeed, many men find that the mentoring relationship at work allows them to heal some of the wounds of parenting; feeling frustrated with their own children, some men turn to their younger colleagues as "surrogate sons."

Daniel Levinson, one of the most careful students of the mentoring relationship, writes that "the mentor relationship is one of the most complex, and developmentally important, a man can have in early adulthood." He reports an intriguing fact from his research: "Mentoring is best understood as a love relationship. . . . Most often . . . an intense mentor relationship ends with strong conflict and bad feelings on both sides."[2]

The mentoring relationship suffers from the same deficiencies and stresses of other male relationships, particularly those of father and son. Notwithstanding its positive aspects, men often act out in the mentoring relationship unfinished conflicts with their own fathers and families. And often the "socializing" that occurs within the relationship serves merely to reinforce the instrumental and silently oppressed side of men. Some mentors can be unconciously destructive of their charges, and some mentees can demand an unattainable or inappropriate love from the mentor, which also interferes with their work. In this chapter I shall explore some of the darker sides of the mentoring relationship and their roots in the tensions of the father–son relationship.

The Father Hunger in Men

Unsure of their own fathers some men search for older, more senior men who will help them solidify a fragile masculine identity, which is usually of the brittle, instrumental sort that emphasizes career achievement and public demonstrations of power and strength. Such identities may lead to a withering of the man's capacity to tolerate his own more receptive, less public, or action-oriented sides.

A powerful mentor may speak to the hunger vulnerable young men have for a strong, all-accepting father-hero, whom we can love and revere unambivalently. "I am that father whom your boyhood lacked and suffered pain for lack of," said Odysseus to Telemachus.

George Vaillant mentions only in passing a striking finding from the Grant Study. Looking back at age forty-seven, the successful businessmen, scientists, and academics he interviewed had forgotten or denied the key role models and ego ideals they had identified with in adolescence. Those figures were replaced by the mentor. He reports a startling statistic: "However, while acknowledging that their mentors were often 'father figures,' the men took care to differentiate these mentors of adulthood from their real fathers. *In more than ninety-five percent of cases, fathers were either cited as negative examples or were mentioned as people who were not influences.*"[3] For many young men mentors truly become the better fathers they yearn for.

The mentor–father connection is exemplified by a lawyer, a physically powerful former basketball star, who has carved out a role for himself as the executive assistant or "chief troubleshooter" for the CEO of a large bank in the Pacific Northwest. Coming into adulthood with a sense of father as weak and mother as too strong and needing an arena in which to express his own aggression, he found the man he identifies as his mentor, the chief executive officer of his company. While explaining his complex and demanding duties to me, he switches from the language of the boardroom to that of the basketball court, referring to a common play where one player screens off an opponent to provide a teammate with an open shot at the basket: "Basically I set picks for my boss so he can get off a good shot." He describes his boss in idealized ways, emphasizing his gentleness and ability to make decisions while standing apart from the fray, buffered by his younger associate. The drama he is acting out at work is that of the angry "protector" for his boss-father, now doing his duty and shielding him from the aggression of the corporation. Much of this relationship with his mentor is rooted in dynamics between himself, his mother, and his father.

He sees his father as "puzzling," a man who modeled an accepting, passive and non-violent approach to life ("My father always cautioned me not to fight back when kids got rough in the school yard") but who seemed dominated by his mother ("He never stood up to anyone, particularly not my mother, and she dumped a lot onto him"). He relishes his childhood memory of the one time his father did assert himself with his mother, during a family drive in the country: "He was driving. My mother was going on and on, bitching about everything. My father turned to her and said 'be quiet.' She shut up immediately." With a mournful tone he concludes the story: "That's the only time that ever happened." The lawyer remembers his adolescence with some shame, recounting angry acts of rebellion that seemed to hurt his father. As I listened to his description of his role in the bank, I wondered if he was now creating a resolution for his own family drama. In the role of his mentor's assistant, he now saves his father from his mother, all the while doing penance for the aggression he felt toward that "remarkably peaceful" man.

As he sits down for our first interview, this lawyer presents his agenda: "I've taken the time for this because I hope in talking with you I may learn something new about myself." As we finish our long, very enjoyable conversations he ends with a question to me: "You are a psychologist. Why do you think my father stood up so little for himself, so little for me?" He left me with the distinct impression that this was the question he wanted, and feared, to ask his own father.

For other men, authorities become the objects of their anger *at* their fathers. Our ambivalence can swing in either direction:

toward loving mentors too much or toward too much hatred of them. One lawyer could not talk of several older partners in his firm without slipping in references to "these clowns I work for." Yet it was the very same men who had voted him into the firm and whose goodwill this man so desperately sought. Yet they, like his father, were figures he could not escape from; they had to be degraded.

The Wish to Be a Good Son During a Time of Social Change

In a time of changing sex roles we look to our mentors for a vision of the future. We want them to testify that the future can work—that it is possible to age healthily as a man, with integrity and strength. Mentors, after all, know us in some ways better than our fathers. They understand more of what the work part of our life is like, the special demands and peculiarities our unique career demand of us, and they understand more of the special character-istics of our work situation—which partners in a law firm will look askance or with approval at this or that approach to a case, what the grant situation is like in our field, how to deal with a delicate tenure case in the university, and so on. We see an idealized ver-sion of them at work, where cognitive, rational, and certain social skills are emphasized.

Often, too, we want them to give a seal of approval to a changed work–family balance. Men coming out of the 1960s may be search-ing for different resolutions to the same work–family pressures mentors struggled with in the 1940s or 1950s (whether to commit to achievement over family, how to make a greater place in life for children, or how much sacrificing he should do for his wife's career) and may be resolving them differently. The younger man needs some seal of approval from the mentor for different choices yet may not be able to ask for or get it. The older and younger man may speak different languages about work and family, about feel-ings and emotions in a man's life.

Here are two examples. The first involves a dual-career couple facing a new kind of career decision, the second a lawyer facing a difficult moral challenge. In each case the man's mentor plays a crucial, somber role.

"Do I Have to Be as Ruthless as My Teachers?"

"I feel like there are mentors to show me how to be a surgeon in the old mold—completely dedicated to my work to the exclusion of everything else, inattentive to other people's feelings and needs, and willing to ruthlessly climb the ladder of success." The young physician stopped and thought for a moment, then plunged on:

"But there aren't mentors, or at least I haven't found them, who can help me become a *feeling, powerful* man, as well as physician."

A physician and his wife, studying to be a doctor also, are talking in the living room of their Brooklyn apartment about a traumatic recent experience. He's a cardiologist and has just finished his residency at a prestigious New York hospital. He's very good at what he does—so good in fact that the chief surgeon in the hospital, a man with an international reputation in heart surgery, offered him a plum: the chief resident's position in the cardiology department of the hospital.

"That job was the first prize in the race," he laughed. "We all wanted it, not for the salary so much as the prestige. It means a lot to me—I've gotten very close to the Chief of Surgery.

"The fact he offered it to me felt like such a vote of confidence in my work." His voice trailed off, as if the wound from what happened next had not healed.

His wife, a few years younger, broke in:

"Except I messed up the works, Eric," she said ironically.

"No, no, Beth," her husband interjected with a wave of his hand, but she seemed not to notice his attempted reassurance.

"I'm finishing up medical school this year and have decided to focus on a subspeciality called pediatric cardiology. I'm particularly interested in microsurgery with seriously ill newborns; it's a very exciting field with the possibility of saving babies that years ago had no chance of survival.

"Anyway, the place for training in this field is Washington— that's where the best work is being done. And last month I was offered a *great* residency at one of the primo teaching hospitals down there."

Now what were they going to do? He was offered a prize position in one city, she was offered one in another. The talented couple faced a dilemma not uncommon these days in marriages where both husband and wife work: Their careers were leading them toward a geographic split. Weekends together, weekdays apart. Two apartments. "We felt like we'd have to sell our car and buy the Eastern Shuttle."

Eric described what happened next:

"We decided that Beth had made all these sacrifices for my career over the years, and now she had this offer that could really get her going in her career. It felt like it was truly *her* turn."

"So I looked into a possible good position with the National Institutes of Health in Washington—not a plum like here in New York, but it would be good enough. But we're still not sure—it meant giving up the chief residency position, my work with my mentor, in effect putting Beth's career ahead of mine for awhile. Last month I went in to see my department chief, this man I've worked with for so long. I wanted to share the situation with him. I told him what we were thinking of doing, asked him what he thought, and said that I'd need letters of recommendation from him."

Later that same day his mentor called him back into his office and gave him a reply. "He told me that the chief resident's offer was withdrawn because obviously I wasn't 100 percent into my work." After a sip of his tea, Eric continued with some bitterness to say, "He hardly said anything at all about my marriage or what he thought of our decision. Isn't that great? It just proves a feeling I had all through medical school: Don't talk to other people about your feelings and indecision." He posed a frightful question: "To make it up to the top in medicine, do I have to become as ruthless as my teachers seem to be?"

Beth said sadly, "I feel sorry for men these days, I feel I have mentors of powerful and nurturing women—even in medical school—but I don't think men do." Beth may have been optimistic. The demands of institutions and the compromises senior women have had to make may take their toll on her ability truly to combine power and caring. I wonder if the younger men who now may be drawn to senior women as mentors will find in them more nurturant models. What does the lack of male models of power and caring mean for the development of these men? Do they come to feel, or are they seen as, in some way deviant or "feminine, Mama's good little boy"?

Eric's mother happened to be visiting on one of the afternoons I spent with the two physicians. She heard part of the conversation I had with her son and daughter-in-law and later in the day spoke with me alone, adding a new dimension to the mentor-father dynamics we had been talking about. Sixty years old, a professor of English in the Midwest, she spoke earnestly about her son and shed light on his unfinished business with his father. She had heard what happened with her son's mentor and was able to give voice to a side of the experience denied to her son. She spoke impatiently: "All right, these older men have never been allowed to have their feelings, they don't know how to nurture.

"But I'm worried about the effect on Eric. He's taking that rejection harder than it appears. I wonder if he won't decide to stay in New York—there is a part of him that truly wants to live up, that wants to be the best, and will do anything to live up to that ideal. That's why Attila the Hun's reaction at the hospital hurt him so much. It was a rebuke—as if he wasn't living up."

After a brief puff on her cigarette, she divulged the family dynamics underneath the mentor relationship.

"Eric feels such an obligation to his father, that's what's going on here. He wants to show him how good he can be. But he's done enough, he's a good son. . . . They had such a terrible time when Eric was in college."

She described Eric's participation in the 1969 antiwar protest at Columbia University and the wedge that this had driven between father and son. Bitter accusations flew between the two as Eric's father, a professor of biology in the Midwest, could not understand his son's rebellion. "He'd never admit it, but I think Eric is still making up for his sins. He seems to want some forgiveness, an okay from his father. But they never talk. Ever since adolescence. And Eric never seems to get off the hook. He can't get the forgiveness he wants from Dad, or from this lousy surrogate Dad he found at the hospital."

As I listened I could empathize with Eric's wish to be a good boy and his silent struggle with that harsh internal voice that says, after the brittle rebellion is over, "You do it Dad's way or not at all." It is a developmental task to get through that voice without having to dissociate from Dad or the best parts of yourself.

Eric's mother continued. "I've talked to my husband, trying to get them to talk. I've told Alex that his life is different from Eric's. Alex didn't have many choices—his father died young and he had to support the family. So that's what Alex has done—worked hard, been very nurturing—but he doesn't talk much to the kids, he showed his affection by giving them baths, he hugs and kisses them, but they don't talk much. He's like most men of his generation; his father wasn't there for him, and now he doesn't know much about feelings. When he looks inside he thinks nothing is there. I'm always the switchboard in the family, trying to hook people up to each other."

Do What You Have to Do!

The second example is a West Coast lawyer in his mid-thirties who has recently started his family. His wife works part time as a music teacher in the Los Angeles school system. He has worked hard to be a success in his demanding trial work. Choosing to become a "litigating lawyer," which he describes as demanding confrontation, means being able to take charge in the courtroom. He was fascinated by "the opportunity to jockey—the game aspect." Yet it has taken its toll, and the arrival of a child has shifted some of his commitment: Is it really worth all the confrontation, long hours, and travel? He is a senior partner, a status he reached in part through the patronage of his mentor at the firm, a man who's made his reputation and career through his knowlege of courtroom tactics.

This example shows how some men unconsciously will turn to their mentors for permission to become more receptive, engaged, and caring, reenacting a drama from some point in childhood when they turned similarly to their fathers. As adults we ask our mentors the most profound questions in the coded language that men use in speaking to each other; logical, rational career questions to mentors often express profound personal dilemmas in the area of nurturing versus performance.

This engaging, articulate man's thoughts turn to a recent dilemma he faced in the courtroom: He became convinced that a witness of his was lying. He was the prosecutor in the case against an unpopular teenager in town, who was accused of theft. Some crucial testimony that seemed unavailable that morning (Who had last seen the stolen goods?) had suddenly and miraculously become available after the lawyer had shared with town officials his assessment that they had a weak case without it. "I came back out a few minutes later, and one of the members of the group said, 'Counselor, I've just remembered,' and then he described to me, in elaborate detail, that he had seen it during that period of time, and it was a very convincing story."

But there was one problem: "I was absolutely convinced that he was lying to me." The lawyer was stunned and confused.

"I went to a pay phone and called my senior partner. . . . He had a lot of experience in this whole thing. I looked to him for advice."

And the advice he got was "to put the man on the stand, ask him questions, he'll answer as he sees fit, and it's up to the defense lawyer in the court to bring out any other aspects of the facts as they exist and for the court to make the decision. My colleague said, You don't *know* he's lying.' "

"From a lawyer's point of view, it's really an intellectual problem, it's like a syllogism almost. You put the pieces together and make a conclusion that comes out in the end automatically."

The advice wasn't terrible advice, but it carried an ominous underlying message: ignore your feelings, ignore your values, and *do what you have to do.*

I wondered if there wasn't a deeper question this man was asking: What do I do with experiences that challenge my values? Can I hold onto myself in my work as a lawyer? Those questions were never discussed between the lawyer and his mentor, and one reason may be that the more emotional, personal themes were disguised beneath career, task-oriented questions. Just as Eric was also asking his chief: Can I be an okay doctor if I give up some of my ambition to my wife? In both cases the coded answer from the mentor could be paraphrased as: "No. To be successful in my eyes, you must perform on the job as I have been trained to do."

The lawyer reports feeling the answer he got was correct, but he seems to protest too much: "It's drilled into us from the beginning of law school, and the Supreme Court makes a big point of this all the time, that every citizen, whether it be a person or a corporation or a municipality or whatever, has a right to retain a lawyer to be his spokesman in court and it's the nature of the Anglo-Saxon legal system that. . . ." And on and on in defense of the advice he received. It's almost as if this man himself was not aware of the more profound question he was asking or of his need to "live up" in the eyes of his senior partner.

The more I listened to men around age forty talk of mentoring relationships, the more it felt as if an important part of life caused both participants in the relationship difficulty: the vulnerabilities of manhood, juggling careers and work, the times of indecision when one wants to shift the balance away from work and toward self (often even in ways that will ultimately be productive to work), the problems of coming to terms with the rest of life (aging, pressures and opportunities from wife and family), and how men evolve more nurturant, interconnected values and express them at work or outside. The nitty-gritty of men's emotional life, of intimacy, in other words. Those aspects of men's lives we seem to have difficulty bringing into our relationship with mentors, just as we did with our fathers. Yet they are crucial to the continued growing up of both mentors and mentees.

A quite well-established internist in Chicago, for example, talked about his struggle to come to terms with the *limits of his power, and the painful reality of mortality*. He told of how upset he got when patients died despite all his efforts to save them. He revealed that he often went to their funerals and found himself at times weeping uncontrollably. Shifting uncomfortably in his office chair, he told me that "sometimes it really helps just to talk about all this."

And to whom does he talk?

"Well, the younger staff, junior officers on the service. I'd never go to more senior physicians, never tell them I go to patient's funerals. They'd never understand, they'd think it was odd." Yet he does talk to younger physicians about his pain, and has been rewarded by winning the teacher-of-the-year award at the medical school where he is on the faculty. I suspect there is a connection between his ability to share his inner experience of the "hard questions" of being a doctor and his popularity with the medical students.

For those of use who grew up during the 1960s, the mentoring relationship may be made more complicated by the unfinished baggage from those tumultuous years. Some younger men distrust all seniority, as if the older generation were corrupt and have no moral lessons or help to provide. So such men will not accept any "parenting" from mentors. The rebellions and sense of betrayal between the generations that characterized the years of Vietnam and Watergate also seem to have left some older men distrusting all youth, feeling that the young only want to change the elegant and wondrous social fabric of the existing order without replacing it with anything better. So they will not help "parent" the young in their efforts to find better solutions than they themselves were able to find.

For those of us who came of age during the 1960s, the slogan "Never trust anyone over thirty" captures the mistrust and rebellion in society and in our families, which may further complicate mentoring. The tear in the masculine fabric leads the young to desire a healing; we want to be good sons for our mentors and, through them, for our fathers. Such an experience, the feeling of being a good son for father, can indeed be healing, but the yearning for it can also be disastrous when unfulfilled.

Separations and Rejections

It was with my mentor that I first recognized the unfinished father issues in my own life. For many men the experience of trying to separate from their fathers colors their relationship with mentors, making separation and rejection critical components of the mentor–mentee dynamic.

I actually wasn't all that interested in mentors when I started my research on men's lives. I talked at length to men about mentors, but that seemed to be more because *they* wanted to than because I did. Older, more senior men weren't relevant to the younger generation coming of age; gray, bland creatures, demanding and unsympathetic—so my conceit went. There I was, still distancing my own father, trying to act as if *he* were unimportant. That act chagrins me, now that I realize how much I depended on mentors for their love, indeed sought them out, and how angry I would be when they wouldn't give me what I wanted.

The day I went to see my mentor to tell him I was taking a year off, I felt absolute dread. It was at a time when I needed space and time away from my academic and research responsibilities. The hardest person to explain my planned absence to was the director of my department, whom I shall call Robert. Leaving would hurt his feelings, I feared. There seemed to be an unspoken obligation to be there. Separating and rejecting seem very hard to sort out at that point. And, too, I was scared to let go of him.

It was a gray early October day when I went over to the department to tell Robert of my plans for the year.

As I stepped off the subway and walked down toward the hospital building where our department was housed, my chest began to tighten. The place looked somber and depressing. Its presence diminished my plans for the year. Given so much suffering in those wards, why try to sort out my pain at all? I felt like a coward abandoning the field of battle.

At the departmental lunch, surrounded by other colleagues, including Robert, all of us munching on our brown bag lunches, I had a failure of nerve. I avoided telling them that I would hardly be around and finessed the topic when it came up. I found part of myself subtly aborting my carefully thought-out plan for the year. I almost started volunteering for *more* work when it was offered. Would I supervise some new psychiatrists? "How about lectures for a new course that needs your help, Sam?" "Sam, let's meet regularly to write that grant proposal we've talked about."

"Maybe, maybe," I found myself mumbling. "Let me think about it."

By the time I got home to dinner that night I was a total ball of what we call "stress" these days. My wife Julie asked me how my day had been.

"Okay I guess. Went over to the department. Staff lunch. Saw a lot of people." I gave voice to my disguised terror. "There's a lot going on over there. I'm thinking of doing some supervision, maybe writing that grant proposal."

There was a plea for help in those offhand comments. In my roundabout way I was silently asking, "Is it okay for me to say NO to all this? I need some support, or my whole year will be thrown away in these commitments I don't want!"

"Gee, Sam," Julie came through. "Don't you think you've got enough scheduled? Aren't you going to leave yourself some time?"

Tears formed in the back of my eyes when she said that, verbal proof of her faith in me, proof that she was on my side. It was more than I could say for myself. Her reply was like a beam of warm light, and in its warmth I could see the self-defeating part of myself that all day had been piling on the work, burying the hope of a calmer, more reflective, joyful year of self-discovery.

Where was the origin of my ambivalence? I could not get the face of my mentor, Robert, out of my mind. He had been smiling at me when I met him in the corridor before the lunch, a puff of smoke rising from his pipe. He was glad to see me. I in contrast felt like the carrier of a dirty secret: I was abandoning him. We would not be spending days together, doing our work together in the same old way.

He sits in his office busily at work, smoking his pipe, thinking, being careful, precise, and orderly.

He was too precise and restrained for me. All I felt was a need to get away, and that felt like abandonment. It was impossible to justify, and I couldn't explain.

For the last five years I had met with him once a week. We analyzed data, then sat around and talked. In my time of need, eight years ago, he was there for me. Feeling dead-ended in a university teaching job, dimly aware that I *had* to find something else, I began desperately writing fellowship and grant proposals.

Then, at the suggestion of a friend, I went to see Robert. We hit it off immediately. My grants to study the adult development of men were funded. Robert was interested, and soon I was working with him in his department. In contrast to my graduate school and junior faculty experience, where encouragement had been meagerly dispensed, as if there were a critical worldwide shortage, with Robert everything became good, more than good enough. Things I said in our talks became nuggets, treasures to be examined and thought out. Robert found my work fascinating. He is an eminent man in the field. Now I was working and studying with him as an equal. His confidence in me was a heady experience. The way he valued me was food and drink I couldn't get enough of. Yet suddenly it felt as though I had to get distance from him.

By an unlucky stroke of fate, that year he was in crisis too. His wife was deathly ill, budget cuts jeopardized his research, and I felt *his* need of *me*.

I wanted to be a good son for him, the good son everyone told me I already was for him. His wife confided that I'm his friend, that he talks at home about what we say at the office. Colleagues, worried about him, ask me how he's doing with all the troubles in his life.

And how is he doing? He's *doing* it: Takes care of his wife, applies for grants, sits patiently in his office, trains more scientists, meets with students, goes to all the meetings demanded of him. How can he do it? Doesn't he want to scream, cry, shout, destroy a few buildings? Where are his feelings? I couldn't stand being around that patient, aching silence.

Robert just endures! His silent message to me was that this is the fate of men, to swallow their emotions, rise above them, and get on with the work.

And in the depths of my soul I realized that to show my love for this man, to be the good son we both want me to be, I'd have to follow his example. We would have to spend the year sitting around and talking about *data*.

Does *he* want to be taken care of? I would wonder. Does anyone take care of him these days? No. He looked haggard and drawn, and seemed not to notice it himself. I would look at him, see so much unacknowledged pain, and feel a terrible sadness. To live with someone who needs caring but will not accept it is a terrible, brutalizing thing. I wanted to talk about about what it is like to have a wife dying, about how to ask for and get caring. How do you accept such misfortune? His answers would have been very significant, given that I idealized this man so.

Could I have said that to him? It felt impossible, as if taboo. I wanted to care for him, hold him, comfort him, but he made that impossible and I felt my own wish to care suspect—the pain too overwhelming and foreign. How do you comfort a father? How do you deal with a wife's dying?

Few pains in life are as intense as the recognition that you want to befriend someone and there's only one way to do it: Give yourself up.

He was in the "armor mode" stage of personal crisis in his life, taking care of his wife, so ill at home, keeping her as long as possible out of the hospital. This caring man just wanted to "get through." Yet how do we do that?

There is a deeper prohibition: *We will not talk about my experience of this*. I submit it is absolutely terrifying to have someone you love in jeopardy and not be able to find out what is going on within that person. And I submit too that this is routine for sons with fathers, and carries over to men's experience of mentors and work.

The day he told me of his wife's illness, Robert made the prohibition clear. He knocked on my door and asked if we could talk for a few minutes. Sitting heavily in the lounge chair in a corner, he came directly to the point:

"Ruth has cancer."

As we talked, he would answer any question I had. She had a recurrent history of it; this wasn't the first incident. Yes, it looked bad, but they were hopeful. He would tell the rest of the staff. He might have less time around the office than he had hoped. Any question he'd answer—except the most important.

"What's this all like for you?" I asked.

He waved his hand as if to dismiss the question. "It's tough, tough, but. . . ." His eyes looked right at me, beseeching, "you understand." What did I understand? That a man doesn't need support when tragedy hits? That I had nothing in the way of deeper caring to offer? That I should not look for holding and caring when I was in pain?

The anger I felt at Robert may have lain in the obligation I felt, the sense of being valued only in terms of what I provided to my mentor. If I lived up to what he wants of me, he'll love me; if I try to be different, he will be enraged. The feeling men speak about of being "smothered" in a relationship reflects the feeling that our personality will disappear under the weight of another.

I believe my mentor got solace from my being there; we both seemed to me to have derived deep satisfaction and relief from my being like a son. Yet there was oppression in that demand, which can never be talked about, perhaps the same oppression women have identified as the objectification they experience from husbands and men as "just sex objects," or with mothers when they feel loved as adults only when they are "finally married." So too for sons.

We want to meet that obligation to endure in silence, to distance ourselves from our feelings and get the job done. The prohibition against talking of it leaves us all holding onto the obligation and trying to get away from it.

I went ahead with my year off, but we couldn't talk together about why I was doing it. What became a productive year was split off from him, filled with accusations of betrayal and rejection on both sides, with unfortunate consequences that were to take years to work out.

Those feelings about a mentor were surely "inappropriate." They may seem so particularly for people who don't like it when adult life gets muddied up with unfinished sadness from childhood. We do need to distinguish how the mentee approaches the mentor. When the mentee comes to the mentor as a needy little boy in search of an all-knowing, all-loving father, both men are put in a difficult position: The mentor may feel angry, constrained, and confused (without being sure why, since the parental overtones to the relationship are often hard to see), while the mentee will easily feel disappointed, guilty, and angry. When both mentor and mentee feel comfortable enough with their feelings, values, and identity—and with each other—to express themselves honestly and to explore relatively openly their mutual vulnerabilities and strengths, there is less difficulty. Clearly that happens in some mentoring relationships, but we must understand that the issue of male vulnerability becomes highly charged for both mentor and mentee from their own relationships with their fathers.

The question is not, Is it "right" to seek parenting from mentors? Given the male experience, it often may be inevitable. The derivation of the word mentor is instructive in this regard. Mentor was Odysseus' trusted counselor under whose disguise the god Athena became the guardian and teacher of Telemachus in his father's absence. Sons will need those transitional male figures to consolidate their identity as men; the price we pay is that father–son dynamics will reappear where we least expect it. Rather than working to keep it out of the relationship, both young and old might do better learning how to tolerate vulnerability better.

During my time away from the department I felt for months like a bad son, and a terrible question shadowed me: How did I ever abandon my father?

My Father, My Mentor

After leaving the agonizing luncheon meeting that day with Robert, I found myself preoccupied with memories of my father and of my angry, guilty obligation to live up to his model:

> I feel bonded to my father by an obligation he willed me to endure in silence. He willed me or I willed myself? I've never lived up to this obligation. Beyond my mentor, the director, stands my father, rebuking me without words by his very life history for my self-centered preoccupation with my feelings. Rebuking me this year, this moment, for not working as hard as he did. He stands before

me, a large man in a business suit, with the weight of the world on his shoulders, responsible for everything, taking care of everyone except himself, his unhappiness, his pain, his regrets about what he didn't do with his life.

Every morning around eight o'clock, my father left the house, very unhappy to be going to his store, and came back at six P.M., exhausted and angry. Angry at customers who came in every day to hassle him about prices or the quality of a job. That's what people seemed to me to do all day in the Bronx: hassle and nit pick. "Oh, the men came with the carpet but they haven't finished the job," or "Shame, this carpet's for sale two cents cheaper at Rug City." Or he would fight with business associates. He continually blamed them for his never having made the adventurous decision, never really "making it big," turning Osherson's Inc. into the multimillion-dollar business he wanted it to be. Like many men it was only later in life that he realized raising a family healthy and honorably was success enough for a man or woman.

But through our childhood he had a dream of success focused on work. And perhaps understandably—like many men of his time he was caught in a generational and historical trap. He wanted that success as a gift to his parents, who had come over from Poland and started the carpet business. In his mind they had gambled and won, while he had gambled and lost. His parents had left the old country and with their own sweat and courage had started a small business and left it to their son. When my father retired, he closed it down. That business, that work was a bond of obligation and love between him and his father and mother. He was the only son, so when he left the army after World War II, there was no hope that he would be allowed to study history at Columbia, in spite of his desire to. There were sisters, smart and energetic, already involved in the business, who could easily have taken it over, but there was no question of that. It fell to the son, the only son, to show his love through his career. He had to carry out the obligation, at the price of his happiness.

Always held in check by the family, my father was provided with an answer to all questions about why he took no risks. "I was surrounded by nay-sayers, Sam. Don't let that happen to you." Chained. If only he had been able to free himself, the myth went, what grand deeds and great light he would have brought to the world. Father unchained . . . who knows what would have happened? He might have had to confront failure, with no excuses. Or sort out feelings, impulses, desires that were just too complex.

So he came home every night tense and angry. He had done his duty at the salt mines of the Bronx and only wanted to "relax," usually accomplished by hours of television every evening. "Relax" was a big word in our family, along with "unwind." It enraged me when my mother would say, "You need to unwind, go away for a vacation." The grim message that carries is that work is the place where you suffer, you put on the tight harness of responsibility. The chains. No pleasure, no fun in work. Then you try to get over it by unwinding. Yet if work ties you up in knots, isn't it likely there is something wrong with the work or how you're going about it?

In our family there was something wrong with work if it didn't exhaust you, make you feel you had been walking uphill all day. Then home was the place you used to cure yourself. You might use TV, eat a lot, or go to bed early. The passive time. So activity and passivity, work and play were placed in arbitrary opposition. Play was passive and couldn't accomplish much. Active, playful creativity and imagination had no relation to life's real problems.

My father feels like a weight on me. In the deepest ways I am bonded to him, in ways I hardly understand. I want to hug him and hold him. I want to take his grief into mine and merge it with mine. Yet I also want to shake him and accuse him. In all his "work" we never had time for each other—I couldn't salve his pain, nor he mine. He never let go. Does that mean I can't?

For the first time I see how much his pain meant to me, how much I wanted him to be happy, wanted in a child's typical fashion to make him feel better. We couldn't talk about those things—so was becoming like him the only way to show my love? To be a good son for him? Imitation is the sincerest form of flattery. An invitation I accepted, and rejected.

I wanted to be a friend to my father, and perhaps the deepest pain was learning that I couldn't be.

My father went to work, I went to school; we were on parallel tracks. I would drag myself to the school bus stop even as he was pulling out of the driveway to commute to the Bronx. How I hated high school! The endless memorizing of dates and facts, the narrow-minded rote and routines of the teachers, lessons that seemed so unconnected with what was important in my life, with what I needed to talk about. He had his customers with their niggling demands, I had my teachers—poetic justice. Like father, like son.

Becoming a man felt like accepting an odious burden of endless work and mindlessness. How I would have liked to talk to my father about that fate, but couldn't or wouldn't! He was so busy, so tired, so depressed, taking care of us all, bearing up so well in the arduous male world, for which my high school was merely the training ground.

Isn't that the point, though? The biggest lesson I learned from my father was that, day after day, he endured. You took what life gave you and you gritted it out. You were able to get the job done. And he was doing that for us, wasn't he, he took all that shit because of his wife, family, children. And is that my obligation to him? To take all the shit that life can hand out?

When it comes to enduring mental pain men are tough. But when it comes to letting go of pain, by revealing it, finding a way out of it, then we're not so tough.

My father didn't—couldn't?—take the risk of examining his pain, his depression. His choice, if you can call it that, was to fulfill his responsibilities as he saw them. Which is what many men do. There is considerable nobility in that, but what is the message to the sons? To live up, you must suffer as I do, willingly. Fathers and sons get so little experience in taking care of each other, in nurturing each other, holding each other emotionally.

I remember one seven o'clock in the morning on a cold winter day in the 1950s. It was time to get up to go to high school. My mother came in to wake me. I said I had a bad cold, could I stay home from school? Her friendly but questioning face. Maybe she knew I wasn't really sick, but she wasn't sure. "Well, okay," she said, and my heart leapt. But I still had to get past my father. So I had to convince us all, including myself, that I was sick. I lay in bed with my eyes closed, pretending that I was sleeping.

My father was dressed for work in his business suit and about to walk downstairs when he saw me still in bed. He came into my room. I felt a terrible dread inside me. I didn't want to talk to him. I couldn't deal with him. He came to the side of my bed. I didn't even open my eyes but acted as if I were asleep. He put his hand on my forehead. Fair enough—sick son, let's see if he has a temperature. Still I didn't stir. I didn't want him to tell me to get up and go to school.

His hand rested on my forehead like a weight. How ridiculous my act was. How could I still be asleep with his hand pressing my head into the pillow like that! I would not deal with him, I would not go to school. Didn't he wonder how I could be as soundly asleep as all that? That sick, we had better call an ambulance. Not a word was spoken. Kind man that he is, he let me sleep.

He walked out of the room with heavy steps. He was on his way to the Bronx, while I looked foward to a wonderful day of pleasure: reading, dreaming, listening to records, thinking, talking to my mother. I heard him plod down the steps. The front door slammed. The car started.

"You little shit," whispered a voice inside my head. "He can take it. Why can't you?"

Odysseus was wrong. It's not true, Telemachus, that your father comes to you only once and forever; you meet him again and again in different guises through your whole life. We relive with our mentors our ambivalence over our fathers' message as to what it means to be a man. Many men learn from their fathers that to be in the work world means to suffer, indeed that manhood itself is a kind of dreadful obligation. With our mentors we will try both to live up to that demand and to be excused from it.

Cannibalism

If the mentor relationship normally ends with a rupture, as Levinson suggests, that may reflect the ordinary difficulty of development: Differentiation and growth are perceived as rejection. One person experiences the changed relationship, perhaps becoming more "realistic" in its emphasis on autonomy and sure-footedness, as a rejection of the other.

Yet, too, perhaps the normal difficulty of the mentoring relationship reflects normal difficulties between men rooted in the father–son relationship. From the mentor's point of view the mentee's increasing independence may rekindle internal conflicts about the older man's *own* choices. If the mentee has a rebellious streak, which may or may not reflect suppressed sides of his mentor, the senior person may angrily reject the younger for decisions that the mentor already renounced in the course of his career.

Alternatively, the mentor may unrealistically, perhaps maladaptively, encourage within the younger person suppressed sides of himself. He may goad the younger man to rebellions that the senior person was unable to carry out.

On a deeper level the separation-individuation struggle the mentor and mentee are engaged in may rekindle for both of them difficult feelings about separation: that to leave is to reject loved ones. Rejecting a line of work or a kind of life-style may feel like a potent rejection of the person himself, particularly because usually neither mentor nor mentee realizes that there are profound paternal feelings of love involved in what seems like merely a work situation.

And, too, the vulnerabilities that permeate the process of growth and development may be too hot for many men to handle.

Is it possible that in some cases the old betray the young, as they themselves were betrayed, by persuading those of us in our thirties or forties to give up our original passions, our sense of outrage, our idealistic motives, or our desires for a fuller kind of life in favor of a narrow horsecollar that passes for "adult maturity."

Mentoring is such a fashionable word these days. It is casually dropped into conversation; many young adults assume they have a mentor, as if you can't be truly dressed for success without one. Psychology and business texts wax poetic about the mentor's importance. Both parenting and mentoring link the generations—a "linchpin" is Erik Erikson's metaphor for this volatile relationship. In the process the old find a way of seeing their ideals and values survive, while the young find sturdy, trustworthy elders to give them a confident view of the future.

Ah, the beauty and perfection of nature and the social order! Behind these texts you can hear Mozart playing in the background: All things fit together in a grand scheme.

Given the complications we've reviewed so far, particularly rapid social change and the heterogeneity of contemporary life patterns, that "linchpinning" of the generations doesn't seem so harmonious. Sometimes when I consider the experiences of my peers, and some experiences of my own, a more violent metaphor occurs to me: a predatory relationship between the generations that can only be called *cannibalism*.

One generation may cannibalize another by stealing its energy, its ideas, and often, literally, what it produces. In graduate school a student or apprentice does work that the senior professor then markets as his own. But that's mild compared with stealing the *energy* of the young by absorbing fresh enthusiasms and passions into meaningless or destructive projects and goals defined by the elders. Within many different institutions hollow reports and meetings lead to no change and are fated always to lead to no change. They can become wasteful make-work created by the senior staff to keep the junior staff busy and to test their loyalty. Can the young candidates tolerate such mind-numbing bureaucratism without blowing the whistle, without calling it into question? Perhaps, without realizing it, the seniors want to create cynicism in the young, the same cynicism they have come to feel in their own impotence, resulting from compromises they have made. Cynicism may be the wrong word; semiparalysis might be better.

Feeling cynical and impotent themselves, the seniors may find the idealism and energy of the young painful to see, though they allow themselves to experience the pain only as irritation. There's a consequent impulse to show the junior staff victim that his work doesn't add up to anything, to engender self-doubt and the feeling of failure. A senior colleague of mine once referred to the imperative that "we must break the maverick horse" as justification for a negative yearly evaluation of a junior professor.

It is relatively easy, too, for the older generation to sour the lively enthusiasms and intuitions of the young by making them feel inappropriate, bad. That goes on all the time in graduate schools and, I am sure, in other institutions as well. In subtle or not too subtle ways, a distaste for the emotional approach is put across: Distance yourself from what you see before your eyes; pay no attention to your inner cues or to any internal dialogue.

I'm amazed at the gratitude of many men in junior positions when they find encouragement to talk about their enthusiasms, and at the shock and doubt when you suggest that the inner impulses are worthwhile, are legitimate, and ought to be reactivated more often than they are. Some who reject the notion do so because they believe personal feelings may not be the most useful or valid measures or data to bring to a question, but many reject it out of hand because the approach leaves them feeling too naked and exposed: It's a freedom they don't want. They prefer feeling resentful and oppressed.

A friend of mine, a sociologist, several years ago wrote a very personal book about the draft, Vietnam, and his experiences counseling black youths in the 1960s. He wrote it after finishing his graduate studies and beginning a successful academic career. The book did not conform to the way he had been trained to work as a sociologist. He sent a copy to his mentor, eager for his reaction, hoping that eminent man would give his seal of approval to this new venture. One day my friend was looking through his mail and found the book returned to him by his mentor. When he opened it, he found this message scrawled across the title page:

"What the fuck are you doing?"

The Cruelty of the Young

Ah, but I protest too much. The young are predatory too. They demand that the old be sturdy (rigid), defined, and tough. They need to believe that, and perhaps they cannibalize the old as much as the other way around. Men in their twenties are above all predatory; they feel pressed to get somewhere, to live up to the challenge of being a man. They must make career decisions and start families to show that they can make it in our society, among other motives. They then get caught in the momentum of those decisions; they want the older generation to testify that it all works, that the choices they have made will bring success and wisdom. They will hardly tolerate it if some really wise older man, who has been through it all, says, "Maybe this way it won't work. We have to start over, and we need your energy and youthful intuition to help us change things."

Perhaps young men will not tolerate the mentors of power and caring that Beth wishes for Eric. Clearly, for many young men, and perhaps women, the appearance of gentleness in a mentor is too loaded, cuts too close to painful wounds not healed from father. We prefer to feel deprived. As the executive said, "I don't like weak authorities." We want to degrade them, and hate ourselves for it. We don't want to see the reality of failure, even ennobling failure, in our heroes. We criticize them if they fail or show "weakness."

The young can be as cruel as the old. Maybe both are equally stuck—unable to see each other, to connect. Fated to distort each other.

Many of the older generation feel that the young are relentless in their efforts to prove themselves, to test and edge out their seniors, to show how big and strong they are. Vaillant remarks on the "crassness and narrowness" of men during the career consolidation phase of their life, which he identifies as usually occuring during the twenties and early thirties.[4] Vaillant summarizes the competitiveness within the mentoring relationship with his story of the forty-year-old man talking about his mentor: "I was the featured speaker at his retirement dinner."

I have a persistent suspicion that the young and old are kept in this dance more out of fear than for enjoyment of battle. In some remote recess of our consciousness we all, young and old, fear that men are not really as strong as they look, and that we have traded something very important, an internal center connected with the feeling world, for our power in the market place.

We need to find ways to allow gentlessness into the mentoring relationship, a place for openess, and the "emotional holding" that males are hardly comfortable with, and that many renounce. Perhaps the young need to allow the old to be themselves just as vice versa, giving up the illusion that if only we do what they say, the old will take care of us and provide us with ultimate security and safety.

Perhaps the fear of a vacuum at the center of the male image, our paternal lineage, makes us want to force our elders to be stronger than they can be. It also impels us to become more, not less, like them, adopting the posture of invincible strength, colluding with the myth out of some primitive terror of revealing the vulnerability at the core.

3

Of Working Wives and Men's Loneliness

A Feeling of Neglect

"I didn't anticipate having this difficulty when she began working, and I'm surprised by it. I haven't gotten used to *the feeling of neglect*."

The handsome lawyer winced at the word "neglect," his right eyebrow arching up as if questioning his mouth's choice of words. He leaned back in his office couch. An articulate, engaging man, he had helped his wife make the shift from housewife to a successful career in social work. He liked the fact she worked and appreciated her paycheck: Her new income was not just play money to him but a contribution to greater financial and career freedom in his own life. Yet when women no longer are what women *were* back in the good old days when moms were moms, it creates problems for men. A primary occasion for men to feel abandoned by their wives is when they go off to work.

The feeling of neglect is a problem not just for men in traditional marriages whose wives go back to work after the kids are grown. Even men who expect their wives to be more autonomous—married later, usually to women who have careers of their own—have spoken of the sense of loss and abandonment they feel when wives have a strong commitment outside the family.

One thirty-eight-year-old economist with young children at home and a wife with a teaching career spoke of always assuming his wife would work, then talked moodily of "a de-emotionalizing of certain relationships. The marriage in the past few years has been less exciting than it was . . . such a thing as an emotional divorce can happen."

A thirty-two-year-old woman, a successful Southern journalist in a dual career marriage without children, said that "my husband and I have a pattern: For several days before I am about to leave on a business trip, he starts to act like a two-year-old—grumpy, sulking around, acting hurt and injured. When we try to talk about it he says he is feeling nothing, but I know that our fights have something to do with my going away."

A serious struggle for many men I've talked with results from holding a self-image of being nontraditional, accepting, and encouraging of working wives, yet finding that they act in angry and distancing ways when their wives really do become more autonomous or less focused on them. In most cases, the husband can't talk about the discrepancy between how he wishes he felt and how he really feels.

In this chapter I look at the impact on the husband of a working wife and the vulnerabilities and pressures that may leave the husband a wounded father, angry and isolated as the family rearranges itself at midlife. To understand the true impact of wives who work, we must set the phenonomenon in its broader context as a substantial change in family life. Often wives begin work or return to work, for example, as their children become more grown up and independent. I believe there is a general experience of male vulnerability at midlife, especially in light of the growing autonomy of wives and children at that time. Both those changes in family life reveal men's disguised dependency on their families.

That is why I use as a central example in this chapter the traditional family pattern in which a wife begins work or returns to work as the children grow up. The discomfort of many men at midlife with the growing autonomy of wives and children in their families reveals most clearly dynamics of loss and change at home with which normal men in more nontraditional life patterns also struggle.

The Traditional Husband at Midlife

The lawyer and his wife, the Hendersons, exemplify a common difficulty for men at midlife, provoked by the rearrangement of their families as adolescent children are "launched" from home to college and the wife pushes for greater autonomy by going—or returning—to work or school. Close to 50 percent of the women in this country return to work as their children get older.[1]

Almost 25 percent of the men in our sample of Harvard graduates from the mid-1960s found their way into the traditional work–family pattern I have called "early starters," in which the man soon after college makes work–family commitments that define him in traditional roles as an ambitious career professional and a father to a family that depends on him for economic survival. While no longer the dominant family pattern in men's lives, it remains an "ideal" one and was the normative pattern by which many of our parents lived.[2]

My data indicate that men at midlife are now struggling with the kinds of "empty nest" problems that used to be characteristic of women at midlife.

The phrase "empty nest" usually refers to the wife's depression and symptomatology around the loss of her main childrearing duties as the family grows up. Yet only a minority of women in most recent studies report such depression and symptoms when their children grow up.

The husband's predicament has become apparent only recently, at a time of changing sex-roles, when women are less trapped in the empty nest. Many women today see the rearranged family as a positive opportunity to express parts of self left behind when they elected to become full-time moms. In their article in the Sunday *New York Times Magazine* on "positive new images for women at midlife," Baruch, Barnett, and Rivers write: "If some middle-aged women see themselves as having been shortchanged in the past, most of them do not think it is going to be that way in the future. They are looking ahead with optimism. Instead of being obsessed with their failure to "measure up" to youthful expectations—as men purportedly are—they are often starting on new ventures with a fresh set of challenges."[3]

Their data indicate that women who can develop well-paying new work roles along with their parenting and wifely roles show considerable satisfaction with their lives, not great loss at the growing up of children. By contrast there is some research evidence indicating that it is husbands who have the difficult time when wives develop commitments outside the family and the kids are launched to college.[4]

A wife returning to or beginning work, particularly when combined with the "departure" of grown children from the home, puts men back in touch with dependency needs and a sense of loss never really mastered growing up. A feeling that the home is being fragmented or destroyed may confront the thirty-five- or forty-year-old man with his yearnings for his mother and father. The grief and anger of the husband at midlife often become invisible, unacknowledged by him and his family; the man subtly resists the changes that midlife brings, experiencing difficulty with the crucial developmental task of evolving new goals and purposes in his life, clinging instead to the shopworn myth of his instrumental power.

On the other hand, a working wife may help free a man from the myth of self-importance and personal isolation that is the core of the narrow, instrumental identity offered to men in our society. A man in his thirties or forties may find that the rearranging family of midlife helps to heal the angry, needy, wounded father within.

Let's examine the vulnerabilities and opportunities the man in the empty nest faces.

The Vulnerable Man in the Empty Nest

Recovering from the word "neglect," Mr. Henderson continues, telling me that "without doubt, the biggest change in my life over the past year" is that his wife has finished graduate school and found a full-time job. His words remind us that as the wife pushes for autonomy and enters the work world, she shifts the affective balance in the marriage, becoming a different person for her husband. Now she's off to the office in the morning, as he is. She meets new people and comes home mulling over ideas and experiences that he knows little of. She is no longer centered on his needs and those of the family, enlivened after a day around the house by the excitement he brings home with him. Indeed, she may now have a new set of enthusiasms, which he does not share. When wives resume or begin careers later than their husbands, there is an irony for many husbands at midlife: The wife feels freshly enthusiastic and eager about beginning a new stage of life (work) just at the time when he is peaking or leveling off in his career. For him career is old hat; for her it's still a marvelous new experience after years at home. He may feel older than his years when around the youthful freshness that an exciting, challenging career commitment has provided to his wife. As the kids are being launched, so too is the wife. For some men it feels as if everyone in the family is going on to something bigger and better at work except him.

The husband and wife are both in a new stage of life, yet the husband may not realize that as clearly as the wife. He may have no way of articulating the impact of the changing family system on him. The husband may feel suddenly competitive with his wife: Is she going to do *better* than he in the domain of life he has always looked to for his self-esteem: work? And there may be secret uncertainties: How does he measure up against the other men she is now meeting at work? The wife is truly gaining a new perspective on the workplace, and the husband may seem less competent and admirable to her now that there are other successful men to compare him with. His self-esteem may be tethered to her daily trips to her office.

It is just this challenge to the myth of the man's centrality that can be healing to the husband, because he is no longer "out there all alone" with no way of testing some of his preconceptions about himself and his work commitments. Marriage can be a great change agent for both spouses—providing ways of learning new defenses and attitudes—if they each have an equal voice within the relationship. A wife with real-world experience and a sense of competence that comes from working may then enter into a dialogue within the marriage with her husband. She may have an increased self-esteem and sense of authority at home that comes from being taken seriously and earning a paycheck in the world of work. Such personal growth may leave her with a more equal voice about the central values and commitments that define their marriage. Her husband is not the sole source of her knowledge about the demands and challenges of the "real world." She forms her own opinions, based on her own experience, about the difficult questions that have traditionally plagued the husband most directly, including how much and how often to put work obligations above family commitments, the importance of career success, or how to deal with the competitive or personally distorting demands of the workplace. As a result, a working wife may challenge her husband's characteristic myths and preconceptions about his work and identity, some of which are quite oppressive to men even as they desperately cling to them. For example, many men whose wives work talk with relief at the sudden realization that the economic maintenance of their households no longer depends entirely on their success at work. That reduces the husband's need to guard his authority in the home and allows him to open himself to more intimate relationships with his wife and children or to experiment with new aspects of self less tied to traditional career commitments. Men also report learning new strategies from their wives about coping with common work problems involving competition and power.

My wife has pursued her career full time, and I've been struck by how challenging it is for me that she understands the work world, confronting deadlines, dealing with interpersonal conflicts, and the dilemmas of success and failure. I found I had much to learn from my wife. She presented a contrast to my tendency to be at times overcontrolling with people; I was intrigued by her approach to work, which seemed less competitive and isolating.

Doug Heath found in his studies of college graduates from the mid-1960s that men consistently ranked their wives as having an equally or more maturing effect on them than their careers.[5] One thirty-eight-year-old man spoke this way about his wife's return to work: "It helped us in our understanding of each other. It was a stretching experience. Overall [it] strengthened us in our relationship while putting us through a period of stress and chaos."

One of the reasons for the "chaos" is that the husband's disguised intimacy needs and dependency suddenly become exposed.

Mr. Henderson, for example, contrasted the way things used to be at home with the way they are today:

"Now something is missing, and I'm not sure what. For a while it was fine. There was a sense of working together, pulling toward common goals. Our friends tended to be my friends, especially when we were much younger and working. The process of becoming a partner takes a long time, it's kind of a contest in a way. She was very invested in that. *I felt adored and the center.*" It is surprising how embedded the go-getter is in his family, a family that *looks* dependent on him, but upon whom he depends as well. He needs the smell and feel of that cozy little haven, reassuring him as he performs in his role as "the force": the protector and provider for his family.

"One thing I wish is that we did things more together as a family, like in the olds days. Go skating on a Saturday afternoon." I wondered aloud what kept him from doing such things. His face saddened.

"Well, as the kids have gotten older they are less interested in a family walk, which is the expression they use. *I have felt a little left out or passed by, unnecessarily.* Partly because Betty's working so hard. She will always try to do things, but she has to plan it carefully. I feel when she's doing it that she's allocated an hour for this and if it lasts two, she starts to feel pressed."

Mr. Henderson spoke with some poignancy about how things *used* to be:

"It was a relationship in which I was adored, and I was the force in everything. I was the breadwinner and I was good around the house. I had the feeling of clear superiority to my wife—who is a very talented, very capable woman." He spoke sheepishly, not without humor, sitting on the leather office couch: "I think it was probably a classic male chauvinist, patronizing perspective."

That ironic picture led me to wonder whether providing and protecting are the way many men enter into the family on which they depend for warmth, good feeling, and security. For many, though not all, men the mode of intimacy that they seem most comfortable with is *taking care of* rather than *being taken care of*. The marriage and family become the place where they find people who they can take care of and feel powerful around, thereby having their own powerful dependency and intimacy needs secretly met.

One "protecting father" described himself as "the kind of father who does not feel like a father unless he is experiencing himself as the fortification in which his children can reside."[6]

Many men who marry early and start families of their own seem most comfortable with that kind of intimacy, which might be called "paternal intimacy." When their families grow up, the children reaching late adolescence and becoming more autonomous and self-reliant, these men have great difficulty focusing on their own confusion and neediness. It's as if, having worked so hard to become powerful and strong, they find themselves without the psychological resources to make the transition into a new stage of life. Men like that may have difficulty with their children's autonomy and attempts to separate, responding with sadness or anger, surreptitiously (or not) trying to keep their kids dependent, usually without realizing it.

Used to seeing their own dependency needs projected onto those around them, they may still want to attend to what their wives and children are feeling (as a mask for their own feelings) rather than what they themselves are feeling.

Mr. Henderson, for example, first introduced his wife's working by telling me that his daughter was more lonely. Only much later did he bring up his own sense of displacement. Such a man may first report his wife has been "really shook up by changes at home," then mention that when she refused to accompany them on a vacation trip—suddenly busy with her own commitments—he was very disturbed because it "broke up the feeling of family."

When our teenage children begin to make their own decisions, to take their own risks, we can no longer protect them from life's dangers in the same way we could (or believed we could) when they were young. The father then becomes vulnerable himself to the consequences of his children's behavior, and may find himself confronted by his own uncomfortable sense of powerlessness and anxiety. Here is one father recalling a dangerous shared moment with his son, when a storm at sea turned into a metaphor for the normal separation process between adolescent and parent:

"It's fun and interesting to see my kids getting older. Some of it is wistful as I realize I'm no longer needed. Pride in them and sadness that I'm getting older. I am sometimes astonished, just bowled over by what happens. Last summer we were cruising around the bay for a period of about five days, just had some really terrible weather. Unexpected, very heavy gales, had to reef at sea, and there were a couple of times, one in particular when my son wore lifejackets and lifelines, and he and my wife had to go forward and drop the mainsail, which was reefed, and you know, 60-knot winds are almost a hurricane and there are seas sweeping over the boat, and he is a very small, slender boy. But he's up there dropping an enormous gaft mainsail and is in water up to his belly button, being pushed hard by a couple of tons of water every time a wave came over. And scared to death, but everything went without a hitch, and there was almost a partnership kind of thing. But if he had gone overboard I never would have gotten him. Really scary."

Confronted by the depth of their vulnerability, many men may feel that their adult sense of self is being secretly undermined by their families. A father who equates maturity with being in control and in charge may have considerable trouble with the late adolescent passage of his children. As he reconnects with his need for his family, becomes aware of his own fears and anxieties, a man may feel he is being pushed toward becoming a spoiled boy, perhaps the position he or his father occupied in his childhood family, or he may feel embarrassment at not living up to the "strong man" image of his own father.

The father too is often strugging with his grief and loss at the "launching" of his children. When the children begin to leave home for college or work, the father may feel that his "fathering" years are coming to a close and may experience a wish to make things "okay" with his sons or daughters without knowing how to make it happen. Wright and Keple found, for example, that many high school sons look to their fathers for instrumental support but no longer turn to them for emotional support.[7] The adolescent child may not look to his father any more for affective support, as the father–son connection becomes distorted and the possibility of rapprochement lies years down the road. So the father may be caught in his isolated, peripheral position in the family, struggling with a loss he cannot mourn as he has to let go of his children. The American painter Fairfield Porter captures some of the midlife father's lonely lament in his poem "The Loved Son." As his grown son leaves home, Porter remembers some of the young boy's earliest partings, and he rightly warns us that if the father cannot endure his regret he will indeed become "heartless." The use of regret is to point us toward our heart's yearning. Porter's yearning is toward the missed connections with his son, the wish for intimacy with the boy that remains unfulfilled:

> When the grown boy turns his back and leaves
> Looking forward to college or even the army
> Glad to be grown up, happy to be gone
> Counting his new dependence as independence

> I think how carelessly I have regarded him
> With what little penetration I have known him
> And have not listened to the pleasant wit
> That marks the shrewdness of his watching mind

The father closes his poem yearning for the "easy intimacy" with his son that the boy will find among "companions of his own age," who without "the baggage of infancy" see each other freshly and,

> In a flash of insight looking in his eyes
> Know the depths of his being and love him instantly.[8]

The father's wish to heal the wounds of childhood with his grown son before he leaves home helps us understand the terror of the father caught in the storm at sea with his son, "scared to death" the boy might drown; the father becomes aware suddenly that his son is on his own before things have been worked out between them, and in fact they may never be worked out. The father may be drawn back to his own leavings as an adolescent and the ways he said goodbye to his father. So as "the loved son" leaves home, the father may reconnect with his yearnings to have been a loved son to his own father.

Consider now the dilemma of many men at midlife: They are stuck because they cannot evolve a new sense of meaning and purpose. Mr. Henderson speaks of feeling "left out or passed by, unnecessarily." Everyone else has something to do, some vision of the future that energizes them—becoming a social worker, going to college. Mr. Henderson seems to experience himself as worn out, just aging, useless, and being left behind now that no one needs him. That is in fact how the "empty nest" experience used to feel to many women. Could it stem in part from the reality that many successful men at midlife are so defined, by themselves and the others who depend on their success, that they truly are stuck in an identity that does not have room for an evolving sense of self? Mr. Henderson, as a partner in a powerful Wall Street law firm is viewed as a stable, successful member of that community. His partners look to him to bring in large fees and to attract new business to the firm. His secretaries and younger associates look to him for work. And his family has depended on him for years for their financial support. Now they may see him as "Dad," the person who works hard, who is successful, who does not talk about his feelings very much. What kind of changing is he going to do?

There is a crucial normal developmental task for men here. Feminists have argued that men have something to learn from women, having to do with the capacity for greater intimacy, empathy, a more caring and interdependent approach to life. Traditional research on adulthood supports that view. The healthy growth of men's personality in midlife and beyond is often described in terms of attributes that our society defines as "feminine." David Guttman writes about the normal shift in men from a preoccupation with agency and power through young adulthood to one at midlife centering on receptivity and nurturance. Erikson's middle stage of adulthood is described positively as the search for ways of becoming interpersonally "generative" rather than personally stagnant and isolated. The Yale psychologist Daniel Levinson reports from his studies of "the seasons of a man's life" that a struggle with the polarities of masculinity–femininity, among others, marks the midlife development of men. He remarks that transitions and change mark men's adult life because "no life structure can permit the living out of all aspects of the self."[9] Note what these theories imply: Men grow out of childhood and into adulthood not "whole" but rather with the sense of self organized around personal achievement and self-action in the world. The women's movement should thus be welcomed in that it offers a solution to a problem in men's lives: the shift at midlife to reclaim parts of self left behind or devalued in the rush to become a man.

Yet that isn't so. The empirical data on male aging, for example, is not reassuring, once we get away from those more "theoretical" or hopeful writings. One study found only one-third of its broad sample of normal men at midlife achieved what the investigators describe as a "transcendent-generative solution" of the midlife passage. Many men remain stuck in a shaky myth of their own power, alienated from the rest of themselves.[10]

While there certainly is resistance within men at midlife to changing or expanding their identities, a resistance we shall examine shortly, it is essential not to underestimate as well the powerful forces from work and family blocking change for men who may partly want to broaden their sense of self.

When I was interviewing men who changed careers at midlife,

one told me: "You know, when you want to make a big change in your life other people will cut down trees to stop you." At first I thought that was an oddly paranoid statement, but over the years its truth has become apparent. Other people depend on us to be ourselves, because their identities and needs are dependent on our being who we are. A man like Mr. Henderson would need to push back against the pressures, external as well as internal, keeping him so well-defined, in order to begin to develop new meanings and purposes that would energize his life and leave him feeling less "passed by." There is an old maxim that no one in the kingdom has less freedom than the king. Many of these successful *paterfamilias* men would probably agree, if they understood the extent of their entrapment.

To push against the familial forces keeping him trapped within his instrumental sense of self, a husband or father risks unleashing the rage he feels and family members feel toward him. The father may feel anger at what he sees as the ingratitude of his family—here he has been sacrificing so much over the years for them in his hard work, and they seem so ungrateful. The wife and children are all going off to what seem like new commitments, leaving him behind. There may be envy that fuels the husband's rage as he wishes he too could move on to an exciting new stage of life. The rage may spring as well from the father's disappointment in his family and the unfamiliar vulnerability he feels—he has given so much and it has come now just to this, his kids leaving and his wife becoming more independent. The rage, finally, may spring from the father's fear of his family. After years of appearing to control and dominate family life, he sees other family members becoming powerful and autonomous. What will they do? he may wonder. Will they seek revenge against "the King" or merely try to expose the nakedness of the Emperor by challenging his cherished beliefs and values? Often children's decisions about marriage or career that don't conform to the father's beliefs are subtle challenges to his power.

The family's rage toward father lies in the years of accommodation that they may have colluded in creating. When children are growing up, father is seen as the patriarch. Family members relate to him by trying to placate or manipulate or cajole him so as to avoid direct clashes with his power. The father may be a hated and feared figure as well as a beloved one. As the family reorganizes itself at midlife, the years of accommodation, having prevented everyone from finding safe ways to disagree directly with father, may fuel the rage that the wife and children feel. In some families in therapy the wife and teenage children often act as if they are serfs rising up against the powerful lord of the manor.

The rage that family members feel also may protect them against their underlying sadness, perhaps at leaving father behind. When the family rearranges itself, the wife and grown-up children may be looking toward the future—at the new career or love commitments that await—and it can be difficult for all involved to acknowledge their sadness about leaving, about the letting go of what was. It is often easier to feel angry than sad. That is true of both the wife's or children's sadness at becoming different from or leaving father behind and the father's sadness at seeing his family change.

In some families there is collusion between the wife and children to continue the deception that the father is "the force in everything." Speaking of this pattern of "protective denial," the sociologists Farrell and Rosenberg relate it partly to the family's anger at and fear of the father:

> As the wife moves toward increased autonomy, she often does so in a delicately balanced climate of deception. Mother and children often form secret alliances—deceiving, laughing about, and simultaneously protecting the husband. The wife recognizes the husband's efforts at maintaining the image of himself as the patriarch. She seeks to avoid confrontations that might undermine his belief in being in control of the family and having their support and respect. . . . The couples seem more intent on not hurting or on protecting each other than sharing experiences.

The husband is thus denied an opportunity to come to terms with his own life. That seems one price of the pattern of paternal intimacy.

> This sort of truce is utilized partially to control the anger felt toward the man by his wife and children. No longer fearful of him, as they often reported themselves to be earlier in the family's history, the accumulated resentment can become an explosive force in the family. It is expressed through jokes among the children, half-whispered asides, and an awareness that "the old man" no longer has the emotional strength to stifle them. This very weakness evokes a sense of disdain, but also of pity.[11]

And what are the consequences in such a family? The disdain for father as he ages sets the stage for the son's terror of male vulnerability. The wounded father is passed on from generation to generation in the fear that underneath the brittle strength of father lies a secret weakness.

The Family as Mother

There is, finally, another kind of loss husbands struggle with when their wives go to work: the rearrangement of the family may touch on separation issues with mother, evoking earlier points in the life cycle when boys had to let go of the caring that mother provided, perhaps before they were ready.

Let's return to Mr. Henderson for an illustration, as he first expresses puzzlement about the undercurrent of sadness in him:

"Shit, I can't believe I'm saying this—a proud, white liberal Democrat. *I'm just not comfortable with this relationship as equals.* I do believe intellectually in what she's done, and I'm proud of it. I like the paycheck she brings home. I think she's happier and productive, I just had no idea what the effect on me would be." With a shy smile, as if cornered, he acknowledges his depression and anger. "I'm 10 pounds heavier this year, and angry about it. I used to run a great deal, but I've stopped doing that. I just don't have the motivation to do it. I feel I provoke most of the arguments at home these days. I'm the one who is unhappy, more frustrated, making demands." His eyebrows arch questioningly again as he returns to his wife: "Betty's happy, the kids are happy."

He speaks like many men his age who tend to group the kids and wife as one unit, himself another, separate. Farrell and Rosenberg noticed that too:

> [T]he most common family constellation is one in which the wife is the central point in the communication network of the family. We repeatedly hear that both the children and the husband see her as the one who "understands them" and who listens to their central concerns. She is perceived as the primary source of warmth and support in the family unit. Her position also gives her an opportunity to form coalitions with the children.[12]

The husband is indeed often on the periphery; the wife becomes Mother to more than her children.

Clearly, Mr. Henderson feels lonelier in the home now. He spoke earlier of feeling "a little left out or passed by, unnecessarily." When he speaks of being "10 pounds heavier," noting that "I used to run last year, but I stopped," he sounds—like many men at midlife with signs of depression—in the midst of a grief reaction, struggling with a sense of loss.

The strongest feeling Mr. Henderson showed all afternoon occurred when he said that his wife's working leaves him feeling "neglected," a word that implies purposeful harm or inattention. He knows his wife isn't purposely hurting him. His goodwill is clear, and so is hers: The marriage counts to both of them. The sense of neglect stems from a more unconscious, deeper sense of something painful being done to him by his wife's absence. So he speaks of being "left out" of his family's attention, *unnecessarily*. He is expressing the sense of *separation as punishment*, the confused feeling of something harmful or punishing being done to him when his wife's attention shifts off him, when she becomes more autonomous and independent.

As Mr. Henderson and I talk, the afternoon sun moves low in the sky. The artificial fire in his office fireplace casts a warm glow against the gray day beyond the windows. He sits with elbows on his knees, his tailored suit rumpled. He hardly notices, deep in concentration, remembering something, pondering it. Then he slowly makes an important association. He comes closer to his truth at age forty:

"My mother died when I was young. Cancer, quite suddenly. Or it seemed all very sudden. Perhaps I'm oversensitive to these things, to my wife going to work, to the house seeming so lonely and empty. I'm sensitive to loss. I want my wife around."

He associates his wife's going to work with the death of his mother. A time when the warmth and light went out of his life, leaving him feeling lonely and abandoned. Not that he treats his wife like his mother—he is a competent, decisive man, able to help his wife move ahead in her life. It is rather that the experience of a strong wife, with interests of her own and a separate identity, evokes feelings associated with loss, abandonment, having someone important leave. For many men our adult families come to substitute for mother, and we look to our wives for what we had to give up in separating from her. Lacking a rich sense of father as an emotional presence in the family, often carrying around instead a memory of father "babied" at home, men wind up in a position similar to their own fathers' even as they strive to be different.

The British psychoanalyst Elliot Jacques reminds us that the life changes of midlife return many people to what he calls "the infantile depressive position," when the world depended on Mother.[13] Given the pressure boys feel to detach from women and identify with their fathers or—if fathers themselves are too "wounded"— with a father-surrogate, I suspect there is considerable grief and loss associated with letting go of mother as a child and home as a late adolescent, before being ready to leave being cared for and to become an "adult." There are few words in English with as much emotional resonance as "home." When E.T. eagerly says "going home, going home" in his scrappy little voice, he is touching the deepest longings of the adults in the audience as well.

When some men make the young adult transition out of their families or origin, wives and families become the repository of home-ness, of mother-ness. Traditionally the route was to marry a helpmeet who would provide a "haven in a heartless world" while the husband worked his way through medical or graduate school, or up the corporate ladder. Like Mr. Henderson, many men remember the early years of marriage fondly as a time when the focus was on the husband and his needs. The young husband has the best of both worlds: being treated as a child at home while creating and propagating to his family the myth that he is independent and "the force." The family, where he could regress and be taken care of, becomes the benevolent Mom, always providing the reassurance that he is the hardworking, achieving man.

Acting It Out: How Men Resist
Their Wives' Push for Autonomy

A wife's going to work may be experienced in terms of the husband's earlier experience of mother. Was the separation from her experienced as a *rejection* by mother, an angry or *punishing* act? As an *unavoidable loss* that had to be accepted with resignation? As a *relief*, sparing the boy the feeling of being smothered by this mother he so needs? The husband's response to his wife's bid for autonomy will be colored by that earlier separation experience.

In most cases the man will be put back in touch with his childlike yearning for his mother and his shame and rage at the wish to be "babied" and taken care of by her. That is how a wife's going to work reewakens the wounded father within our hearts. A man may feel determined to avoid the passive dependency his father displayed in the family or may try to live up to the rugged ideal of a father who seemed never really to "need" his wife. In either case the man is put back in touch with wishes that leave him feeling a sense of danger—we might be abandoned or deprived again. Since many of us can't talk of our sense of loss and betrayal, we act it out.

An ex-Army officer, for example, told me in glowing terms about how close his family was, how important it was to him to be a good, available father, and how supportive his wife was to him as he faced some key business decisions. We sat alone in the living room of his elegant New York townhouse one winter afternoon, surrounded by the evidence of a warm family atmosphere. He insisted on getting out scrapbooks so I could see pictures, proudly telling moving little stories about each person. I would have recommended this man for the pulpit, he seemed so gentle and caring, settled into a mutually supportive relationship with his wife.

Yet she, some time later and also alone, spoke haltingly about her carpentry work, which he hadn't even mentioned, and about his angry response to that increasingly important part of her life. Her hobby since college had been woodworking, and she was trying to turn it into profitable part-time work, with some success. But her husband erupted whenever he came home from the office and found her at work in the basement. He called her work terrible and said no one would ever buy it, and she ought to be ashamed of herself for wasting her time and other people's money on her products. She isn't sure, she says wearily, if perhaps he isn't right and she should stop.

When a wife goes off to work, some men will feel betrayed by her, others abandoned; some feel like failures themselves, others will feel intrigued and curious. Men may respond to their changing families in several different ways:

1. Rage and anger, a threatening posture either subtle or explosive to enforce the *status quo*, like the ex-Army officer/minister

2. A sad or passive-manipulative posture, exemplified at times by Mr. Henderson's struggle

3. Curiosity and eagerness, seeing an opportunity for mastery and growth, which Mr. Henderson also exemplifies

4. Avoidance, by retreating into work or by defining the changing family as "my wife's problem"

5. Becoming overly instrumental at home, trying to solve the "wife's problem" and thus subtly to undercut her autonomy

In fact most men adopt combinations of those approaches, intertwining an openness to change with a resistance to it. Let's examine two instances where husbands are dealing with a wife's push for autonomy within the marriage. Each illustrates how men act out their anger at their wives; in the first case within the marriage and in the second, by fleeing to work and avoiding the wounded father in his own childhood.

The Man Who Insulated His Wife's Study

A middle-aged couple is sitting in my office, having come to see me for counseling. The wife is a perky woman in her forties, her auburn hair arranged in a neat bun. She is back getting a master's degree in education. Her husband is the owner and president of an executive placement agency. Their youngest son has begun college this fall, leaving the house empty of children for the first time in more than twenty years. With the intent of celebration and a sense of drama, husband and wife both took time off to fly with him to his college in California.

They dropped their son off, getting him set up in his new home in the freshman dorm. On the flight home she chatted eagerly of the new semester about to begin in her graduate school. She felt the trip home was a monologue:

"All the way back to Boston my husband moped and seemed withdrawn, and we really couldn't talk. I pressed him, but he just said that he felt sad and didn't know why. It bothered me that he was so down, because I felt ecstatic. Here was our last son set up in college, childcare was done! Now I could do what I'd wanted to for quite a while: concentrate on graduate school."

Graduate school was a big step for her. She was nervous about leaving her house during most days of the week. She most of all wanted to get the house organized and clean before beginning classes.

So what does her husband do? He begins an enormous, dusty home project in their town house: to insulate the walls and ceilings of her study for the winter. The walls come down, tools everywhere, dirt eagerly infiltrating the entire house. He pooh-poohs her when she suggests she'd rather he didn't go to all the effort, and here she is trying to clean up. Soon she becomes overwhelmed by the mess and loses hope of having things neat and orderly before her classes begin the next week. She hasn't wanted really to interrupt him, because maybe the project would make him feel better. But the mess is driving her crazy, the dust settles faster than she can clean, and soon the whole thing is making her feel more and more angry.

She tells him they have to talk, and one weekend afternoon in the fall they sit down.

"This house is driving me crazy, you're always working on this project, not talking to me very much, but I think you're upset and I think a lot of it has to do with my starting classes and Davey's going off to college."

"No, no, there's nothing wrong with any of that—it's all set, right, you are going?"

"I mean," she replied insistently, "your *feelings* about my going to work, and all the kids gone."

"Oh. Well, I just want you warm for the winter. It's going to be cold, and when I think of how cold the house gets," he laughs, "you sitting here studying and shivering. Honey, I just want to keep you warm for the winter."

A gleam suddenly appears in the wife's eye.

"Well, dear, how about you? Are you feeling it's getting colder at home these days?" she asks archly. He was feeling cold and was trying to keep his wife warm.

As he talks about his feelings, a picture begins to emerge of his obsession to insulate her study. The youngest son was becoming an adult, making the father feel older and more obsolete. Ironically that son, very close to his father, had talked on the ride down to college about eventually going to graduate school in business and becoming an executive like his Dad, which only reinforced the father's sense of rapidly being superannuated, the younger generation nipping at his heels. To add to the outdated feeling, his wife seemed to be leaving him too, taking on a new role, starting a new life without him.

"I feel stuck," he tells her mournfully, "everyone is out doing all these things, and *I'm just plodding along, treading water by myself.*"

Here again is evidence of how stuck the husband is within the traditional arrangements of sex-roles. Since he has been the breadwinner all these years with his wife at the center of the family, his reconciliation with his children, the process of letting go of them, is blocked. It is that much harder for him to acknowledge to himself or his family that he is feeling the need for new directions. He has never learned how to pay attention to his needs and feelings, much less put them into words for his wife and kids. He depends on his wife for that. Sitting and thinking about the therapeutic task ahead of the three of us in couples therapy, I become aware of an irony: It is his wife who has arranged for him to come here, a place where we may begin to talk about feelings. That makes it still part of her agenda, not his.

"But what about the insulation project?" his wife asks impatiently.

"Well, do I have to spell it out?" he complains in an exasperated tone. "It's felt to me all year as if I'm losing all the warmth in my life, the kids gone, the house empty, and now you off to school."

"So your impulse was to keep *me* physically warm in my study, when *you're* the one feeling cold and lost? That makes me so sad to hear. All these weeks, instead of caring about you I've just gotten madder and madder." She laughs. "You haven't gotten any warmth back from me, just heat."

Though looking uninvolved, disconnected, and private, *his* desire to insulate *her* study was an attempt to deal with the relationship losses he was feeling. It was a symbolic effort to heal a loss nonverbally. It expressed his anger at his wife's starting school and an unconscious attempt to stop her by disrupting the house and complicating the transition ("I'll make such a mess that you'll never get organized"). It expressed the penance of someone who fantasizes he has to make up for a personal failing ("I'll make things better, now will you stay?")—again, that male equation of women's autonomy with punishment. And the insulated study offered the symbolic hope of retaining the warmth and love in his life.

This example is but one of many in which a man becomes instrumental and attempts to take care of a woman when her actions have actually left him feeling secretly in need of her care. Many observers have noted that men are most capable of intimacy through strength. Being powerful, in control, "the force in everything," we learn, is the way to be close to others, particularly women. When others shift their attention, the bond of intimacy, it is not surprising that some men will associate that with the failure of their efforts. At some deeper level of fantasy it is as if the wife is going to work, going off, because the husband is not good enough. Such feelings may be the residue of the earlier separation struggle boys experience with mother, in which their detaching from mother and identification with an instrumentally strong father are unconsciously experienced as the result of something wrong with themselves. If the little boy had been good enough, he may feel, he could have stayed embedded in the female world.[14]

When we decode the actions, the message the husband was signaling by his efforts becomes clear: "I need to keep the warmth in my life, and you—my wife—are it." His busy, seemingly detached project beat out an SOS as if in a Morse code of the heart.

In this case the husband and wife were able to bring into focus the fact that both of them were experiencing a changed family world and that new patterns of caretaking and support within the marriage were necessary. Shortly we shall consider various ways the couple in a changing marriage can adopt new patterns. First, though, let's consider a case in which the couple has greater difficulty acknowledging the changed circumstances of their marriage, now that the wife has gone to work and the children are almost "launched."

Mr. Alvarez: The Need to Tame a Wife

One way for men at midlife to become emotionally impoverished is to locate their own emotional struggles in others, often wives or children, rather than within themselves. Men may attempt to avoid the feelings created by changes within their families by working harder at their careers.

Mr. Alvarez, a high-tech executive in Silicon Valley outside San Francisco, at age forty-two faces a commonplace struggle with his wife, which he can see only in terms of their separateness and her neediness. They have been married about fifteen years and have two children just entering adolescence. He sees himself now as a "person on the way up." Trained as an engineer, he is on the verge of moving to a position of greater responsibility and independence either in his present company or with a competitor. He has been in his present position for several years, during which he has resolved a number of tricky production problems in his company. His division is now running smoothly, and he is looking forward to the new challenges that an anticipated promotion will bring. He also wants his wife to have another child, and that is where trouble has surfaced in the marriage.

Through young adulthood this man has been pointed toward career success. He married a woman whose readiness to take care of the home and take responsibility for childcare promised to contribute to that success. He mentions a fair amount of self-questioning after leaving home for college and remembers a strong desire to marry. He married within a year of graduation on the rebound from a broken relationship that had left him "very upset." He describes his bride as a "strong, attractive woman." Yet the roles in the family were clear. With pride this man says, "I've always been the leader and she the follower." Despite that heroic portrayal of himself, he depended on the family as a stable, friendly, known entity from which to confront the confusing ambiguities of the postcollege world, particularly while starting a demanding career in business.

The couple had children quickly, and he took a position in San Francisco with a multinational corporation. At home he is the boss, and the discipline is strict. He says, "I get mad and shout when things don't go the way I want." He values family life and doesn't like anything to disrupt it.

That arrangement worked well through young adulthood, but over the last few years, he acknowledges, he and his wife have been "fighting more openly." He says, "I'm worried about my marriage, it is more hostile than in the past." His wife doesn't want another child, although he strongly does, and he is confused by her unwillingness. She wants to find a job, which confuses him too, because "we don't need the money, my salary is more than adequate." His wish for more children, doubtless coming from many sources, seems to spring partly from a hope to maintain the *status quo*.

As he talks of the future, he keeps returning to the worry about what his wife will do now that the kids are approaching the teens and seem so independent: "They're very mature, it's almost as if they were twenty years old." He suffers the fate of the person who must control everyone around him: The mirrors he creates are unsatisfying; the routines he creates become a prison. Not only does he identify their marital distress as solely his wife's problem, he also perceives his solution—for her to have another child—as the only one of choice. He feels "bored" in the marriage and says that "the problem is that she doesn't want to change." Yet the changes he wants from her are *his* changes: The main problem he stresses is that she seems not to be in favor of his continued advancement in his career. The position he is in line for involves considerable travel and time away from home. She is not in favor of his taking on such duties. "She gets afraid from my job changes," he says. Her side of it is that because he is around so little she has little time or support from him to pursue anything out of the house. When I asked how they deal with this, he replied, "I soothe her."

Mr. Alvarez presents a picture of conflicting directions of growth for husband and wife. He constructs work and family in this way: Career is primary, and family is a support or adjunct for him in his advancement at work. The wife, in his mind, has no separate existence, no legitimate demands of her own to make. He seems uninvested in helping his wife change. He reports feeling concerned, but says that their current difficulties have "all worked out before," implying that real changes are not necessary.

Clearly, his portrayal of his wife as "scared of change" smacks of inaccuracy and projection: He also had trouble with the last large transition, from home to college, using marriage as a means of coping with the new demands young adulthood brought by setting up a new, transitional home different from, yet like, his parents' home. Most of his success and advancement have been at work within the context of a stable family. It's not a huge leap to wonder if Mr. Alvarez may be having some unconscious difficulty himself with the empty nest transition.

His parents' relationship seemed to have prepared him poorly for this phase of life, with little evidence of negotiation within their marriage. He remembers his father as "very dependent," while "my mother did all the housework. . . . She always complained to us about my father." Nor did he seem able to ask about his father's side of the story: "My father and I left one another alone." Mr. Alvarez is without an image of an engaged and vital father, able to cope with family transitions and change. That may help us understand better why, during his own family rearrangement, Mr. Alvarez seems more comfortable focusing on his ambitions and plans at work while ignoring how his wife is changing, preferring that she change only in the ways that fit his needs and plans.

The sense of himself as the Man In Charge must be much more comfortable than any similarites to the Needy Father he knew as a child. If his wife is scared and needy and wants protection, that is certainly preferable to *his* feeling that way, even if it means not seeing that both he and his wife are changing, facing a new reality as the primary commitments of young adulthood are waning. *Both* spouses need to find new meanings and purposes to move into the future; both probably feel some combination of eagerness and trepidation over the work–family balance in their lives; both face the challenge of reassessing the past, of sorting out what was important that will be left behind. Both need to assert confidence and to nurture their self-esteem as they let go of their children and assess their roles as parents and caretakers. If he is unable to address the situation with his wife, a husband pays a price, as does his wife: a hostile, frustrating marriage, and becoming too work-centered and isolated himself.

When we last spoke, Mr. Alvarez was eager to tell me about his new plans to set up a computer franchise separate from his executive responsibilities in a different company. The changing family environment seemed to be hardly on his mind, even while the tension in the marriage had yet to be resolved.

Men in these traditional family environments often seem intent on "taming" their wives, keeping them under control. The women seem to represent an indispensable but potentially uncontrollable element in their lives. I wonder if men's need to keep their wives under control lies rooted in their earlier needs to "tame" their mothers. Consider Mr. Alvarez's devalued image of his father: His mother complained to her son about him, she was subtly in charge, and Mr. Alvarez distances himself from his father, an enigma he couldn't solve. Yet the old man has that "wounded quality" in this memory, as if to the young Mr. Alvarez the family became the place where strong men become weak. So we can see why he would distance himself, retreat to an instrumental role, at the first sign of his own neediness—"weakness" vis-à-vis his wife; she must remain the weak one to reassure him. It's as if his mother was too powerful; in a subtle, unarticulated way, she threatened the boy's vision of masculinity. Perhaps he is now controlling his wife in the same way he came to deal with mother: getting his needs met in a surreptitious manner, in a way that allows him to look strong while being taken care of.

For such men, who experienced mother as intrusive yet indispensable, the empty nest experience in midlife replicates that childhood dilemma: How do you hold onto someone you desperately need without becoming overwhelmed by them? While that male struggle is revealed most clearly when the family rearranges itself at midlife and the husband is threatened with the resulting losses, many men experience such a tension throughout any intimate relationship.[15] The tendency to become instrumental and distant in times of need haunts men throughout family life, since a man may lose his wife (albeit temporarily) many times—for example, upon the arrival of children as she becomes preoccupied with mothering, or during fertility problems, as she becomes centered on her own pain and sense of loss.

Helping the Husband in the Empty Nest

The wife may be in a better position than her husband to recognize that her working profoundly affects him. She may become so involved in the demands of doing her job that she forgets her impact on her husband. Yet both spouses need to pay attention to the husband's irrational yet real neediness and anxiety about his wife. For example, the thirty-two-year-old Southern journalist who told me about the "regressive effects of my business trips" on her husband described how preoccupied she'd become with packing and preparing for her frequent trips, so that she paid little attention to her husband several days before she left. "It was very hard for him to say he wanted time with me then—that he felt left out." The wife found that if she could identify what was happening and point it out to her husband, they could talk over their mutual needs more directly. "If I verbalize it we can talk about it, but if I don't, often nothing happens, he can't talk about it, it feels too immature."

The problem with the wife's taking too much responsibility for drawing out the husband, encouraging him to talk, is that she is put in the position of taking care of him again and may feel, as one wife confessed to me, "as if I'm doing the work for two people in our relationship." If there is too much asymmetry in the relationship, with the wife doing all the emotional work and not feeling cared about enough, she will feel resentful. So while my comments focus on the husband's experience, we must remember that the couple needs to find ways for the wife to feel taken care of as well, and for the husband to take responsibility for expressing clearly, not manipulatively, what his needs are during a time of family change.

It is often helpful for the couple to talk about the man's irrational fears, which are often fears about his wife (perhaps in working she will find him less attractive than men she will meet in the workplace, or maybe she won't be able to take care of herself on business trips and "something will happen to her"). For many men it is very hard to talk of the fear of losing their wives when they become more autonomous.

The couple should pay attention to the husband's sense of shame, often over experiencing uncomfortable feelings that seem out of control. That shame is related to men's belief that they must be strong, must have all the answers, and if they feel confused or needy it is someone's fault—either their own or their family's or the therapist's. Many men at this time are scared that their neediness will overwhelm them or their families if they let it out, so they feel it's better not to acknowledge it at all.

There is often anger that the couple hardly understands, and it can help to talk it through. Particularly in the early stages of the "second journey" of his life—the post–dependent children/working wife phase of his adulthood—the man may struggle with a sense of betrayal by his family. He may feel that he's worked so hard and gotten so little back. Their own anger may be frightening to many husbands.

Underneath their anger, though, lie a deep sadness and loneliness. Couples should remember that many men would rather fight than weep. Learning more about that sadness is often a necessary step to redefining a vision of oneself and moving on into the future with confidence.

Husbands and wives need to pay attention to the sense of loss and unfinished business the husband feels, often with his children: What are the tensions and conflicts he wishes were resolved now that time seems short? Some fathers need to do a lot of talking and sharing with their teenage sons and daughters at this time, not in the instrumental, authoritarian mode they may be most comfortable with, but rather by sharing their own confusion, their experiences with their children, how they faced and resolved life choices that their own children now confront. As Farrell and Rosenberg point out, "adolescent children and their middle-aged fathers confront similar identity issues. Their simultaneous attempts to confront these issues may exacerbate the difficulties of both, while also creating the possibility of mutual support."[16]

Similarly, the husband often needs to talk about his own father: How did he age, how did the old man deal with getting older, with a changing marriage over time? The man may find a yearning for more contact with his father or mother reawakened as he feels boyish at this time, or he may have great fears of aging into the negative image of his own father, becoming passive and dependent upon a powerful wife. Talking such wishes or fears through within the marriage may help the husband come to terms more maturely with those possibilities.

While husbands at midlife often see themselves as different from their wives and children, the irony is that they truly share a common bond with their families. Each is facing the task of redefining himself or herself in the world: The wife struggles with exploring new options, her feelings of insecurity in venturing beyond the confines of the mother role balanced by her curiosity about new possibilities that await her. The children are launched into college, confronting choice and possibility, identity, career, and intimacy questions. And in truth, those are some of the same questions that the father confronts anew at midlife: What balance of work and intimacy do I want? What are the central values and purposes that will fill this new stage of my life? How do I maintain my self-confidence and self-esteem through this time of change? The father himself, with or without the help of his family, may work to make himself more isolated or resistive. Yet the crucial task in most rearranging families is to see that *all* members really are going through a shared experience of self-exploration and change.

Vulnerability and Rage: What Not Being Able to Have Children Tells Us About All Men

A Silent Sorrow

One day soon after my son's first birthday I was on the phone talking to another father, hoping he'd provide me with provocative quotes for an article I was writing on becoming a father. He was a lawyer whom I had never met, having obtained his name through a friend. He told me forthrightly how he had experienced his son's childhood as a healing period. A Vietnam vet for whom the destruction and brutality of the war had been a painful experience, he took several years off to care for his son while his wife went to medical school.

We were having a cozy talk about being fathers, exchanging gossip and trading happy, familiar memories, when suddenly the man's words startled me:

"Before we adopted Adam, there was a particularly hard time in our marriage."

"Adopted?"

He chuckled. "Oh, I didn't mention that? Probably because it no longer matters—Adam is my son now, and that's that."

He went on to explain: "We tried to conceive for several years and never did. That was a very hard time. We wanted kids so badly, and Pat, my wife, never got pregnant. The doctors never did find out for sure what was wrong—whether it was her or me or what. All those tests, and they didn't find anything really clear-cut. There was a time we wished they'd find some medical problem already, so at least we'd know."

He laughed at the irony in his statement: the wish for a problem just to provide an answer.

I knew what he meant. Julie and I had experienced three miscarriages before the birth of our son. One out of every seven couples in this country are involuntarily childless; about one in five experience significant reproductive difficulties at some time in their lives.[1] We know a good deal about the turmoil women experience when couples are infertile but much less about men. For both spouses it is a time of considerable stress in the marriage, as well as personal emotional vulnerability.

Through the faceless telephone the lawyer and I chatted on about infertility, suddenly brought closer together by our bittersweet bond. Our shared experience made us part of what one husband referred to as the "secret underground of men who've gone through reproductive difficulties."

The last of our miscarriages was more than two years ago, yet I could still feel the desperation, loneliness, and powerlessness of those years. Few experiences have been as powerful and instructive to me. Although I didn't realize it at the time, the miscarriages were most directly responsible for the period of journal-keeping and introspection that began at the time; I needed time to sort out my own pain and confusion about the "reproductive difficulties" we were experiencing. I didn't see it that way at first, and for many months my journal was filled with work issues and memories of childhood, but then more feelings about the miscarriages started to appear. What strikes me now is how much I was centered on Julie and how difficult it was to sort out my own feelings, to accept them. Reproductive difficulties—infertility, miscarriage, abortion, stillbirth—catch men by surprise. They seem to happen to women only: One researcher has called men "phantom figures" in reproductive dramas.[2]

One obstacle to learning more about the male experience of infertility is the emotional withdrawal of men who experience fertility problems. Scientists and filmmakers often report that it is hard to find men who will talk about the experience. A recent dissertation by Dr. Tracy MacNab of Boston is a compendium of information on the subject, yet one comment not in the report sheds a special light on things. "Getting men to talk to me about this subject was difficult and demoralizing," he writes in a private moment. There was such resistance.

MacNab explains more in the dissertation. He provides an elaborate description of his search for men. His review of the literature had led him to conclude that "most of the statements we have about men and infertility are inferences, assumptions or myths."[3] Thus he wanted to interview directly men who had experienced infertility. He sent letters to people known to him through friends and colleagues describing his research, his personal interest in the subject, in a reassuring manner and asking for referrals, then sent a follow-up letter. At the same time he contacted numerous gynecologists, urologists, endocrinologists, fertility clinics, general medical practices, and university health services, as well as Resolve, the national organization for infertile couples. He responded scrupulously to concerns about anonymity, providing assurances of good intentions. Overall he distributed over four hundred questionnaires in this manner and one hundred more through his personal network.

The outcome? You would think he was distributing typhoid. "Three months after all of the above stages had been accomplished, fifteen of the initial questionnaires had been returned."[4] Clearly something was making men reluctant to come forward and talk about their experience. MacNab's comments here are as important as any of his statistical findings: "The medical clinics explained that their average male infertility patient did not return for a second appointment, often avoiding even the simplest evaluative procedure. [A] urologist stated that the men who he dealt with were usually so devastated that they could not talk about what the experience meant to them."[5]

Why? What lies behind that emotional withdrawal of men? Many factors are clearly at work: emotional isolation, shattered dreams, a sense of failure, and a challenge to self-esteem.

The lawyer I talked with on the phone spoke of familiar feelings:

"All you try to do to create life is suddenly beyond your control.

There is a sense of futility experienced for a long time." Having children expressed a new kind of creativity; not being able to conceive affected his view of himself and blocked the development of a self he valued. He went on to explain:

"Infertility means coming to grips with disappointment. In our early thirties, our work developed, my wife and I, we had a big success orientation. There is a self-centeredness of life when children are not involved." He spoke of his hopes attached to the unborn child, of a new evolving self. Looking back, "from a personal standpoint things seem empty in life before parenthood."

For the husband a terminated pregnancy is a loss, and it makes the relationship with his wife stormier. It poses a challenge to the marriage and causes psychic stress for both spouses. Reproductive problems may plunge a man into experiences of helplessness, powerlessness, and rage that he hardly anticipates or understands. As with most family events, the man experiences the change in his marriage within a context of loneliness and isolation. Finally, the experience of infertility informs us about the experience of growing up male. From it we can learn how violence and love become intertwined for men.

As with all family crises for men, we are back to the unfinished business with fathers and mothers. The man's experience of his father as distant and remote from the affective experience of the family or as having been overwhelmed by it provides the grown son with little reassurance that he can understand and explore his own complicated feelings during such experiences as infertility. The tendency is to stay outside the pregnancy event, as father stayed outside the "woman's world" of reproduction and pregnancy. Our tendency to retreat to an emotionally remote, instrumental stance haunts us when we try to reduce the isolation we feel and get support, particularly from other men.

The changed marriage and volatile mix of love and anger we feel at our wives during this time propel many men back to unfinished business with mother, too. As a man struggles with his neediness and his wife's struggles to maintain herself during the crisis of infertility, he reenacts some of the ways in which he dealt with the demand placed on him as a child to grow up and separate from mother. As the changing family of midlife brings many husbands back to a sense of losing mothers, so too does the experience of relationship crisis during infertility and pregnancy.

Only after the birth of my son did I realize how angry and guilty I had felt after each of the miscarriages. Actually all three blurred together, melding into one long period of grief and loss, like an out-of-control canoe ride through white-water rapids that lasts thirty seconds but is remembered as taking at least three hours. How hard I worked to "save" our baby by taking care of my wife, as if in some magical way I could prevent with my own strength, my own protectiveness, the miscarriages from happening.[6] How little I knew afterward about taking care of myself, how easy it was to say "My wife is very upset" in a hushed, knowing tone, but how hard it was to know, or say, what I was feeling.

Yet the miscarriages ultimately were a healing event, helping me to come to terms with my rage and vulnerability. They helped me make some decisions about my work and love life that I may not have made if the crises had never happened. The miscarriage and fertility issues my wife and I experienced slowly helped me re-evaluate the kind of work I do, why I do it, the role of intimacy and competitive issues in my life, and how I relate to women (my wife in particular).

With the help of my wife, the miscarriages opened up a very reflective and extremely productive period of my life. Yet I am still astonished how much conflict went on within me, kept in silence during those years. The musing of one man stands for many men: "I wonder if I threw myself into my work to hide my feelings about infertility."

In this chapter I shall draw more fully on my own journal material and tie it together with the increasing research that has begun to appear on the infertility experience of men.

A Cocoon Threatened

The day of our first miscarriage, Julie was five weeks pregnant and everything seemed fine. All my life my biggest fear about sex had been of getting someone pregnant. Now that we had decided on it and were pregnant, as far as I knew, nature would just take its course: Nine months later, out popped the kid. Wrong.

At the office one day, busily at work on my research, I got a call from my wife, usually so confident and strong, now in tears.

"I've been spotting all morning. The doctor says I may be miscarrying, and I'm going over to his office."

No time to talk about the bleeding. I hopped on a crosstown bus to join her at our clinic. As I stared out the window, I suddenly felt lonely. My frantic mental efforts to test the sturdiness of my fantasied cocoon of invulnerability and good luck ("nothing *really* bad ever happens to me") were stymied by my fear that the cocoon had finally, at age thirty-three, slipped away. Years later I would be struck by a conclusion from a study of men's adaptation to infertility: "Men who have experienced infertility have lost the secure and reassuring sense of statistical normality."[7] The city bus crawled across town, the driver seemingly determined to take last in a snail race. Sitting there I wondered, "What the hell *is* a miscarriage?" I hadn't yet learned that one in five pregnancies end in a miscarriage, the premature delivery of a fetus before it can survive on its own. Since the odds of reproductive difficulties increase with age, that is a familiar problem to those in their thirties who delay parenting until the biological clock nears midnight, then find themselves plunged into a shadowy world dominated by the question of whether they'll be able to have kids. "From the 1960s generation to the Clomid generation," a friend sighed at a Christmas cocktail party that year, as a group of us (the "underground connection") sat talking about fertility drugs with the same fervor that twenty years before had been devoted to a different kind of drug. The infertility rate among women aged 35–39 is 24.6 percent, according to the National Center for Health Statistics, almost double the 13.6 percent rate of women aged 30–34.[8] At age twenty the percentage of pregnancies ending in miscarriage is only about 12 percent, according to one authority, and by age forty the figure has increased to over 30 percent.[9]

The Wounded Husband

The doctor was examining Julie when I arrived. As I walked into the room he was removing a surgical glove streaked with red. Our attempts to make life suddenly seemed to be mixed up with blood and violence. I sat in the corner behind my wife, who was stretched out on the examining table, partly covered with a sheet.

She smiled at me through teary eyes as I took her hand. The doctor looked thoughtful, and we waited for his verdict:

"Well, at this point we don't know, we can't tell whether you are miscarrying or not."

"Don't know," we echoed incredulously.

"The cervix is closed, which is a good sign, the bleeding has stopped, and the fetus may be fine. We just can't say yet."

In reproductive problems there is rarely a definitive diagnosis, which adds to the anxiety and sense of being out of control. Not being able to experience any bodily signals himself, since the theater of this drama is his wife's body, the husband will often become all the more focused on her body. What's going on there? What are you feeling? He may become dependent on her for reassurance, which is hard for him to ask for because he (and usually she too) looks to *him* to be strong.

In truth there is a delicate task here for both partners in the marriage: Each needs to be able to be needy and dependent *and* to be strong for the other. The dilemma for the man is that he often gets messages to be strong or to take care of his wife when he himself feels a nameless anxiety and doesn't know what questions to ask about this foreign, feminine world inhabited by women (his wife, nurses, other mothers) or strong men (the doctors, who always act in control).

One of the most difficult tasks I faced—and I have heard about this from numerous men—throughout the period of miscarriages and indeed during successful pregnancy was to take seriously my need for reassurance, to find ways to ask my silly questions, usually rooted in a deep need, to tolerate my intolerable fear of seeming foolish, silly, or out of control emotionally. It often felt easier to compete with the medical staff in acting instrumental and controlled. "Okay, now, what's to be done? Medication, humph, humph." Husbands really do have a split allegiance: emotionally connected with the wife and fetus, with all the feelings engendered, but also asked (not inappropriately) to be strong and able to mediate between physicians and wives, who are usually presumed to be too emotionally involved. Is one allied as a feeling participant with wife or as the in-control caregiver with medical staff? The husband is often expected to be there for his wife. So little is known about the man's experience of failed or successful pregnancy that he receives hardly any encouragement to be vulnerable and to deal with his fear, rage, and sadness, unless one counts the fervent encouragement from childbirth instructors or nurses (women, note) to "be sure to ask whatever questions you have to!"

I ultimately came to see that the division of our marriage into me as the Strong/Controlled/Protector-Defender and Julie as the Weepy/Emotional/Expressive Partner (the pregnant one) didn't wash. I often overreacted, becoming too competitive with or distrustful of the doctors or caught up in my identification with the fetus, while Julie was able to see things more clearly. One of the things I learned was that I could let go and experience my feelings of sadness and vulnerability while Julie could be there for me, just as I could be for her.

The husband will experience both internal pressure and social expectations that lead him to assume an armored, emotionally isolated posture. Dr. MacNab, who has interviewed numbers of men struggling with infertility, writes, with some irony, that "traditional gender roles are alive and well in our society." He advises that "it may be very useful for men to be able to support their wives without themselves becoming overwhelmed by the emotional aspects of infertility (at least in the early stages)," yet he goes on to note his finding that "men report feeling trapped inside this image of invulnerability."[10] MacNab notes that men's attempt to live up to the expectation that they will face any situation without complaining or requiring support for themselves may serve initially to preserve the husband's sense of hope and maintain the energy necessary to continue with life tasks through the disappointment of infertility. In the long run, however, that psychological mechanism becomes dysfunctional to men's wellbeing: They become socially isolated, often growing distant from their wives. Medical problems of the husband that may underlie the infertility may be left to stagnate, and often the husband finds no community of peers with whom to discuss his experience. Men's self-protective emotional withdrawal, MacNab concludes, "in some cases . . . even leads them to avoid the very medical procedures that might more accurately diagnose and treat the problem. The price of loyalty to this role is a large one."[11]

For some couples struggling with infertility a pattern of protective denial occurs in which the wife continues to assume that she has the problem even after the husband has been found to be sterile. In his discussion of couples' response to infertility, Schecter indicates that in such cases the wife is often protecting a fragile husband:

> [The wives] intuitively felt that such a deficiency would be seen by husbands as severely affecting their masculine ego and so . . . were willing to assume the defect. The acute sensitivity of these women to potential narcissistic hurts in their husbands often led to delays in requests for adoption of a child. So many women . . . feel definitively that they have a number of children plus one (their husband) to care for—and their reality-testing frequently is extremely accurate.[12]

As he finished the examination, our doctor was encouraging. "Let's keep our fingers crossed and hope for the best. I'm going to schedule another checkup for you in a few weeks." He was sympathetic. "There really is nothing more to be done now."

So we took our hopes and went home.

Miscarriage as Loss

A counselor has noted that "people may dismiss grief over the loss of a fetus because they assume not much has been invested in it. . . . But attachment to an infant begins long before birth."[13] To a man the fetus may represent a future hope, an unarticulated but nonetheless real vision of himself as a father. I did not at the time formulate this in words, but the baby represented a vision of myself as lifegiver and caregiver, a different kind of working in which I would be less tied to the rewards of the public world and more centered in the private world of family. In this world a more caring, centered self could evolve. That is one kind of loss—a loss of a vision of self—men struggle with during reproductive difficulties. As the articulate lawyer told me over the telephone, "work seemed emptier, less important after I realized that I wanted a baby." Dr. MacNab has noted the frustrated "wish for children [that] has real roots in the development of male identity." As a counselor of men experiencing fertility problems, he advises that "we need to allow men to take account of and responsibility for these important wishes."[14]

The husband often has formed a real attachment to the fetus and may become understandably lost in his own fantasies about the fetus. We picture it kicking, moving, alive, and familiar to us even before birth. With modern technology many expectant parents do see and hear their babies in the womb. Ultrasound, a kind of miniature television, now provides *in utero* moving pictures of the baby. One man, reflecting on the "very sad year" of his son's stillbirth, wrote: "[A]t this same hospital [where the stillbirth occurred], with the same equipment, a few days before Christmas, we had watched with mingled awe and pride as the screen showed a constantly moving black and white pattern in which (with the doctor's guidance), we had been able to clearly see our four-month-old son's well-developed body: legs jerking, arms moving, heart pulsating with steady regularity. Tonight, as we watched stupified, there was no pattern, no picture, simply an empty screen."

And, too, we may overidentify with the fetus, projecting our own vulnerability onto it, thereby intensifying the sense of loss and grief attending a miscarriage. The hormone progesterone secures the implantation of the fetus to the uterine wall; there was some question whether low progesterone function early in the pregnancy was the reason for our miscarriages. During those long weeks of not knowing during each miscarriage, I could picture the fetus only a few prenatal weeks old clinging to Julie's uterus with tenacious progesterone fingers. I mobilized all my energies to save them, to turn back death: Surely if I did everything around the house, and got Julie to spend hours in bed, and took care of her, surely they would survive. Looking back, it seems to me that some of that expressed my own sense of fragility and loneliness in the world, my terror of the void, of separation. Males grow up seeing women as the wet, moist source of life. Boys must renounce mother psychologically at a relatively early age in our culture. Men carry around an unfinished sense of vulnerability and loneliness from their childhood struggle to show their independence from mother even as they yearned to stay longer in her warm presence. There are many life events that trigger a sense of Mother Leaving, and that can tap the special rage and sadness, the particular male vulnerability about separation. Miscarriages, abortions, and still-births are cogent examples.

The Husband's Anxiety: Doing Penance

Well, we did as our doctor advised. We hoped for the best, but it didn't matter. Seven weeks later Julie bled again, and an ultrasound X-ray revealed the fetus had indeed miscarried. In fact, it had stopped developing by the fifth week.

So we were plunged into the medical world of tests, machinery, and the human body made manifest. My healthy, strong wife was poked, prodded, examined, and X-rayed. Here is a terrible kind of powerlessness for men: watching or hearing about medical tests, examinations, all invasions of your wife's body.

When there are infertility problems men are asked to experience their wives' bodies in a way different perhaps from any previous way. Women's bodies have strong meanings for men, carrying with them connections to life itself, being held, being dropped. That is a highly charged part of life men are suddenly being asked to look at, and what they're being asked to see is mother's body being invaded, life ending, fetuses not holding on.

Julie and I were plunged three times into the world of modern medicine, filled with its technological marvels. It is not easy for men to watch their wives going through all those procedures while nothing is being done to themselves. That is the opposite of how things are supposed to be, how they have been: *We're* supposed to suffer while *they* watch and comfort us, not vice versa.

When I imagined my wife laid out on the table in the hospital for a D and C after one of the miscarriages, with various metalic probes and feelers penetrating the most private, mysterious parts of her body, I felt as if violence was being done to her. Isolated, tired, besieged by medical sights and sounds entirely unfamiliar, it's easy to become confused. Was I responsible for her pain? Why wasn't I fulfilling my manly function of bearing that pain, protecting and defending my wife? How dare I feel, in some cowardly part of me, relief that I didn't have to go through it all?

Dr. Tracy MacNab informs us in his study of men's response to infertility:

> For many men it was very difficult to watch their wives go through the medical interventions. In all of the cases . . . where extensive surgical or pharmocological procedures were used, the wives received the majority of this medical attention. The men described worrying about the side effects of fertility drugs, standing by while their wives underwent surgery, or watching with apprehension during artificial insemination procedures. One participant remembered his extreme anger when the exploratory surgery that he had disapproved of turned up negative results.

Several men did mention positive reactions to the medical establishment. Through experience and study of the medical literature on
infertility, they developed a sense of equality with their physicians. "I
saw doctors as more human and fallable." This led to a sense of col-
laboration between doctor and patient that gave the patient a sense of
empowerment.[15]

Men I've counseled during fertility problems of different kinds
often have the hardest time coping with their fears for their wives.
The husband may just be plain *scared* for his wife—worried that
she may wind up physically injured from the medical interventions
or gynecological difficulties causing the problem, or else frightened at seeing his wife in emotional turmoil, her struggles with
disappointment, depression, or anger. Some men fear their wives
will never recover from the sadness or psychological pain they
feel.

Many men struggle as a result with guilt directed at their wives
during fertility problems. One observer of men at abortions has
noted that "guilt is a frequent emotion. Men feel responsible about
getting the woman in trouble. . . . Many wished they could trade
places with their female partner."[16]

Men will tend to feel overly *responsible.* Here are men quoted in
a study of miscarriage:

Paul: "I kept thinking. . . . I don't ever want to put her through
this again."

Tom: "Vicki was terribly upset and having a lot of pain, too. I
wanted to rescue her or take away the pain, and I couldn't do a
damn thing except watch her cry."[17]

This difficulty at seeing your wife in peril is not confined to fertility
problems. After the birth of his son one man, who was happy and
proud to have helped in the delivery, said to me with a trace of
shock in his voice, "This is the first time I ever saw my wife in such
pain."

At one point in my journal I wrote about my fears and my wife's
struggle:

*I keep feeling I want to apologize to Julie. For not protecting her
better, as if I should have been able to prevent the miscarriages, as
if it were my fault. I mean, what do you do when you find a note in*

the garbage written by your wife that says, "The third time this happened, I felt totally alone in an alien world. What's the point?"

I know this is normal grieving and disappointment. Julie is basically fine, she's just giving voice to the part of her that is frightened and despairing. And I don't search through her garbarge all the time, we do talk over these experiences.

We have talked a lot about it all. She started working full-time this year and in some ways it's been a godsend. She's told me how good it feels to be working, to keep her mind off the frustration we're both feeling. But of course, where does she work? Running an after-school program for kids! So she's surrounded by small, soft children, at their best, playing all afternoon, then she watches parents pick them up and drive them home each day at five. Great! What a way to get your mind off it!

Seeing Julie adrift on the sea of emotions that the fertility problem engenders drives me crazy. I can't get my mind off her and all she's going through, I want to take it away, make it not happen to her. Idiotic, because I can't take it away.

So every day she goes to work, gets enmeshed in the bureaucratic infighting of her job, thinks about pregnancy and whether she's really living up to being a woman. And I support her and watch her and she watches and supports me. But that's it, isn't it? Beyond a certain point Julie's sailing her own boat through this emotional tempest. Maybe I grow up slower than others, but there is a loneliness here I am unaccustomed to.

During the three-year period of our miscarriages I danced around myself in a conflict with fears of my own destructiveness; the pain and physical vulnerability of my wife tapped early currents of terror and guilt about my capacity to hurt those I love. I did a lot of penance during those years, as if each miscarriage were a mark of my own evil, were in some dark fashion *my* fault. As we'll see, I suspect reproductive difficulties tap men's childhood conflicts around feeling capable of doing violence to those they love.

The Invisible Husband

Given those struggles with loss, vulnerability, and fear, let us consider the special kind of male isolation husbands experience during reproductive difficulties.

In our innocence we told everyone we were pregnant the first time within days (minutes) of finding out ourselves. We then had to tell those same people about the miscarriages. I'm amazed now to remember how hard it was for me to focus on what I felt even when people asked. I kept wanting to *do* something, to take care of Julie, to make her feel better. I was helping her up and down the stairs, carrying every single grocery bag up to our apartment long past the time when it made any difference. She let me do all that for a while, but finally she got annoyed and said she didn't need such "infantilizing."

A man will often retreat to an instrumental approach during those emotionally trying times: focusing on the wife, trying to do something effective, taking care of her, and suppressing his own feelings. Julie cried a lot; that was okay, people expected her to. Then they'd turn to me and ask, "And how are you, Sam?" with concern in their voices. But my stiff-upper-lip hand-waving would soon lead them back to Julie. My act and their expectations were fully in synch.

In addition, people from whom you expect support often surprise you. One thirty-three-year-old lawyer told me of a phone call from his mother. "She called soon after our second miscarriage. We were exchanging pleasantries when her tone suddenly changed. Impatiently she blurted out: 'Steve, stop getting Joan pregnant!'"

He looked at me with astonishment and explained: "My own mother believed I was forcing my wife to get pregnant against her wishes and perhaps at the risk of her health. I became furious and I challenged her right on the phone, explaining that if anything it was Joan in her mid-thirties who felt pressed to have a child. I was feeling constant grief. Then my mother came to her senses: 'Oh, I'm sorry. I was just expressing womanly concern for Joan, I didn't think how it must feel for you.'"

With so much attention and expectation on the wife, it is easy for the husband to become invisible. A man whose wife miscarried told one investigator that his sister, who had had a miscarriage herself and was therefore in a good position to empathize, avoided talking to him about what he was going through because it was "too personal."[18]

Arthur Shostack found in his study of men and abortion that 40 percent of the men talked to no one but their wives.[19] That can put tremendous pressure on the marriage to contain the husband's intimacy needs at this difficult time. The wife is also struggling emotionally, and there are many pressures that change the husbands relationship with his wife. There is the changed sexual relationship that difficulty conceiving brings with it, as the couple has to schedule sex to maximize the possibility of conception or is told to avoid sex while recovering from a miscarriage, and so on. Feeling like members of a trained animal act following the commands of the medical ringmaster is not the best recipe for spontaneous sexuality. Both husband and wife are struggling, too, with challenges to body image and self-concept. It is easy to become alienated from our own bodies and then, slowly, from our spouses'. Because of reproductive difficulties and medical interventions the wife may feel unattractive or not female and nurturing. The wife may be struggling with her anxiety that "real women have babies, they don't miscarry," reflecting a wounded sense of her femininity. She may feel betrayed by her own body. She may feel irrationally angry at men, after feeling poked, prodded, and yet dependent still on the medical establishment. The husband in turn may feel unmanly because of their difficulty in conceiving. He may have his private, irrational nightmares of responsibility to cope with: A miscarriage may tap, for instance, the secret wish and nightmare of the young boy to cause damage, to wreak havoc with the penis-weapon. Both spouses may struggle with their anxieties about commitment, as well as a fear of letting down the other person. Why are we married if we can't have children? Will my mate still love me if I can't have children? There is so much anger and frustration around infertility, often due to undiagnosed problems or pointing to remedies that may or may not work, that it is easy for the couple to pour out their frustration, disappointment, and anger at one another or slowly become withdrawn and isolated from one another, at times unconsciously to protect the other from that irrational anger and disappointment.

The challenge for the couple is to develop new caretaking patterns with each other. The husband and wife have to balance their wish to "just get through all this" with the real need both have to reassure and comfort each other during a difficult time, feeling cared for when frightened and helpless. Among the many ways to take care of each other during a difficult time, I want to emphasize the importance of the husband's and wife's relationship to each other's bodies and their own. Often couples will get into fights and conflicts about sex—feeling distant from each other—when really they are battling about feeling loved, feeling that their bodies are okay and haven't turned against them or become repulsive to the spouse, feeling the reassurance of being touched and held when hurt. And we shout at each other about that through the megaphone of sex.

I believe a principal source of isolation for men during times of reproductive difficulty lies in the nature of their connection to other men. I found with men friends that chances of being heard easily slipped away, and yet it was probably men I most wanted to talk to. Having a chance to talk over frustrations and fears with a friend of the same sex may take some of the pressure off the relationship with one's wife. Yet infertility problems may be difficult to talk about; their link to sexuality may raise competition or embarrassment among men. "Other people do not understand" is a complaint often reported, or the feeling that "there's something wrong with people who can't have children."[20] Yet beyond the competitiveness and distrust, isn't there a need in most people for some validation from one's own sex?

The man may find himself confronted by his childlike yearnings for validation or approval or a moment of special connection with his own father, and he may feel as an adult with other men a similar feeling that it is inappropriate or unsafe to talk about the confusing mix of vulnerability, hope, and disappointment that infertility brings with it. In talking with men about infertility I often have the impression that they would like to talk to their fathers about the experience more than they do, even though that wish usually goes unacknowledged or unexpressed.

In order to provide support to each other men will have to overcome their discomfort with "emotional holding," with the silences and hesitations that have to be overcome to talk about the frustration and pain of abortions, miscarriages, and similar matters. We have to overcome our tendency to want to *do* something too quickly, mistaking becoming instrumental for providing emotional support.

After the last miscarriage, a close friend called as soon as he heard the bad news. This guy had helped us move our furniture into the house we had bought a while before.

"I'm sorry about the news, Sam."

"Yeah, it's hard, but we're doing okay."

He asked about Julie. I told him she was back at work after taking a few days off.

Silence built up on the phone. Clearly uncomfortable, perhaps mistaking the silence for the end of what I had to say, rather than the beginning, he told me warmly:

"Shit, Sam, I wish I could *do* something for you guys—help you move your furniture, anything to help." Neither he nor I could say that just listening, validating appropriate emotions, was a form of help.

Cutting through this tendency to be instrumental, stay armored, to view caring and human connection as something we really don't need, to devalue and deny our human qualities— that's what can come out of the encounter with infertility. By presenting us with an insoluble problem, one that we can't turn away from, it can humanize us, as can many family experiences. It confronts us with our vulnerabilities in a way we may be able to see. We can learn the same lesson at work, but it is often more muted: We can rationalize and protect ourselves from our failures, and we often feel invulnerable.

Reproductive difficulties can help heal the wounded father within our hearts by leading us to understand that pain and vulnerability are a part of life, not a badge of failure. A man can come to see that he can do everything right, try as hard as he can, be ingenious, alert, and smart, and life can still knock him on his ass. He may learn the reality of his interconnection with those he loves: the importance of comforting and allowing yourself to be comforted. He may come to see, slowly, that to be able to comfort and love someone else you must be able to allow yourself to be comforted and loved by them. Those who can barely tolerate pain in another person haven't been in their own pain freely touched and held and helped to heal.

Scenes from a Marriage During a Miscarriage

Let us focus now on the internal psychological conflict men experience between neediness and rage, rooted in our developmental experiences growing up male, and rekindled during the stress of infertility problems.

For us the crux came when our doctor suggested the fertility drug Clomid after our third and last miscarriage. I had a lot of reservations about its safety. One morning in the midst of our indecision our gynecologist, Dr. L., returned my call to him. He was also the fertility specialist at our clinic, and Julie suggested I call him to try to get some resolution to my feelings about Clomid. Julie had talked to three friends who had taken it, all about her age, who were then either pregnant or had already had children after using Clomid. She had found them reassuring. "Honey, they're all intelligent people, not just technology freaks who will lie down and let the Medical Establishment roll over them."

Dr. L. was very courteous and patient on the phone. He explained that he had tried me the day before, after my phone call to him, but I must have gone out. He put to shame our jokes about unsympathetic doctors; we had made bets on how many times I would have to try him to get through. Just once, it turned out.

"Mr. Osherson, I can reassure you about Clomid."

He thought at first I was worried about the impact of the drug on the fetus and explained that Clomid is given during the five to ten days before ovulation and is out of the body before conception. All it does is act as a trigger for the pituitary gland's action thus boosting the progesterone output during the second half of the menstrual cycle.

"Your wife would have an amniocentesis anyway, because she is over thirty-five, so you can be sure there are no congenital defects in the baby." Okay. But what I was finding so difficult to explain was my anxiety about the long-term effects on Julie. Everyone was so baby-oriented, I felt like an oddball saying that my real concern was for my wife. One day, as we left our clinic after yet another examination and some preliminary discussion of Clomid, its risks and advantages, our nurse, herself pregnant, looked at Julie with a knowing expression. "You'll do anything to have a child, wouldn't you?" The nurse was expressing a hidden bond between women. I was stunned, and I knew too that I *wouldn't* "do anything" if that included potentially severe danger to my body. Now that I have a child I feel differently, but at the time, pre-baby, I felt uncomfortably pulled along by what felt at times like my wife's primal desire to reproduce. A resentment at the baby focus ran through me as I talked to Dr. L.

"She may experience some discomfort in the ovaries," he patiently explained.

"How about long-term effects?" I rushed on. He sounded so patient and calm, I felt a cauldron of fears. *He's a year younger than me*, I realized with a shock, *yet I feel about eight years old.*

"Well, it's been given in Europe for the last twenty-five years."

"Have studies been done to prove its safety?"

Well . . . no . . . but he felt very confident it was safe. He then gave me some other facts that looked reassuring but basically involved leaps of faith, e.g., Clomid was originally used to treat breast cancer, so how can it be carcinogenic? (But how about radiation and chemotherapy, which destroy cancer but are themselves Enemy Number 1 of anyone who is healthy?) Yet I was getting his point: Clomid solves a short-term problem, but we just don't know about the long term effects, though everyone is acting as if we did. Dr. L. was sympathetic—he had even found time to call me on his day off—and I could sense he wanted me to be confident, but at that point all I could think was that you can be led down the garden path by a sympathetic guide as well as a hostile one. His willing friendliness, though, was a relief. At the end he said, "You know, you want to have a baby, don't you, and you're both in your late thirties?"

Julie was in the living room when I got off the phone. We sat on the sofa in our favorite position, our feet intertwined.

"You were on the phone for half an hour! Amazing. Did it help to talk just the two of you, man to man?"

"A little."

"I would like to go ahead and try it. Are you willing?"

"Mmmn. . . . I guess so. He said the odds are high that we'd miscarry again without it."

"If I didn't have any feelings either way, would you try again without it?"

"Maybe. We might go to other doctors, look around more."

"Look it's my body and I have no faith in acupuncture and herbal remedies, and doctors who say they have the answer when they have treated two people. Dr. L. has seen hundreds. Do you feel you could be optimistic about the Clomid? I feel like it's the first ray of hope I've had in six months."

"Yeah."

Her voice hardened.

"Look, I need reassurance. I'm terrified of another miscarriage. Don't make me the guinea pig for your anger against traditional medicine. I need hope."

"Well, Christ, I do too, but I don't want you to do something that will harm you. Or the baby. I have some rights in this too." It's her body, but I'm connected to it. Men today face a delicate situation when dealing with reproductive decisions. Many women argue angrily that it has taken generations to gain control of their bodies, and now men's entrance into the reproductive domain of life may erode their control over "our own bodies." Yet men are emotionally connected both to their wives and to the fetus, and they will suffer emotionally if they do not feel as if they have a voice in the decision-making. Nothing though, will engender more anger from women when discussing reproductive decisions than the argument that men have "rights" too. Reaching equitable decisions about whether and when to have children is one of the greatest challenges a marriage will face.

"We both have rights here," Julie countered. "But you can't trample me. Have you been able to come up with any decent alternative?"

"No. I need more time . . ."

"Well, we don't have it. If we're going to start the Clomid this cycle, it has to be taken next week. I feel okay about it. In fact, I feel good about it. There are always some risks one has to take. And I need to be optimistic about this. I'm scared we're going to get polarized into me for it and you against it."

Looking at the situation at that point, I felt she was right. Clomid looked like our only real choice. I'd already spent hours on the phone exploring alternatives, but none of them seemed solid. The physician president of one New Age Health Foundation gave me a long account of the millions of problems his "herbal specialist" could treat—everything from brain damage to hangnail—but when I reiterated that the problem was miscarriage, he rambled: "Oh, well, yeah, uh, let's see, there's this herb from China, and this forty-five-year-old woman from Maine who has had many miscarriages tried it and it worked with her. Look, why not come in and try it? If things don't work out, we won't charge you."

Was that the crux of it? There is no answer. Underneath all the techniques, confident explanations, routines, good cheer, and optimism, no one really knows for sure. You pays your money and you makes your choice.

Okay, so things felt out of control. We're on a jet plane with no pilot. What made things particularly difficult was the feeling of being alone, out on the edge. At the time I wrote:

There is no place for my terror in all this, my rage and fear as I stand around and watch Julie's body become a battleground, stand around while she is drugged, and given a D and C after waiting two hours in the emergency room during our last miscarriage, and she stays overnight while I drive home alone through the dark city streets. . . . Underneath all the calls to doctors, talks with friends, questions about how is Julie there is my terror screaming to get out and nowhere for it to go, I am surrounded by faces telling me everything is safe, fine, has been used for years, all those smiling faces telling me just to be calm. Telephones, guidebooks, pills and procedures, but what about our feelings, they have not been invited to the party.

*   *   *   *

So I picked up the Clomid from the Community Health Plan Clinic's drugstore one day. Big blue ones, 50 mg. The girl rang up the sale, and I got out my wallet and handed her a big bill. "Oh, no, sir," she smiled at me, "your wife's insurance covers this." Cheerily, "Isn't that great! Gee, the whole thing only costs you one dollar." Wow, I wondered, and an arm and a leg?

*   *   *   *

About a month after Julie started taking Clomid, things came to a head for me, and brought on feelings of helplessness I can only associate with being a child, perhaps with the last time in my childhood when my love, neediness, and anger were so fiercely welded together.

Julie was away that weekend, both Saturday and Sunday, at a required departmental workshop. I felt cold, abandoned. I thought about going to our place in New Hampshire alone. Instead I decided to work on an article. Nothing came of that either. I couldn't focus on the writing. In the afternoon I set out to buy some clothes I'd needed for a while but bought nothing, just wandered around Cambridge until evening. It's odd—I wanted to give myself something, some sustenance, a shirt, a record, a book, anything, but couldn't get myself to do it, as if I were undercutting my own efforts to feel better.

On Sunday came an upsurge of pain from my right knee, which took me by surprise. It had started a few years back, after two decades of running. I'd been seeing a physical therapist to sort out the problem. The knee is generally fine if I don't run on it. But that

Sunday I was walking with a friend, and the knee started aching merely from walking. Not only that, but my back started hurting too. I was grousing about it to my friend, himself a runner, and he said, "Well, Sam, I feel for your knee and all, but not for your back. I think that's just psychosomatic. You've always been sensitive in the back." He was trying to be reassuring but failed to empathize: Mental pain wasn't part of the equation for him. Men will often somaticize their pain as a way of getting comfort when they are hurting mentally. We present physical complaints when we are seeking emotional nurturance and reassurance.

For the rest of that weekend I was obsessed with fear: Was my body falling apart? What if my back suddenly went, with all the symptoms, shooting pain down the legs, numbness in the feet? Immobilized in bed for days on end . . . ?

Julie got back Monday morning, but I was still depressed, and by the time I saw my last client, about 8 P.M., my back was really worse. Perhaps all that sitting, listening to clients, had done it.

Then Julie and I started sparring before going to bed. I was really grumpy, pretty impossible to be with. I got out all the paraphernalia I had developed over the years to deal with muscle pain, all of which drives Julie crazy: hot pad, extra pillows, oil to message the muscles the way the therapist had shown me. Julie was trying to read in bed before going to sleep after a very busy day, and there I was setting up a battlefield hospital. If I could have figured out how to strap myself into traction I would have done it. I was mumbling about the relative virtues of ice versus heat on joint problems when she reached the end of her rope. Peering over her book, she said:

"Are you sure it's such a big deal? I mean, I've strained my back in exercise class and it goes away in a few days."

I was pissed. "Great, thanks a lot, that helps! How do I know my back isn't falling apart like our friend Alice's?" (She was struggling at that time with a disc problem and spent most of her time in bed.)

"But you take great care of your back," offered my rational wife. "You're too sensitive to your body anyway. Look at you with all those oils and treatments and books. Are you in the running for hypochondriac of the month?"

Well! That was the limit! Mustering all the hurt, guilt-making tones I could, I said reasonably, "Look, why can't you just reassure me, or at least have some sympathy. I am in pain, you know."

It worked. A pained look came over Julie's face. "Yes, I know, you're right. When I have ailments you just take care of me without criticizing. How many times have you rubbed my back, let me just fall asleep lying on your chest while you soothed me . . ."

We kissed and made up; we were both tired and turned over and went to sleep. Yet we had just danced around several dilemmas. How do you make your anxiety known to someone who is busily trying to keep her own similar feelings under control? Perhaps Julie didn't really want to hear me at that point, even in the childlike way I was asking for comfort, because my pain and fear were too disturbing for her. And about that childlike way I did ask: Part of me didn't really want to ask. I harbored a secret anger that she didn't massage my back, make the pain go away. But I *would not ask*; my resentment was an old pet I didn't want to give up. How do other men ask for help of an emotional nature—not financial or career advice, but simple holding and caring? When we were growing up, such neediness so often led to embarrassment or a sense of failure that now men become self-punishing or punishing of others when they feel helpless and needy.

The next day, still in a terrible mood, I went to see Michael, my physical therapist. I was fuming.

"Here I've been coming to see you for almost a year now, and where am I? In as bad shape as ever." I described my variety of aches and pains. Petulantly I demanded, "what can I do about my back?"

He saw the death-warmed-over look on my face, took a deep breath, and said, "I want to talk about your back and your knee. But I think we need to begin with a massage. You sound like you're in real pain. How about if I massage and you talk?"

The feeling of a hand on my back, working on the hurt, trying to take it away, felt almost like forgiveness, an invitation back into the human race. It reasoned softly with the rage I felt against Julie and at myself, and with the fear I felt at that rage. It was also telling me that what lurked in darkest consciousness could be admitted to the light of day.

There are so few times when men actually touch and hold each other. Michael's response to my obvious need validated for me the pain I felt; and it was particularly important that this response came from another man. The theme of wanting to be held emotionally by other men keeps coming up in men's accounts of their emotional growth. It has nothing to do with homosexuality; it needn't be a physical holding. It is an emotional holding. At some men's workshops the participants hold each other's heads in their hands, silently. *Holding* the other person's pain. Being taken seriously emotionally by another man means that you feel less un-manly for feeling so deeply about an event.

"Sam, are there any things going on right now that are possibly getting focused in your back and knees?" Michael wondered aloud.

The trail, of course, led right back to the past lonely weekend when I felt adrift on a piece of ice, with no warmth in my life. Julie and I had been cut off from each other emotionally, while we each struggled to keep our anxiety under control. That's the price of get-ting through all the tests, doubts, and decisions we'd faced. Neither wanted to rock the boat with difficult-to-handle feelings. Couples can be very good at "getting through," but then you lose what Julie calls the "grease" in human relationships, the grease that comes from making contact on the deeper emotional and physical levels. And I'd been cut off from Julie by my own anger at her as well, a primitive, irrational, and childlike anger that I could only glimpse in myself out of the corner of my eye before it scurried away out of sight. If I didn't want to see it, I surely didn't want to write about it. I'd rather have done anything else, like fall asleep for a few days. Anger at someone you love can drive you crazy:

Admit it: part of me is mad at Julie for being 38 and having prob-lems carrying a child to term. Part of me wishes she were 24 years old, like those attractive women I teach every day in graduate school. Yet how can I feel this about Julie, with all she's had to go through for both of us, all the pains she's taken on while I just stand around and feel sorry for her and myself? That last exam she had, for example, a hurtful biopsy of uterine tissue to test for something. Biopsy—autopsy, Christ I can't get that imagery out of my mind. I was there to support her, hold her hand. On the wall was a chart of the female reproductive system, all in clear detail in black and white . . . and then we're supposed to be romantic about it later.

Something in me wants a young womb, unsullied by doctors and needles and the sadness of failure. A part of me still cries out: that is what women are for, the image of perfection, beauty; ten-sion-releasing, not tension-making, bringing softness and ecstasy into your life, not scaring you by being sick, leading you into the realistic nightmare of blood, internal exams, and reproductive charts, into a world that has never been yours. Walking past news-stands we are constantly reminded of what women are supposed to be. They smile at us, movie stars, young actresses, singers, beauty and pleasure that could change your life, not with love as we know it but with a transformation into eternal bliss.

Does every man have trouble coming to terms with the reality of women as opposed to the illusion that within the love of a woman lies all we need to get along, to take us out of the mundane? Compared to this illusion, hyped up falsely and forever by media merchants, every women, as a friend once said to me, is ultimately a disappointment.

Ridiculous, absurd. I'm furious with myself for even momen-tarily harboring this illusion. The whole thing comes at me like a boomerang returning to its owner. I accuse myself: "I got you into this, Julie, I'm sorry." In the next breath I accuse her: "You got me into this."

Into what? Into the hard work of keeping a relationship going, of having to nurture and support each other, of weaning ourselves away from our illusions of how easy adult life would be.

There is something so childish about this helpless, poor-me stance; the rational side of my mind sees it as resembling the be-havior of a little kid who's been abandoned, who's lost the sole source of nurturance in his life: his mommy.

Such is what I wrote in my journal during those days. Similar thoughts ran through my mind in Michael's office.

"Can you understand," I said to Michael, rising up on one elbow from the massage table, desperate for my confessor to allow me my sins, "that I can love Julie *and* be angry at her?"

Michael nodded in agreement and said, "Sam, you're a *man*; has it ever occurred to you that you may be holding some of your pain in your knees and your back. Is there some way you can get the warmth you want from Julie? Tell her you need some time to talk together and that maybe what you have to say will sound like a kid for a few moments but you want her to listen anyway, there are things you need to get out."

"Easy for him to say, he doesn't have to do it," I thought, as Julie and I sat talking over a glass of wine later that evening. How the hell was I going to tell her about this pile of sludge that had built up? *"This ain't the time,"* an insistent scared voice kept whispering in my head. When is the right time? *"Some other time."* And I felt so sleepy.

"How's your back feeling?" Julie asked.

"Better. Michael really helped. And I need to talk to you about some stuff," I hurried on. "I feel like there's a backlog of shit that's accumulated."

"Okay. Uh, is this really heavy? If you're going to get really critical of me, start a fight, I don't want to hear it."

"Honey, I'm upset—it's okay, we don't have to be frightened, we're both having emotions about this pregnancy thing. If we talk, it'll help to see them through."

"Yes?" She looked at me hopefully.

"Yes, getting upset now will help us, not hurt us. And it's not just me. I feel you haven't been around—hardly at all—emotionally—and I want you back. I feel so strung out. Cold, tired, empty. Listen, let me just try to say what I have to: I'm scared. Scared for you, scared for. I need you. I want to feel close to you again."

"When you say it like that, it's okay. I've been so scared myself I haven't even wanted to talk about it. Look at me. I feel like crying again. Why don't you ever cry?"

"Oh, I do. You just can't see it."

"Okay," Julie laughed. "It's as if I worked through all my fears weeks ago and now want just to bull through this pregnancy thing, and now you're scared. Before, you seemed confident. I hate to hear it from you today when I'm trying to be in my 'army mode,' just get through. But talking like this really helps, honey."

We went on for a while, and then I said, "You know, I guess I'm not as reconciled to your taking Clomid as I thought."

"I really feel okay about it. We're both maybe too sensitive about our bodies; I think my cells can handle this stuff."

"Well—"

"You know, I don't think I'd take it month after month at 100 or 150 mgs. Does that help, to know we haven't indiscriminately decided I should keep popping those pills? I want to try it this month, but not for months and months."

"I hadn't thought about that; it does help to look at it that way."

"You worry about something happening to me, don't you?"

Her comment felt like a sudden release, freeing me from a dark internal night I had been adrift in for days.

"Yeah, yeah, I do." I had to work to keep the tears at the back of my eyes.

"You know, I'm pretty strong. I come from a healthy family. So did your mother. You worried a lot about her dying, too, remember? About her smoking, when you were a kid, and how she still smokes. Remember what you told me once about how angry that got you as a kid, and all of you in the family, you all felt it was so dangerous."

Jesus, I thought, she's cutting to the heart of the matter. My mother's health did obsess all of us, and it centered, not surprisingly, on her smoking. We all tried to stop her—my brother, my father, me. She was always stopping, then starting. When I was ten we had a long talk about it one night, and she gave my brother and me her last carton of cigarettes and we happily threw it off our porch into the woods. But she soon bought some more. There was such energy focused on my mother in our family—that she be safe.

"Babar!" I yelled to Julie.

"What? Those kids' stories about elephants?"

"Yes," I said, as the memories flooded back. "I've always hated the entire series of Babar books. Whenever I see them in a bookstore or in somebody's house, I cringe. Those rotten books are terribly popular, but I hate the guy who wrote them because of one story. In the very first book, Babar's mother is killed by a hunter while out walking with her young son. It's horrible, I can still remember the pictures, there's Babar with his mother, all nice and cozy, out for a walk, full of love. Then this hunter shoots a gun, and Babar's mother goes down. There's a picture of her all crumpled up. I can't tell you how much that affected me, it still does, even thinking about it—the gray of her skin, all crumpled and dead. I just can't describe the terror of it—Babar's mother dead . . ." Strange how, when you really cry, the tears seem to roll down your cheeks like soft, liquid boulders. How vitally important mothers are to young children, how fearful we can be of losing them—a separation every boy must master his own way. Is it ever *really* mastered?

"Makes me want to cry too, Sam," Julie said reaching out.

"It was so unfair. Why did she have to get killed in that story? And poor Babar left all alone." I exclaimed: "The mother was so big and strong and then she was dead. I mean, an elephant, you can't get much bigger and stronger than that! Killed by some stupid jerk who didn't know what the hell he was doing."

Mothers are extremely powerful figures for adults as well as children, and men transfer lots of fears about them to the women in their lives. I suspect there's a part of every man that is sure he cannot exist without the warmth and emotional supplies of a woman and is in terror of being abandoned whenever he is really separated from her. What can we do with men's rage at being abandoned, starting at an early age? Perhaps in our need to defend and constantly protect women we are trying to tiptoe past the rage we feel if they leave us too much alone. Separation and violence seem so interconnected in men's minds.

The child psychologist Dr. Bruno Bettelheim urges us to pay careful attention to children's fairy tales. "[T]hese tales, in a much deeper sense than any other reading material, start where the child is in his psychological and emotional being. They speak about his severe inner pressures in a way that the child unconsciously understands, and—without belittling the most severe inner struggles which growing up entails—offer examples of both temporary and permanent solutions to pressing difficulties."[21]

What "severe inner struggle" does the Babar story describe? The young child's struggle with his or her anger and rage at mother, the fear that his violence will harm her, the child's fantasied *sense of responsibility* that his rage will harm mother. Babar, after all, leads his mother into the trap, she was out taking him for a walk. There is a key page: the scene of Babar weeping over his dead mother, the hunter running toward them (a decidedly phallic hunter with his mushroom-capped, circumcised head). This story charts the male life course in a few simple pictures. After the death of his mother, Babar runs from the hunter and finds himself in a little town far from the lush, timeless, maternal jungle he inhabited. And in that town, so many things interest Babar! Especially the grown-ups he sees, the male elephants in fine clothes. He buys some too, and then looks like an idiotic elephant dressed in spats and a three-piece suit, taking lessons from teachers, and generally joining the world of automobiles, department stores, and schools, of doing and accomplishing. Yet "he does often stand at the window, thinking sadly of his childhood and cries when he remembers his mother." I bet he does, but just the same he gets on with the job of becoming a good little male elephant.

What we see here is an enactment of the boy's struggle to separate from mother. Note that the separation is accomplished through violence: Babar grows up with the murder of his mother.

Who's doing the murdering? Society, Dad, the asexual "civilized" schoolmarm who takes him in—or is it Babar himself? All of those forces really, but at root the tale is describing an inner fantasy within the young boy, in which he leaves behind femininity for masculinity by "destroying" mother: degrading and rejecting femininity, and hyperidentifying with masculinity.

The renunciation of women is an essential part of accomplishing a successful male gender identity. Yet when the female world is so vitally important to the child, the masculine world represented so heavily by machines, information, and instrumentality, so divorced from the feminine world of holding, caring—how much of a wrench for the boy is it to leave the feminine world behind, the wet, soft, timeless world of the body, of the preconscious, of the imagination, all the sides of life attributed to women by men, and which we all need to be able to be nurtured, nurture, and feel rooted in humanity? When emotional holding and caring is a feminine task and masculinity is activity and conquest, the male child is put in a precarious position in having to identify with that image of masculinity. We accomplish the "developmental task" of identifying with our fathers by murdering the feminine within ourselves. It is the residue of that struggle that I suspect leaves men feeling that deep down they are basically destructive or "unlovable" and that leads us to withdraw emotionally and become silent when we are vulnerable. We resolve never to feel that neediness again. And we carry around the wounded father within: that angry, sad residue of the struggle.

A greatly overlooked aspect of men's psyche is their fear of doing harm to or being hurt by those they love. Many men I've worked with and talked to carry within them an unexamined feeling, often never verbalized or acknowledged, that they are destructive or violent. A key issue for men in their thirties and forties is what to do with the unconscious rage dredged up by the experiences they are having in the family. Talking with your wife about both the rage and the vulnerability can help. Otherwise it is difficult to be present emotionally if you are secretly frightened that there is a demon inside trying to get out.

Losses that can't be tolerated or adequately dealt with often result in idealization; we glorify in a false, desperate way what we have lost in order to hold on to it. How much of men's attempts to make women into Madonnas, soft healing creatures of the imagination, may be compensation for the early losses of nurturance in our lives? A poster in a travel agency window says it all: a beautiful woman sitting seductively on a white beach in a soft nightgown, the warm green sea mirroring her flawless skin. In bold letters above the picture: "Club Med, the Antidote to Civilization."

We renounce our neediness for women, for the caring, tactile contact, and for pleasure they represent to us, but we can never escape the need, so we try to hold onto them and get our needs met in disguised ways. Yet when we are emotionally vulnerable we feel the rage and fear of having our neediness exposed.

That is the consequence of a childhood pattern in which mother is the emotional caretaker and father a distant, instrumental figure. For men today family life is disrupted not just by painful events like infertility but also by joyous ones like successful pregnancies and the transition to parenthood. And in each case we need to pay attention to the husband's silent struggle with his neediness and rage.

5

The Empty Urn:
Do Men Get Pregnant Too?

A Husband at the Amniocentesis

During the seventeenth week of pregnancy my wife and I arrived at the hospital, clutching our forms, to keep our appointment for an amniocentesis. After three miscarriages we had finally made it past the first trimester. Yet we were still treading lightly on our hopes, afraid of again being disappointed. I walked through the hospital entrance as if on tiptoes, not wanting to attract attention to ourselves.

An amniocentesis involves inserting a needle through the woman's abdominal wall into the amniotic sac to take a sample of fluid containing cells discarded from the fetus. Cells obtained in that way allow for genetic testing for birth defects. Although considered a routine procedure for pregnant women over thirty-five, an amniocentesis has risks. A miscarriage may be induced, but, particularly as the parents get into their late thirties, as we were, that risk must be weighed against the increasing possibility of birth defects. (We had engaged, too, in a more terrible, ultimately futile mental calculus: If there was evidence of birth defects, would we agree to abort? After four years of trying to have a child, we were about ready to take whatever we'd get.) The amniocentesis felt like the last hurdle: If all went well, we could finally permit ourselves to believe in this pregnancy.

At the hospital we checked into the radiology department for the test. The receptionist smiled at my wife, showed her where to change into her surgical gown, then looked at me and warned: "It's all right if you want to accompany your wife for the test, but remember, if at any time you feel faint, please leave the room. Last week we had a husband who fainted during the procedure, hit his head, and caused a big disruption. He had to be taken to the emergency room." She spoke so scoldingly, I almost apologized for him. Was he tall? I wondered. Did he have far to fall? Knees buckling, head hitting the floor. How embarrassing. I realized I had never seen a grown man faint. Her tone, and a sudden tightness in my stomach, stopped me from asking what could happen during an amniocentesis that would cause a man to swoon.

The amniocentesis took place in a small room, hardly bigger than a large closet. We were in radiology in the first place because an ultrasound is used during the amniocentesis. An ultrasound, also called a B-scan, is a piece of machinery that uses sound waves to project on its monitor a picture of the fetus inside the womb. Knowing the precise location of the fetus in its dark cave lowers the possibility of injuring it when the needle is inserted. The ultrasound, though, had shadowed us throughout all our pregnancies. It had been the constant harbinger of bad, then finally good, news. Two years ago in this same room an ultrasound picture in the twelfth week of our first pregnancy positively confirmed a miscarriage. The picture on the scope told the story without mercy, as the doctor explained that "the embryo stopped developing after the fifth week; right now there's nothing really there." From this room Julie went for a D and C at 2 A.M. while I drove home alone through the dark city streets, still wet with rain. Walking into the room for "the amnio" brought our unborn babies to mind, and a superstitious residue made me worry for the living cargo my wife was now carrying. The room seemed unchanged, a typical hospital room—insistently functional, decidedly unsentimental. I recognized against one bare wall the metal table and chairs where we all had sat while the doctor gave us the bad news.

Julie, draped in a yellow smock, lay on the operating-examining table. The ultrasound technician adjusted the equipment and then sat in a chair near my wife's head. In walked Dr. L., the doctor, our gynecologist, dressed in his white surgical uniform, a quiet, soft-spoken man. His delicate, dark Asian features clashed with the metallic angularity of the machinery packed into the room, with the harsh blankness of the white hospital walls. He had been our doctor since the second miscarriage and throughout this pregnancy; both Julie and I feel considerable affection for him. He smiled, chatted briefly with us, and then donned his white surgical mask.

The doctor stood beside Julie, feeling about her stomach area. The technician was seated near the top of the table. There was no place for me to sit except down near Julie's feet, in the corner. Julie raised her head and looked down the table at me; she seemed about 6 miles away. She smiled encouragingly at me and asked, "Want to hold my toe?"

So there we were, toe to hand.

The ultrasound technician turned on her machine. There on the screen appeared our baby, difficult to make out clearly, but surprisingly large and well-formed. The baby is so well-developed by this time that it's often possible to identify its sex from the ultrasound picture. We didn't want to know, hoping to preserve the surprise.

"Okay," the technician informed us, "the baby's on its head." Crowded around the fuzzy screen of the ultrasound monitor in the darkened room, the technician in front of her device adjusting buttons, we could have been inside a submarine gliding through the ocean's depths.

The technician found the exact location of the baby to ensure that the needle would be inserted away from it. Amazing—one piece of technology was protecting our baby from another. Previously I had come to hate the ultrasound for its unrelenting judgments of failed pregnancies; now I loved it for its protective power. The technician looked about twenty-five years old, and her red hair tempered the whiteness of her nurse's uniform. She took a ballpoint pen and made an X on Julie's belly, marking the spot where the doctor should insert the needle. Then, the machine switched off, she sat to the side of the table, her hand gently resting on Julie's forehead, reassuring her, while she waited for the doctor to begin the procedure. My wife's toe was still firmly in my grip.

First Julie's belly was heartily splashed and painted with an orange antiseptic solution. Then a local anaesthetic was applied, and the procedure began. The doctor, creases around his eyes reflecting concentration uncensored by the surgical mask, slowly inserted a sheath where the technician had marked her spot, then a needle delicately through the sheath. He gently allowed the vacuum inside the syringe to act as a pump to pull the amniotic fluid up. But the large barrel of the syringe remained empty: No fluid rushed in to fill it. A dry well.

Very quietly, the doctor signaled the technician to turn on the ultrasound again. The technician swiveled in her seat and switched it on.

"Okay," she advised, pointing to a spot on the screen, "you've penetrated the muscular wall of the uterus; you're not in the amniotic sac itself." There was a slight pause, then she said softly:

"Move the needle 1 centimeter, medially."

"Um, medially? You mean to the left?" the doctor asked uncertainly.

For a dreadful moment I wondered if this man was truly competent.

He moved the needle, inside its sheath, 1 centimeter to the left. No fluid. Another dry well.

"The uterus has contracted and moved away from the needle," she explained. Smart uterus. "The wall is cramping." That word again, "cramp." It's remarkable how some words become frightful to you at particular times in your life. Their sound echoes in a room like vultures circling overhead. Cramps preceded all the miscarriages. "You feel like you're cramping slightly, as if you're having your period," Julie once told me, describing the onset of the miscarriages.

The technician reached over and placed a long finger on Julie's belly. "Right there," she instructed the doctor, indicating where the needle should go. Her wedding ring glistened in the dull hospital light.

The doctor seemed unaware of the tension in the room. To me it was as if I were deep-sea diving, the pressure trying to cave in my chest. Yet he seemed unaffected, his attention totally on the procedure and the womb in front of him. He hardly looked at us. A friend of mine who lost her baby soon after an amniocentesis was convinced that the doctor had botched the procedure and injured the fetus or the placenta with the needle. There had been blood in the fluid as it entered the needle. I fantasize punching our doctor in the face if such evidence turned up today, knowing I'd never do that. Yet how much rage would I feel if we lost this baby, no one to blame for "reproductive difficulties," nothing to do? Is there a way to quantify that kind of rage? Is it more than a centimeter long?

The doctor held the needle in front of him, preparing for a third attempt.

The needle looked enormous. (Months later "Doonesbury" was to feature Joanie Caucus's amniocentesis, in which the doctor jokes that "we are just now wheeling in the needle from the other room.") My wife was laid out on the table with a doctor sticking a thick needle into her, a long metallic spear penetrating close to the baby, unknowingly in danger within a secret sea. An image of whales, of harpoons being shot into whales at sea. A line from a book on ships I had once seen, perhaps as a child: *The mother whale is pulled closer to the factory ship.*

Sitting there, I could not get images of violence and sadism out of my mind. I was in no danger of fainting, but I did want to cry out, to stop the procedure. My wife and the fetus, I felt, were intolerably vulnerable. And, too, I wanted to cry at my own vulnerability. Life suddenly seemed to me very precious, and very fragile.

Simply watching was perhaps the hardest part. I wanted to do something, to protect Julie, the baby. Yet there was nothing to do, except to hold her toe and support her with my presence. I felt for the husbands who do faint. Trained to do, to be instrumental, we must just watch. And yet we don't ask for help, for the reassurance routinely given our wives. Instead we sit silently, looking composed. And faint.

While we waited for the doctor to insert the needle again, another doctor walked into the room through a door on my immediate right. Why is he here? I wondered. Is there an emergency no one has admitted to? Perhaps doctors have a secret button on the floor like the one bank tellers press during a robbery, to call for help without alerting any of the customers. This doctor was about my age, short and neat-looking. He was dressed in street clothes, suit pants and a striped shirt, with a beeper dangling on his belt. As he closed the door he looked down at me, sitting in the corner, holding my wife's toe. He smiled and introduced himself: "Hi, I'm Dr. Phillips. Just wanted to see what's going on here, whether I could be of help." So saying, he slid by me carefully and walked over to join his colleague, our gynecologist.

As he passed I had a strong impulse to ask: "Would you hold *my* hand?"

I wanted to be touched, to be reassured. The air was so heavy in the room, the time so heavy. Had we been there two days or three? I forgot to breathe, felt empty. I wanted tactile contact, I suddenly felt an ache to be held, supported, to feel less alone, and I wanted that from a man. I wanted another man to legitimate that it was okay to feel scared, to care so deeply about the outcome. But I didn't ask the doctor. I refused to ask. I was afraid I would embarrass him, was scared myself of looking weak or silly. As that other man walked by, my body withdrew, I felt far away from my skin, armored in my hard shell of male toughness. A rock. Momentarily aware of my need for touch, I felt a familiar anxiety. Is it possible for men to imagine comforting each other without fearing homosexuality?

A nurse would have held my hand, but that felt regressive: Traditionally it is always the nurses who do that. The female nurse comes over to hold the husband's hand, speaking soothingly, "It's okay, there, there, would you rather wait outside in the hall with me?" Mommy leads the scared boy away from the men's work. Or there's a sexualized element, as if the man is saying, "Hold my hand, will you baby? Gee, you're cute when you're nurturant!" The seductiveness of male fragility. Perhaps it will always feel infantilizing or sexualized to ask for such help only from the nurses, until men too legitimize that kind of caring.

The two doctors conferred momentarily. Then the needle went in again. Suddenly a clear, slightly yellowish fluid flooded the chamber. Amniotic fluid, looking like urine. One cylinder was filled and then replaced with another. That one too was filled, ensuring enough fluid for the tests to be done. (Tests that were to reveal a baby as healthy as modern science could certify; twenty-four weeks later our son was born, three weeks overdue.)

"Very good fluid, clear and healthy-looking. No blood, an excellent sign," our doctor explained. He then left the room in search of forms he needed to complete for us. The technician took Julie's hand, moving up to look into her face. She reached over and reassured, "Now all that was perfectly normal. The fluid looks fine, the ultrasound shows your baby is developing just as it should. It often takes several tries to get the sample. Nothing went wrong." Julie looked dazed, and her head and arms were shaking slightly, as if she wanted to cry. But it was clear she had taken in the woman's words. The technician stroked Julie's head. It looked as though all the anxiety my wife had been feeling wanted to burst out, like flood waters straining to smash through a dam. "Do you believe me?" the woman asked in a sisterly fashion. "Yes," Julie answered, looking away and laughing, gently wiping a tear from her eye.

I went over to my wife and held her head in my hands, glad it was over. Suddenly appreciation for this technician and our doctor filled me. As we were leaving I took the doctor's hand and shook it, exclaiming, "Thank you!" He looked at me, smiled back, and replied shyly, "You're welcome, Sam." He spoke my name so softly I almost didn't hear it. It was the first time in two years that gentle, reserved man had called me by my first name.

The Emotional Vulnerabilty of the Husband

What is it really like for men to enter into the reproductive cycle, a part of life that has traditionally been reserved for women? The vast majority of births now occur with the husband present, and the rate of increase in men choosing this experience is striking. In 1973 27 percent of fathers were in the delivery room when their children were born; by 1983 79 percent of fathers were present, according to one national survey.[1] Men are not just "present at the creation," helping to deliver their children in hospitals or during home births, but also are accompanying their wives for doctor's visits and tests during pregnancy.

That phenomenon is clearly to the good. Research shows that the development of a parenting identity really begins prepartum, and the father's presence in the birth process can strengthen the bond between father and child and between husband and wife.[2] Yet, too, there is a darker side to modern pregnancy in that many fathers-to-be experience considerable emotional vulnerability.

The Boston University psychologists Abby Stewart and Nia Lane Chester compared twenty expectant and new parent couples and found that men's scores on a TAT measure of emotional adaptation to the environment were lower during the pregnancy than after the birth of the child. The opposite was true for the wives: New mothers showed a significant drop in adaptation level when compared with pregnant mothers. Stewart and her colleagues suggest that men may experience the pregnancy as signaling the main transition or change in their life, "whereas the women seem to experience the actual birth of the baby as the major transition."[3]

For many men the pregnancy of their wives stirs up powerfully ambivalent feelings which may be intensified by their inclusion in the feminine world of Ob-Gyn. Many men experience a renewed struggle during pregnancy with their own masculine and feminine parts of self, as well as a sense of loss (as well as joy) imagining and anticipating what the fatherhood role will be like for them. The vulnerability that results from being confronted by such confused, angry, and sad feelings drives some men out of the family as powerfully as it draws others in.

There is for the modern husband first of all a sense of entering a feminine world. The obstetrical-gynecological service in most medical centers reflects "maternalness." The carpeted floors and soft chairs and couches, all decorated in cheery primary colors, are punctuated by newborns back with their mothers for an early postpartum visit or by large, round pregnant women, a few accompanied by their husbands.

The husbands will enter the medical center with little confirmation from the environment that they too are in a time of change, since it is the women who are pregnant. The women are distended, round. The other husbands look little different from any other men encountered on the street. Often they sit reading magazines, or looking over work, having just come just from the office.

As we waited in the doctor's office for our first pregnancy checkup, I remember my wife glancing distractedly at *New Yorker* cartoons. I sat thinking about a client appointment scheduled later in the afternoon, looking at my watch and hoping I could get this visit over with soon enough to leave time to prepare notes for my lecture that night. My work felt like an anchor to hold onto, mooring me to a more familiar world. There was an uncomfortable feeling within me as I sat there preoccupied. I wanted to be quiet, hushed, remembering schoolmarms who scold, not wanting to attract their attention. I wanted to impress with my composure. Hey, man, I'm cool. Yet underneath it all lay a primitive fear or anxiety about women. John Updike writes about men's estrangement from the "dark, wet swampy world of women," and Joan Didion refers to the "water world" within which women live.[4] Pregnancy brings us back to that secret sea, the women's world that men renounce in growing up.

During pregnancies, we gain a different view of a woman's body, not as a sexual playground but rather as a source of life. At our first appointment the nurse gave my wife an internal examination while I waited, holding our coats, in the corner of the room. At the end the nurse turned to me offhandedly while taking off her rubber gloves and asked:

"Sam, have you ever seen Julie's cervix?"

The question caught me flat-footed.

"No, no, actually I haven't."

"Would you like to come over here and take a look?"

The notion of looking, really looking at the interior of a woman's reproductive system touched a primitive fear. Such a foreign, dark, mysterious canyon, leading to where, exactly? The nurse's thoughtfulness, though, provided an entrée into the pregnancy. I asked my wife shyly if she'd mind, and she replied laughingly, "No."

The nurse stepped aside and helped me identify the round, doughnut-shaped muscle deep inside the vagina, which served to protect our growing baby from the outside world. My wife's cervix reminded me of a powerful, strong confident clenched fist.

The husband now sees a powerful view of womanliness as life-creating and strong. The wife becomes "full" with the baby within. Ob-Gyn often reveals women taking care of women, their ability to hold life and each other. Watching the lifegiving nature of femininity can stir up a man's wish to be creative in a "feminine" way.

Decades ago the psychoanalyst Edith Jacobson reflected on why so many men in the course of analysis seemed to express almost stridently a *disinterest* in conceiving and bearing children. Her conclusion was that "men's conspicuous disinterest in having children of their own regularly proves to be a stubborn defense against a deeply repressed envy of women's reproductive capacities."[5] And indeed, psychologically minded anthropologists have created a rich literature examining the fertility myths and rituals that foreign cultures have developed to help males ward off and contain the feelings provoked by women's fearsome and mysterious capacity to create life within their bodies.

We don't have to buy the notion that the man wishes he had a womb to see that the man may have a wish to take care or nurture likewise, in a fuller way than he has learned to, to recontact those "feminine" parts of himself, and that he may see such caring as "feminine." For some men that can produce a painful struggle with their own feminine and masculine identifications. A study we made at the Simmons School of Social Work involved interviewing a small number of husbands and wives during pregnancy. The research staff heard husbands repeatedly talk of work-related concerns or choices, reflecting a symbolic concern about their own ability to be generative or nurturant themselves. The staff concluded: "Womb envy, feeling left out, frustration over their inability to share in the sheer creativity of pregnancy and birth were expressed in almost every male interview."[6]

For some men the loss of potency in the face of a pregnant wife can be too much. In her book *Babylove*, Joyce Maynard provides us with the description of a man struggling with such a plight:

The thing about a champagne drunk is, it doesn't last long, but while it lasts, far out. Normally Mark would prefer beer. But this stuff isn't half bad.

He's sitting on the bank of the Contoocook River, out behind the plant where he works. Used to work. He has sixty-three dollars in his pocket, from his last paycheck. The rest went for the champagne. Which is mostly gone now.

He's thinking about his son, who is five months old today. He's remembering the day Mark Junior was born. Sandy thinks the reason he ran out of the delivery room was the blood. She always blames him for that. She says he ruined the bonding.

It wasn't the blood at all. He had seen plenty of blood and guts, deer hunting. What he couldn't stand was the look on Sandy's face. She didn't even look like Sandy anymore. She could have been his mother, could've been his grandmother. Could've been a man, in fact. Mark had never seen anyone in that much pain, working that hard before. It made him feel like a jerk, that it was his wife, and not he, working so hard. Nothing he ever did in his whole life mattered, compared to that. And since then, it's as if she knows that too. He used to think she was so delicate and fragile. Now he knows that it is just a trick. She humors him, like he's a little boy. She knows, and someday his son will know, that when it came down to it, Sandy was the strong one. Mark just stood out in the hall throwing up.[7]

Growing up thinking that men are strong, women are weak; that male power is conquest; that strength alone resides in the outer world can lead to a true existential crisis when confronted with the power of pregnancy. Many men look inside themselves and wonder if they can nurture too.

Men's more intense involvement in their wives' pregnancy, then, can stir up feelings about their own creativity, their ability to hold life as men. Often I was to think of female holding, at the center, symbolized by the life my wife sustained within her pelvic girdle. What, I wondered, is the male analogue of the cervix? Of labor? The questions became more troublesome: Can I as a man nurture and hold others as a woman does? I wondered about the ways in which we may "hold" others emotionally, sustaining and nurturing each other. That evocative or receptive holding seemed very different from the problem-solving, opinionated, instrumental kind of caring that felt for a long time *masculine* to me. The search to become more "holding" of others was to play itself out in my work as a therapist and researcher.

The life within a wife's belly presents still another set of disquieting feelings: Many men identify with the fetus and find their own wishes to merge with a perfect, all-caring mother reactivated. Many men I've talked to report a feeling of disconnection, an internal sense of depletion, emptiness mixed in with the joy they feel before the birth. That feeling often comes late in the pregnancy, taking many different shapes and textures. One man, who worked about an hour's drive from home told of worrying his wife would give birth when he wasn't there, becoming obsessed in the last weeks that he worked too far away from her. *Disconnection*. Others experience a more visceral feeling; some men report feeling cold through the last weeks before birth.

During our last trimester I often felt empty, drained. One gray, bleak February day, awaiting our overdue baby, with an hour free between patients, I lay in my office chair and imagined myself as an empty urn tossed into the snow by Roman soldiers, lying stolidly in the foothills of the Appenines. I felt colder than the weather called for; searching purposefully through my closet I found a soft, wooly poncho I rarely wore. I went right for it and bundled up, feeling instantly warmer. With a shock I remembered it was a gift from my mother, brought back years ago from a trip to South America. I recognized my wish to be taken care of, warmed, by a maternal figure. I needed to spend a great deal of time not only supporting Julie and preparing for the birth but also retracing the sources of warmth and fullness in my life.

Being with a pregnant wife, watching the growth of life within her as she becomes a "full" maternal figure, may rekindle within the husband an awareness, however silent, of how well he was held when young. It may ignite his own tactile desires, his sense of skin, of bodily warmth, his yearning to be held and taken care of. For many men those sensual, tactile experiences were long ago put aside, the diffuse connection to the body broken in the passage to manhood, with sensuality channeled into the genitals.

As the wife becomes bigger and bigger in the extreme of her pregnancy, the world may feel lonelier and colder. Our own emptiness is put in bolder relief. Hence the wisdom of the Couvade ritual among primitive tribes, where the husband retreats to a hut and enacts the symptoms of pregnancy. He is filled up by miming his wife's reality, completed by the social customs and rituals offered him as a pregnant man.[8]

The questions about what it means to be a man and our own deepest wishes to be cared for are intensified because there are ways in which the husband really does become more dependent and needy, even as he is told to be, and expects to be, the strong, supportive man in the family for the woman who is "with child."

For instance, modern pregnancy puts many men for the first time in a situation where they have to collaborate with women (occasionally doctors, always nurses and midwives), often in a one-down position and a novel situation. Not used to being vulnerable and dependent on women or cooperating when needy, many men will try to make their primary alliance with the doctor or will need to put down the nurses even while they are being taken care of by them. For some men used to treating women during the work day as secretaries and subordinates, dealing with an Ob-Gyn nurse can be a threatening experience. From the nurse's perspective, the appearance of men may touch unexpected chords. Many Ob-Gyn nurses entered the field because they wanted to work with women. Many are highly sensitized to women's and feminist issues—and now they find husbands there too.

The husband is sometimes closed off from information that the wife possesses sheerly by having the pregnancy in her body, so that she receives more tactile bodily cues as to what is happening. He must often rely on her to tell him information he wants to know. Often the husband will find himself powerless to affect the situation. Feelings of helplessness and powerlessness are commonly reported by men during pregnancy.[9] Men may talk about "feeling like an observer." A thirty-six-year-old male social worker remarked about having a mere "reactive" role in the pregnancy: "She was the one changing physically. She was the one on the roller coaster. . . . There was nothing I could do to make her feel better."

The husband too watches his wife get enormous amounts of caring and attention, which can intensify his own wishes for the same. The spatial arrangment of husband, wife, and nurse or doctor in most medical encounters is such that the man is put on the periphery. The wife will be on the examining table, her feet in the stirrups, the nurse or doctor standing, attending to the wife. The husband will often be sitting or standing in the corner, holding the coats. Throughout our visits (though not during the birth) I felt on the edge, the periphery, while my wife lay in the center.

Up to a point, that is as it should be: The good health of the wife and fetus is the primary concern. Yet the degree to which many husbands become emotionally "invisible" during the pregnancy affects the health of the family and the course of the pregnancy.

Without idealizing the "sisterly" bond created because women are more attuned to each other's concerns, the husband in this situation will have to express his fears and anxieties more openly. That may leave him feeling uncomfortably vulnerable and angry at showing such need to a woman in a female situation, where women could turn on him, making a fool of himself. Those are adolescent preoccupations that many men never outgrow. Other men may find themselves with feelings of being a much younger boy, needing Mother.

At the end of our three-month checkup the nurse asked, "Are there any questions?" Her tone conveyed both a brisk efficiency and a willingness to reassure us. It was our first appointment with her since the miscarriages, and the farthest we've gotten. There were a million questions I wanted to ask, all shilling for the fundamental one tugging at my heart: How can we keep this pregnancy from miscarrying? The only real question, in other words, was the one for which there is no answer. Instead I found myself asking: "Will sex during pregnancy cause harm, er, increase our chances of miscarrying again?"

That question carried with it, like an armored Brinks truck hauling its unseen treasure of gold bullion, all my hope that this pregnancy would not once again end in sadness and grief. *That's* what I really wanted to say: how scared we both are, stepping out again, having our hopes engaged. Sex is an appropriate topic for men to show concern about. Fear of loss is not.

Listening to the nurse ask, "Are there any other questions?" the open-ended caring implicit in the question, despite her tone of medical efficency (artfully, she managed to convey both messages at the same time), I felt like a little kid about to show a splinter to Mother. Having learned to hold our pain in, we pay the price. The nurse answered my question about sex reassuringly; my fears of loss remained hidden. I refused to make myself vulnerable to that nurse, refused to let her take care of me, refused to do the hard work myself of asking for her help, threading my way through the medical put-off, the efficency of our HMO, her unease at working with husbands.

I felt like a five-year-old, an adolescent, *and* an adult all at once. Sitting in that examination room looking up at the nurse, standing there all composed and pretty in her white uniform, my anger became palpable. I was unwilling to admit how out of control I felt, to admit my fears of hurting the fetus through sex, of not being able to shepherd this developing baby to life, how much it mattered to me that the baby make it. I would not admit such things to this perky blonde thirty-year-old. Memories of girls in high school flooded my mind. Girls, adolescent, standing near the school entrance in formidable herds talking hushedly among themselves. As a teenager a line is drawn between the sexes.

There's the rub: This vulnerability, feeling like a leaky bag of hopes and fears, while the woman seems all composed and competent, can produce true rage in men. *The silent wound:* Having learned growing up as men to suppress our neediness or dependency, not having learned how to deal with it maturely, we get angry when suddenly confronting our vulnerability again. An old demon comes back to haunt us. And where is our neediness exposed most regularly but in relationships with women, during the new, demanding transitions into marriage and parenting?

I wrote in my journal during that time:

Tremors within the male psyche during pregnancy. Women's bodies as a foreign world from which I have been separated first as a boy then as a man. Now I'm supposed to treat it as familiar turf. No change. Memories of mixers, dating bars, sex as predatory, sex as competition to prove my worth, sex as salvation for my soul's loneliness. The womb a mysterious, dark, steamy bog in which I am now lost. What is my role, what am I to do in this pregnancy? Girls as rejectors, taunters, judges, tempters. Now let's work together!

The real-life vulnerabilities and sense of neediness of men during pregnancy also lie in the recognition that they have become dependent on the fetus. As we noted in the previous chapter, research indicates that many men are strongly bonded with their babies even before they are born. It is our vulnerability we feel too: How much we care about the baby, and how little there is to do except let nature take its course. Except for practicing the breathing and birthing techniques to be used, there is little to do in the last trimester. The husband may want to *do* something, to perform, to safeguard what he needs and loves as he's been taught to do as a man, yet there is nothing to do. He must sit and wait. We are brought into touch with what Gilligan refers to as the "tragic" dimension of life: that our vulnerability and connection to others cannot be hidden behind impersonal actions and instrumental decisions.[10]

Men do not, of course, actually carry the baby. Their deep connection to the fetus, however, makes pregnancy for many the first time in adult life when they find themselves actually letting life emerge slowly, patiently, caring in that "feminine" way, not by dominating the situation or conquering it but by letting it emerge, feeling the texture of one's own vulnerability, respecting the uniqueness of one's connection to the other (the fetus, one's wife) as a mortal, limited human being. In having to care without being able to conquer, we may learn to tolerate our vulnerability and that of others, to respect it a little more.

A man may feel empty and vulnerable during pregnancy too because of the real-life problems men face in evolving or anticipating a fulfilling image of themselves as father. We've already seen that many of the social cues the man receives say that it's the wife who is pregnant. Yet it is extremely important that the husband think about himself, rehearse, anticipate himself in a satisfying, full way as a father, in a way that feels emotionally connected to the infant, enfolding, as a *male*. Thinking about yourself holding the baby, playing, taking care of him or her, will counter the sad emptiness that pregnancy can evoke.

The husband during pregnancy may struggle with the feeling of not knowing how to nurture and father in a fuller way. The feeling of emptiness in men during pregnancy may arise from the expectant father's feeling of being pulled away from work by the deep yearnings a pregnancy evokes at a time when work itself serves as a reassuring "anchor" in a new world. One must have faith that the self as nurturer can fill the void created by slowly letting go somewhat of the work-centered, instrumental self. Within each new father is a struggle to evolve a sense of self as *caring*. Throughout our pregnancy I had an image of my newborn infant close to my chest, his head resting on my shoulder. The deep fear was that I would not hold my child well enough, that I would drop the soft package I was responsible for, literally through lack of strengh. Yet the fear was metaphoric as well. There are many ways to drop a child; not being there psychologically for him is one. The fear of not being able to hold him paralleled a struggle in many relationships: that I wouldn't allow myself into his world, that the connection between us would be broken by work commitments that I would allow to pull me away.

The problem is that many expectant fathers may receive messages from the social and work world that play on our fantasies of being a bad or "frustrating" father. When a man makes public his wife's pregnancy, at work or among friends, he may experience an undercurrent of loss and depletion coming from them. Of course, the initial reactions are "Oh, how wonderful for you!" or "A baby, great!" Yet starting a family means *displacing* work commitments and friends in your life. It means choosing the demands of a child over time spent at work or going out with friends. Without realizing it, people who depend on the husband at work may want to ensure that his commitment to their common work is not affected by the new baby. Friends may feel rejected or hurt. It's as if they all are saying *don't leave me!*

As a therapist—dealing with basic issues of separation and

loss—revealing to clients that I was taking two weeks off because my wife and I were having a baby produced strong feelings of loss and anger. Many clients come to therapy because they feel at root unloved and unlovable. Some clients responded as displaced siblings, others as jilted lovers. Did they count too? Would I have time for them? Each responded in terms of his or her particular character and conflicts, yet each did react, and the cumulative wave of feelings—of loss, of my kicking them out, of not being good enough, of not *really caring*—ricochetted back in terms of my own fear of what I would become as a father.

A thirty-year-old man, single, having great difficulty establishing a relationship with a woman, had over the years developed a humorous, yet deeply felt, way of making connection to me. Each week before entering my office he would stop on the threshold, look at me, and say, half sarcastically, "time for the Sam and Ted show," a reference to our therapy as a kind of TV talk show I hosted. That was his sardonic, affectionate way of describing therapy, so different from the sports-oriented, less personal kind of connection he was used to making with men. Soon after I told him about the baby and my brief "paternity leave," he came up the stairs, stopped, looked at me, and said sadly, "No more Sam and Ted show."

A week after I told a middle-aged woman about my two-week break and the reasons why, she began mentioning how cold the office felt. The woman had never mentioned the temperature in a year of meetings, but now she wondered if I could turn up the heat, the office seemed so "chilly."

So in addition to the good feelings people have toward the husband, there may be a sense of loss and displacement provoked by the husband's becoming a father. Men of older generations were protected from those subtle undercurrents of reaction by the Proud Papa role: Because the expectations were not that the father would heavily alter his work and social commitments (although many of course did), there may have been less sense of competition among friends, work, and family for his time. The father would therefore receive fewer messages that he was abandoning others in becoming a father. For men today, many of whom are expected or want to be present in the family, there is a basic tension between his concern to be a nurturing father and the message the real world may beam back at him: You are uncaring for leaving us for your family.

Staying Safe with Sex and Work

Reflecting back on his experience, a thoughtful new father in his mid-thirties pointed out that "men no longer have the old role to retreat into during pregnancy; we've lost the chance to pace in the waiting room nervously away from it all. Now we're supposed to be right there with our wife giving birth, but we haven't really defined what that new role, that new experience is like."

Within our society the traditional division of labor served to protect men from the pregnancy experience. Our fathers needed only to look strong and in control, strutting proud as a peacock in the waiting room while their wives and the doctors "delivered" the baby. In that way the man's anxiety was contained.

The Couvade ritual among primitive tribes contained the husband's anxiety, rage, and sadness in socially acceptable rituals. The "pregnancy symptoms" that the husband mimed provided him with social support and a way to express his own participation in the experience, while his withdrawal to a physically distant location separated him from the family and thus protected all participants from his rage and jealousy of the wife and newborn. Men today are left without ritualized ways to express either their participation in the pregnancy experience or the distanced social role of Proud Papa in the waiting room.

So what happens? I suspect many men sexualize their interactions with women or become highly instrumental to assert their power or control during the pregnancy experience.

First let's look at the sexual feelings of husbands during their wives' pregnancy. Family therapists know that pregnancy and the first years of fathering are a delicate time for couples. The sexual attraction of husbands to other women is a standing joke in many couples; therapists are familiar with marriages in which the husband becomes involved in sexual acting-out during the wife's pregnancy.

For some men sexuality becomes a grounding, a way to define their role in the pregnancy experience. Their sexual role as the impregnator of women may be a way for them to assert their creative role in the experience.

And sexuality may be a way a man reduces the terrible vulnerability and helplessness around women—his wife and the nurses, for example—which he feels in the pregnancy situation.

During the points in our medical examinations when I felt the most vulnerable, I often found myself also physically attracted to our nurse. In the examination room one day the nurse, my wife, and I had been discussing vitamin supplements during pregnancy. She turned to Julie, still lying on the examination table. As I sat in the corner I thought how attractive she looked. A cute turn of the nose, lovely, smooth-looking skin; slim, tan legs extend demurely below the hemline of her white, oh-so-professional nurse's uniform. She listed the vitamins my wife would need during pregnancy. I found myself wondering what this woman would be like in bed. It was as if Richard Gere had waltzed into the examination room, replacing me. Vast spaces of my mind surveyed this woman, even as I listened half-intelligently to my wife's questions to her. I imagined her in a singles bar. I walk up to her in this imaginary scene and start a conversation, feeling an attraction between us. She turns her head flirtatiously to me, smiles . . . Through all this the conversation about food supplements and diet droned on; I even participated in it, as if my mind had dual tracks.

My musings about that nurse as a potential date in a different life were innocent enough, clearly under control and subordinate to my knowledge of myself as a rational, responsible, concerned husband. They probably emanated from many sources: the silly wish to be free of the web of hope, attachment, and potential loss in which I now lived my life, for one. From the demands of marriage and imminent fatherhood to the free and easy life of the single male. Yet the sexual undercurrent to the fantasy was so strong. I wondered about the many cases of men who become involved sexually with other women. Perhaps that tells us something about the male experience of sex as an assertion of power.

In my fantasy I was no longer a vulnerable husband, tightly bound by my hope to the life growing inside my wife's womb and to the reassurances of nurses. No, now I was a powerful sexual male, not a vulnerable male needing help from this competent woman, the nurse. Instead, in my mental gymnastics, she became, through the power of phallic sexual fantasy, the one attracted to and dependent on me.

So perhaps the grasping onto a phallic sexual attitude toward women is one way in which men cope with the vulnerability they feel during pregnancy, a way of restoring an imbalanced power relationship unfamiliar and unacceptable to men, in which they are dependent on competent women.

Clearly many men need to find a way out of their vulnerability. A second escape route lies in retreating to a rigidly instrumental role in the pregnancy situation. The husband may feel reassured when identifying with the doctors, becoming an expert, and focusing narrowly on what he has to do for the wife, who is the needy one. One father of two children responded to his wife's pregnancies each in similar fashion, attempting to move from a position of "outsider" to that of "expert." Instructing, part time, a prenatal class for expectant fathers enabled him to assume an instrumental, authoritative role in a domain where he was otherwise a passive observer. (Ironically, this person reported that time away from home to teach this class became a source of conflict between him and his wife.)

Many of the social cues will push men toward trying to act instrumental and in control during pregnancy. In many childbirth classes the focus is on breathing techniques to control pain and anxiety during the birth process itself. The husband is put in the role of "labor coach" for his wife, focusing on his role as support and aid in carrying out the mental focusing and breathing techniques learned in class. Such procedures are excellent aids during the birth process, but many childbirth classes don't provide much opportunity for the husband to explore his feelings about the pregnancy. He stays bottled up in the "coach role" alone.

And there is the lack of male models. Consider that the other males in the situation are usually doctors, models of competence, power, and control. As men we communicate restraint to each other in that silent, nonverbal way: "We men are taking care of things." The bond of male competence often unites the husband with the doctors. The husband may feel "feminine" or deviant for having uncharacteristic needs and feelings, which he will then keep bottled up behind the competent pose.

The husband's search for an instrumental place in the pregnancy may create tensions within the couple. One woman, who had been through a grueling thirty-two-hour labor, revealed with annoyance that "the medical team acted as though they were teaching him to become a doctor. . . . He was into the scientific, the biological and the educational. The doctor let him examine the placenta and showed him everything that was going on in the room. When the baby was born, my husband didn't even kiss me. He didn't do anything. I was disappointed and bothered by his reaction. He was more or less looking at the baby and watching what the doctor was doing. Then it was all over." Since the medical staff must cope with the husband's needs as well as the wife's, the presence of the husband increases the complexity of the birthing event.

Another husband exemplifies the self-imposed expectations and social pressures on men to act in more traditionally masculine ways in the delivery room. He proudly reported that he had cleared the corridors to make a path for his wife to the delivery room. "I fell right into it. I knew what had to be done and where we were going. There were some trays and rolling carts in there, and I'm going right along in stride, and I walked in and started pushing them out and asking them where they wanted this and let's get this show on the road."

Often men will find "professional" ways to become more nurturing. An increased involvement in work may compensate for the sense of isolation and the uncomfortable questions raised about male power. One new father told me, "I felt often during pregnancy that I was searching for a 'pseudo-intimacy' with people at work." Yet the yearning for intimacy is not false. The husband is often practicing a more nurturant and receptive posture, trying to express a caring attitude that is blocked by the way he sees himself or by the expectations others have of him.

In our study at Simmons we noted the numbers of husbands for whom the wife's pregnancy raised unconscious questions about their own creativity. For several subjects, work or work-related activities or special projects served the function of involving them vicariously in a process from which nature had excluded them physiologically. For them work projects and goals became a "symbolic pregnancy." One thirty-five-year-old scientist with a wife seven months pregnant talked at length about a professional paper he was working very hard to finish. He came to regard it as "a parallel pregnancy . . . in a sense, to finish my paper before the baby arrives."

Work may become one way in which men symbolically pursue their unanswered questions about gender identity. A social work graduate student whose wife is an actress selected a topic for his graduate thesis during her pregnancy: a study of whether creative people are more or less mentally ill than the rest of the population.

Advice for Pregnant Couples

Pregnancy can be the time when a man finally grows up, overcoming his jealousy and resentment of the creative power of women and beginning to explore how he too can nurture and care in a fuller way than he has before. A man may overcome too some of his resentments toward other men and his ambivalence about being a man, thereby allowing himself to take a stronger, more assertive role with his family.

Here are some thoughts on what may lead the husband in that direction:

Don't be afraid to ask questions, to get information, to make your vulnerability known. Try to get beyond age-old expectations that nurses and doctors will magically take care of you, and know what you're thinking. Remember their discomfort in dealing with the emotional needs of men, and try to reach out to them. A tremendous empowerment comes of no longer having to be silent.

Express your feelings to your wife, remembering that you and she will not always feel exactly the same. The wife's reaction to her pregnancy and her husband during pregnancy is important in shaping the husband's involvement. One recent study by Feldman, Nash, and Aschenbrenner reported that the wife's reaction to her pregnancy was more predictive of future fathering patterns than the man's own reaction to the experience. The personality traits and maternal role she carved out were useful in predicting paternal involvement: Wives who became introverted and withdrawn while pregnant had husbands who were less satisfied with fatherhood postpartum. We can hypothesize that the quality of husband–wife interaction and communication in that situation had something to to with the development of paternal identity.[11]

Allow yourself to feel your ambivalence. Your life is changing; pregnancy is the first step in the enormous life change into fatherhood. All large life transitions involve changes in identity and take time to negotiate. The transition to fatherhood is no different. What changes seem most difficult? What are you *losing* and what are you *gaining* in becoming a father?

A good starting point for men during pregnancy is their unfinished agenda with their own fathers. Consider how well held you felt by your own father. What do you feel his expectations were for you? How do you hope to be similar to or different from your own father? How about your mother? Have you come to ask for things from your wife that you feel your mother didn't give you? What are your hidden agenda and secret expectations about what you are entitled to from your wife?

Reach out to other men. I think it is of great importance to find sources of social support from other men: new fathers and old fathers, as well as friends without children. I have been struck by the isolated position many expectant fathers get into—not turning to other men for help, to talk over what they are feeling. Partly this reflects the problem men have in dealing with each other: We don't get a lot of support and insight from each other. Women will cluster around at parties discussing mothering; sometimes women with babies will strike up conversations at supermarket checkout counters or in the laundromat. In that way they are passing along the folklore of mothering, helping to socialize each other into a maternal identity. Rarely do men do that for each other.

Among men the sad reality is that after having a child they are often less available to each other than before. The added press of childcare on top of the demands of work, marriage, and self makes us more insular and isolated.

At a recent conference entitled "When Therapists Become Fathers," one of the main points that emerged was the loneliness involved in the transition to parenthood. The meeting was filled with intense conversation and disagreements abounding; it went way over the alloted time. Several men wanted to go out to lunch afterward to continue the conversation. Hesitation. One man said sheepishly, "I don't know if I can take the time, I'm supposed to be home to take the baby at one." Another: "I can't take the time for lunch with you all. I only have this one day away from the family, and I want to attend other lectures."

One doctor revealed that he had recently joined a group practice composed entirely of physicians who had recently had children. The work situation had formed itself partly for the very reason that all the men shared that experience of being fathers. He wanted to feel support and understanding from his colleagues at work.

Often men don't reach out because they feel like failures for their confusing angry-sad feelings. They may think other men don't go through such experiences. Men get beaten down too by impossible expectations, feeling that to live up to the male image they can't admit to their fears and insecurities.

Imagine yourself as a father. What does it feel like? How will you be a similar parent to your wife? How different? Imagine youself holding and carrying your child.

Remember too that given the current state of male–female relationships, many women today are angry at men and will resent men who claim a place in the pregnancy experience. The sexual-political undertow adds to the difficulty in finding a fuller place within a mutual event (a pregnancy) that most men and women feel happens primarily to the woman. Yet the fact that only the woman experiences the unique reality of being physically pregnant need not detract from or negate the fact that the husband needs information, reassurance, and support as he explores this mysterious part of life and constructs for himself the new role of Father, a major life transition.

6

Fatherhood as a Healing and Wounding Experience

Soon after the birth of his first child, the author E. B. White wrote to a friend: "I feel the mixed pride and oppression of fatherhood in the very base of my spine."[1]

We come now to fatherhood in our survey of men's struggle with the wounded father. The grown son often becomes himself a father. Children have always ignited the emotional lives of their parents, yet today there is a special intensity to many men's feelings about becoming a father. Our knowledge of the price we pay for remote fathers makes us want to father differently. Many men bring considerable goodwill and a desire for change to the task, yet we also live in the real world of traditional social pressures, reality demands, and internalized expectations. What is the transition to fatherhood like for men today?

E. B. White wrote the words quoted above in the mid-1940s, yet they remain an apt description of the ambivalent feelings men experience in becoming fathers. In this chapter I focus on those mixed feelings, particularly the healing and wounding aspects of fatherhood. For many men becoming a father creates an internal struggle with the needy child and the wounded father within, leading to a flight into work. For other men fatherhood can mean the development of a more complete sense of self and a healed relationship with with one's own father, as it provides a new perspective on his life. I believe our feelings about our fathers are a key for men in evolving a fuller role for themselves as fathers.

The transition to fatherhood is one of the most significant in a man's life. The Yale psychologist Daniel Levinson sees the transition to fatherhood as a "marker event" in a man's life.[2] Many men compare its impact on them to a very different marker event: the death of one's own parent. In both bases one feels the mixed dread and liberation at being called upon by life to grow up.

There is much writing today about how important bonding with the father is for the child. In this chapter we'll see why the transition into fatherhood is important for the man's adult development and how it is an ongoing process that extends years after the birth of our children.

The Father as a Needy Child

Mr. Baker is a confident businessman in Philadelphia, the head of a chain of food stores. He is thirty-five years old. His wife is a stockbroker. There is a two-year-old boy at home, and I asked him what life had been like for him since he became a father. He began in an upbeat fashion:

"Life's a little different now than it was before, it's just a real pleasure. I mean we are enjoying it. My wife is real busy right now." After taking several months off after the birth of the baby, she had gone back to her demanding job at the brokerage house.

"Children take a tremendous amount of time and effort, and she had expected that she would be able to have the baby and continue working, and not have it make any difference. What she did was wear herself into exhaustion."

He became silent as he turned a feeling around in his mind. Then he said, "She pays a great deal of attention to our son. Things were fairly blah by last spring. There just wasn't much excitement, and there were just a number of demands. Our son does take more time." He hesitates as he gets to the point.

"I think it took, there was a time actually, when my wife had to get the right balance of our son, the new baby, and me the old baby, sort of thing. I probably felt left out a little bit. . . . If things had continued the way they were, and if we hadn't been able to talk about it, I can see how people break up."

Note that Mr. Baker started out talking of the "real pleasure" of having a child and wound up focused on the "blah" of it all. His words, similar to stories from other new fathers, left me wondering: What is it about becoming a father that leaves men feeling like needy children?

First of all, the transition of wife to mother and the presence of a dependent infant brings the husband back in touch with his own hunger for being taken care of and held, which has been pushed aside in the rush to become a man. Watching a baby at the breast, holding and carrying his baby, and changing diapers revive our own earliest memories and sensations of what it was like for us to be taken care of by our mothers and fathers. In order to develop a true identity as a father, a man must draw on his own memories and feelings of his mother and father. That can create great conflict if the man had to give up too quickly his own wishes to be held, to be cared for. The press of those wishes can be very disturbing to a man whose sense of self hinges on a doer-provider identity.

The psychologist Louise Kaplan notes that "a man's fatherliness is enriched as much by his acceptance of his feminine and childlike strivings as it is by his memories of tender closeness with his own father. . . . When a man becomes a father it is particularly important for him to regain emotional contact with his history of once having been a child and a son to a mother and father."[3] Yet such contact may be painful to some men. A lawyer once described his difficulty coming home and playing with his children because it reminded him of his father, who "was always acting like the infant in the house." What he is saying here is that adaptively regressing with his children puts him back in touch with his resentment at his father, the way the old man took over too much space in the house and seemed to give him so little. Another man was even more direct. He told me that "whenever I give to my daughter I get angry at how little my father gave me."

Kaplan comments that "many men who have been well-nurtured in early childhood cannot revive the memories and emotions associated with good mothering, because in our culture the values associated with masculinity require that male children renounce their ties to the mother and reject dependency and neediness."[4]

A new father may feel a lot of anger he doesn't understand, from which he may need to protect his family. On the other hand, becoming a father may heal a man's relationship to his own body and some of the rage that he feels. An infant holds the father as much as the father holds the infant. He or she restores the father to his own body, through a touch, a searching mouth, two big eyes, an eager grasp, a strength palpable beneath the baby softness. Talking to fathers, I have been impressed with the importance of the tactile connection between father and child.

Having a child may put the father in contact with more nurturing parts of himself as a male. Holding one's child, feeding him, carrying him, feeling the strong, monkey-like grip around his shoulders, the soft-strong body clinging to his as if father were now the Tree of Life, a man may feel life-giving in a new way. The poet Robert Bly may have felt similarly when he wrote to his ten-year-old son, "the kind man moves closer, loses his rage."[5] We identify with our children and in giving to them heal the resentful sides of ourselves that have never felt well enough taken care of.

Other men I've talked to say that becoming a father has helped them locate and actualize the nurturer within. One Vietnam vet, now a successful lawyer, spent four years as a househusband after his son was born: "I was trying to get over the war, to become a sane person in an insane society. My son taught me how to do that."

There are also real changes in the marriage that can leave a husband feeling like a needy child. Parenthood begins in conditions of deprivation as well as joy: Sleep patterns are disrupted, sudden new demands from home complicate established commitments to work, the home itself becomes a more demanding place, and the man's relationship to his wife grows more demanding as well.

For many men home carries with it connotations of being taken care of, a place of rest and relaxation from the demanding public world in which many of us live our lives. Surely most men know that the home is not there just to take care of them, and that their wives need caretaking too. Yet becoming a father means that the home changes in ways that touch on our wishes to be mothered.

The husband is displaced from the center of his wife's attention by the newborn. The dyad becomes a triad, and a lopsided one at that, as the mother–child bond seems to outweigh the mother–father one or the father–child bond.

Many men feel a sense of exclusion, wanting to be involved from the beginning and feeling uninvolved. "There is no relationship closer than that of mother and infant breastfeeding," a man once said to me with longing. "You can't get any closer than that." Some men feel unable to break into the tightness of the mother–child bond. Yet the task of making a place for oneself in the family as a man is a crucial task for new fathers.

New fathers lose their wives in more subtle ways. For example, in families where wives stop working or change their work commitments, the husband's and wife's lives may be thrown out of synch with each other.

Consider Mr. and Mrs. Abrams. He is a computer engineer who tells me about the "conflictive pressure" he feels in his life as we sit in his office, surrounded by "functional-modern" decor, the windows overlooking the rolling hills of Westchester County. Since the birth of his daughter his wife no longer works. Mrs. Abrams had a full-time career as a corporate financial analyst. Now she has changed, and so has their marriage. She left her position as a corporate analyst and "has chosen to stay home and be a full-time mother. She feels she's made some sacrifices to do that." So he confronts a different situation when he arrives home, different from the interested, supportive wife who in years past had the time and energy to relax with him and talk about what their work days had been like:

"She feels at the end of a week, and I think with good reason, that she's put in a long, hard week, and she's had full-time responsibility for keeping this one child interested and entertained. So when Sunday comes around and she's been sitting at home all week, being a babysitter, what she wants to do is get out of the house and do something at the same time that I want to sit down and relax."

In many couples the husband and wife are psychologically out of synch with each other in quite profound ways. The husband usually retains primary connection with his work and career commitments, while the wife, at least in the first months or years of parenthood, cuts back on her work. For many women who developed competencies in the work world, the pull back into the home as they become mothers can be quite disturbing.

My impression is that both men and women today underestimate the difficulty of the transition into motherhood for women who have grown up expecting they'd be able to combine career and family, determined to avoid their mothers' fate of being "just housewives." In several recent studies of new parents the wives report that the primary negative impact of the child is on their work life; many expressed surprise at how disruptive motherhood is to their careers.[6] In such cases the wife may be struggling with the fear that her adult self has been undermined as she spends most of her time at home with a child. Her husband's relatively intact commitments to the "adult world" through his career may fuel a wife's understandable resentment and jealousy of his options. Feeling that she has been "swallowed up" by mothering, the wife may have less patience and less desire to "mother" her husband in the traditional ways that she has. As Mr. Abrams tells us, his wife feels she has made "sacrifices" in becoming a full-time mother and wants to get out of the house just as he comes home.

The problem is that the husband often comes home expecting or wanting to relax after working hard all day. Of course, even if Mrs. Abrams agreed to stay home it would be hard to "relax" with two young children. Mr. Abrams speaks of how "disorderly and out of control" the house seems to him. Many men have told me the family becomes chaotic when children arrive. It demands affective skills, patience, and tolerance for the seemingly ceaseless and at times nonnegotiable demands of children. Having depended on the home as a support system to nurture him in his day-to-day struggles in the public world, the husband may feel betrayed and abandoned by his now demanding wife and family.[7]

The Development of a Paternal Identity

Like many profound life changes, becoming a father is a process that extends over time. Many of the fathers I interviewed in the Adult Development Project had children between ages one and five, yet it was clear that the development of their sense of being a "father" was still going on years after the birth.[8]

One of the tasks in the development of a new identity is the exploration and integration of the mixed, complex feelings we experience during a time of change. Many new fathers find themselves without clear guidelines as to what it means to be a father, besides providing financially. A wife has to evolve into a mother, but physiological and social cues help the woman to discover what it means to be a mother, serving to reduce somewhat the great anxiety that the woman might feel about being good enough. We underestimate the isolation of the new father. If the husband has depended on the wife to interpret family experiences for him, the wife's attention to the newborn may deprive him of that ally, simply because she no longer has the time or energy to serve that function. The social isolation of new fathers from other men, a problem that begins in pregnancy, is likely to increase during fatherhood as we become more family-focused and struggle with heightened time pressure. So the husband is left alone with many unexpected feelings amidst a home environment that suddenly seems out of control.

One new feeling is the engrossment of the father with his child. The phrase "engrossment" refers to the deep psychological bonding and fascination the father feels toward his newborn.[9] But there is an underside to "engrossment." We can feel drained and weary ourselves, with little time or energy for ourselves either alone or with our allies, our wives. It is easy to become so focused on the child as to forget that you and your wife have separate existences and needs. Some studies show a decline of 50 percent in husband–wife interaction postpartum.[10] I remember how much of our time and energy we both focused on Toby when he was born, and this sad, angry, jealous part of myself. A few minutes of talking over coffee at a café with my wife would help.

It's easy to underestimate how much colder and lonelier the world may feel to men once they become fathers. The father may become preoccupied with being able to support his new family and may struggle with conflicting commitments outside the family. For about the first year I remember feeling tired and more fragile with less energy for outside worldly pursuits.

Shifting values and priorities provoked by becoming a father may also leave us feeling vulnerable. The birth of my son lessened my interest in the traditional ways I had learned to feel good about myself. Suddenly taking care of business, doing all the maintenance work my career required—keeping in touch, exploring new possibilities, keeping my salary secure—all felt too draining. I yearned to stay home with my new boy and watch him, to be absorbed into the cozy family scene taking place between mother and baby.

The depth of feeling a father can have toward his child can also be disturbing. Unambivalent love can be a novel and uncomfortable feeling for a man used to a single-minded pursuit of external, observable, provable goals reached in short order, the kind of goals careers usually provide. The striking realization that there is another world beyond work and public success can be unsettling. One can suddenly feel very vulnerable if one's main efforts have been to master the public world, to search for security, success, and safety in the fame, salary, or goodwill of powerful people that commitment to career may bring.

Most men feel ambivalent about how much time to commit to the family, and that is a source of distressing emotions. Men I've talked with report a dual-track problem, unaccustomed to having so much feeling tied up at home, but also being pulled to work. It felt to me for a long time that when at home I was thinking of work, and when at work I was thinking of my family. A teacher said the same thing more poignantly when he talked about taking care of his infant boy: "I love being home with him, watching him crawl across the floor, playing together. There is such a challenge of responding and watching his brave, tentative explorations of the world. Yet too I find I often can't stop thinking about work. My mind sometimes feels like it was brought into this world for the analytic, orderly tasks of work. The slower, more languid play-work of taking care of my baby feels at times like molasses I can't get to stay in my hand. He crawls, plays some by himself. Shall I get a ball from the other room and roll it toward him? Shall I leave him alone? I find myself reading the newspaper while he plays alongside me. The two of us in parallel play, different sandboxes. Except then a few hours later I am back in my office, and my mind now plays another trick on me: I struggle to pay attention to what I'm doing but now I can't keep my mind off my boy! Suddenly I want to be home with him, away from the office I now find strangely barren."

Finally, the postpartum home can become a place where the husband feels uncomfortably secondary to his wife. In many families the wife and husband collude to make her the "family expert" to whom he has to turn for guidance and help. Because she is perceived (often correctly) as the one who has done reading on childcare and "knows what to do," the husband will defer to her about decisions. The wife may feel overburdened in this situation, but the husband too is giving up power and may go along with decisions that he doesn't feel really a part of. Here is one man talking about the key decision that his wife would leave her work and stay home full time, a choice that meant he had to supplement his income even as she felt some loss at letting go of her career: "She had every intention when we had our daughter that after a couple of years she was going back to work, to continue her career. And she did a lot of reading about bringing up children, and what was important, and she came to the conclusion that it would not be a good thing for our children for her to abandon them for eight-plus hours a day while she went off to a job." Note the choice of words: It was *her* decision to stay home. One senses not that he disagrees so much as he feels outside, distant from the decisions that dramatically affect his life.

The wife-as-family-expert pattern is a big trap for many husbands, because it also makes it more difficult for them to establish a comfortable sense of themselves as fathers, and when they turn to their wives it is often as a little kid would turn to his mother, needing help to cope. Many new fathers did in fact as children experience mother as the one who knew what was going on in the family and father as incompetent or absent. Taking a more active role may feel inappropriate or risky to the new father.

Among many new couples the husband needs to spend time by himself with his new child in order to develop a real sense of "fatherliness," and the wife needs to allow the husband the opportunity to experiment with that role and seem vulnerable when trying to master what had been a feminine role. For a while after my son was born, I had to practice diapering on a teddy bear, because I was so frightened of hurting him by sticking him with the pins.

The Wounded Father at Dinner Time

Often the husband–wife skirmishes attendant on the father's daily return home from work are a microcosm of the tensions that keep the man on the periphery of his family.

Let us return to Mr. Abrams, the computer scientist with the disorderly home, for illustration. He tells me with a clear tone of sadness and pain in his voice that "we've had periods of several months where most of the time one of us would be mad at the other."

Could he tell me about one of those times? He had no trouble thinking of an example: "Well, last night. A fight." His mind turned to that tricky transition from work to home, often between 5 and 7 P.M., a potentially explosive time for many couples:

"We had plans to go out and had to leave at 7:30, I got home at 6:30, and I went upstairs to change my clothes, came down, and asked her what the schedule was for dinner. Did I have time to pour myself a drink, sit down, and read the mail before we had supper? She said, 'I've had such a bad day, I haven't had time to plan a schedule.' " There is a poignant tone in his trying to understand her exasperation: "It was clear that she felt I was asking her for a planned out schedule at a time when she really didn't want to have to think one out."

For men, this transition at the end of the day from work to home presents the problem of shifting gears. After a day of being rational and responding to a million demands from people, you arrive home and with little respite are plunged all over again into a new sea of demanding people, your wife and children. At workshops on work–family stress at large corporations the problem of shifting gears repeatedly comes up. "I'm walking up the stairs after putting the car away and I hear my wife through the front door saying excitedly to our kids, 'Here comes Daddy, here comes Daddy!' and I think 'Oh, no!'" The workshop participant went on: "Of course I want to see my kids, but I want a break. Instead, when I open the door there they all are waiting for me." He can see his wife's perspective too: "She's been home all day, wants some relief and help. But it's like all the work I've done during the day doesn't count at all; I'm handed a bill when I walk in the door."

What often happens at those moments is that both husband and wife assert their neediness. The wife is exhausted from taking care of the children, and the husband is tired from the demands of the day. The problem today is that since there is often no clear agreement on how much childcare is the wife's work and how much the husband's, there is an unstated tension over who is doing more and who is getting more.

Often, too, the husband is revealing the adult psychological residue of his childhood experience of his own father. If father was allowed to come home and escape the demands of family life, the man may feel entitled to the same prerogatives. When confronted by his wife, the man may then feel humiliated, unmanly, or cheated of the opportunity to enter the family in the same way Dad did.

The demands of shifting gears can, though, be healing to the man's understanding of his father's own behavior. One executive who is very committed to being home on time at night to play with his young children told me that "after a few months of pulling into the driveway at 6 P.M. and feeling like I wanted to sneak away for a few private moments after a hard day's work, I finally understood why my father walked in the door all those years and headed straight for the liquor cabinet. I've always felt so rejected and angry at his distant behavior in the home, like he didn't have time for me. I'd wonder whether he preferred a vodka and tonic to me. Now I see it didn't *really* have anything to do with me—he was feeling overwhelmed and scared. He put that drink up like a wall between us. I can understand why he was that way without being just like him myself when I walk in the door."

In terms of the family, the problem can be approached, on the one hand, if we think of 5 to 7, or whenever father (or mother) comes home from work as a *transitional time*. Father has to be integrated into the family and provided with time and space to do it. That's often what sitting down and opening up the newspaper was all about. Providing a momentary space, within the family but slightly apart, allows the person to cool out from the day and adjust to the new circumstances of being home. Men will sometimes do that on the way home, sometimes stopping for a drink, but that has grave dangers, as alcohol often becomes the fuel for bitter family fights when he arrives. One man told a workshop that "things got much better when I stopped having a drink on the way home and just went and got a donut and coffee."

On a deeper level, though, both husband and wife at these moments need to validate that both are needy, that both persons' daily experiences are worthwhile, and that no one will have his or her needs met entirely. The couple faces the challenge of both caretaking for each other and also meeting the needs of their child.

What's in It for Men?

It's essential to remember that men have much to gain from tolerating the discomfort of getting into their families: It may help the husband to work through his own anger and to let go of his fantasies of being perfectly taken care of by his wife-mother in a way that allows him to become more nurturing of others.

A prominent Washington lawyer, for example, shared with me his belief that since becoming a parent, with a wife who also works, he had become a far more sensitive and empathic person. Over the past few years this man, Mr. Shea, has become much more available to the younger associates in his firm, in fact making a career change as he became the senior partner in charge of the career development of associates and junior partners. He seemed quite attuned to the emotional needs of those around him; that seemed in part to account for the success he had in a firm where younger lawyers wanted to work.

But at first I got things backward, displaying the cultural stereotype in assigning priorities. I mused to him: "Would you say that what you've learned in being a good father to your associates you've been able to bring home too?"

His reply was quick and direct: "No. It's more of the reverse. *What I learn at home is what I apply here.*"

And Mr. Shea went on to talk of his wife and kids, modestly but forthrightly. His wife had developed a demanding job for herself in university administration, now that their children were in elementary school. "The main thing is that I just can't assume any more that she is always ready to listen to me let off steam or complain about something or use her to relax. I've become much more sensitive to just where she's at. And often I have to sort of hold onto my stuff, until she is more receptive." So he had to struggle and really look at his wish for support, his desire to be taken care of—which had been hidden to him because he was usually secretly taken care of by his wife when they were childless. Confronting his own disguised needs may make him more sensitive to the younger associates' needs and their ambivalence about revealing them.

"I'm definitely here less and home more than last year. I give her support."

"How?"

"Just being around helping with the kids, doing errands around and about the house. Just being there to listen and to hear problems, both her emotional things and the objective problems about what's going on in her department, and what's the best way of handling the situation." He found much for himself in those new situations. Without idealizing this man, we can say in a sense he was learning how to be a father: a father to his kids, a father to his wife, and a father to his younger associates; an empathic figure who attends to the emotional needs of the situation, who can provide by taking care of the human needs of others, not just through his paycheck. At age thirty-five, like many men, he was finding what it meant for him to take care of others, and it involved abilities different from those he was familiar with.

"Okay, this isn't book learning, but it's definitely personally stretching. Instead of saying, 'I want to go off and do something for me,' it's saying 'stop,' knowing that this situation calls for a more mature approach at this particular time. Just stop and rise above that immediate need, and do something constructive in the situation."

Mr. Shea is reflecting back on a process over which he has achieved some mastery. Yet when he talks about the "immediate need" he wants satisfied and hints at his temptation to do something less than "mature" and "constructive" when he arrives home to his busy family, he is referring to the child within himself provoked by his family—his wish for his wife to support *him*, for example, not vice versa. He too talks of shifting gears at the end of the day, arriving home from work, where two screaming kids and a tired wife await him. What "old stuff" is stirred up for a man by that common scene? For many men the wish is to yell and scream oneself, not to be in the authority role as Daddy. Kids stir up our wish to regress to their level, and if we've had to "grow up" as men too soon, we can feel resentful and envious of children's freedom, abandon, and carelessness. After all day in the authority role, some men cannot bear their repressed playful sides. They see in their children the way they used to be, and what they had to give up. So often acted out in the family dramas between 5 and 7 P.M. are men's silent rage at how hard they have had to work and their repressed longing to be a kid again, to have someone take care of them.

The lawyer stopped and laughed.

"When you come home and the two kids are screaming and your wife is swearing, one approach is to say 'the hell with this' and go to a local bar or something. The other approach is to take a deep breath and pick up one of the kids and try to do something with her or him, and say "Hi, how are things going?' "

In taking such a "deep breath" and picking up your children can lie a healing of the rage and sadness that men experience in what they have lost from their own childhood. That is not to deny that parents don't simply wish at times for some peace and quiet and a respite from their fatigue. However, in terms of the long-term effects of close involvement with one's children, I suspect we are just beginning to realize how much positive personality growth men have been denied by their lack of truly involved, emotionally nurturing participation in their families.[11]

But some men, to continue the metaphor, will not "pick up" their children. They distance them and cannot hold them or their wives emotionally. Let's look more carefully at what makes it difficult for some men to take the deep breath that would enable them to become confident fathers.

The Renewed Struggle with the Wounded Father

Taking that deep breath Mr. Shea describes is difficult for many men, because in developing a sense of fatherhood we draw on our own experience of being a son to a father. Many men cannot summon up a sense of fatherhood separate from the wounded image of father they carry around.

A man may fear or wish to become the image of his own father. For example, carrying within them an idealized image of their fathers as either powerful and judgmental or saintly and even-tempered figures, some men may feel robbed of their family's idolization of them as faultless fathers. Goldstein describes the wish to become the "knight in shining armor" who enters the family "only when he wants to, unencumbered by the ambivalence created when excessive expectations are not met."[12] Such men may feel quite vulnerable assuming a realistic masculine role in which wife and children can both respect them and criticize them for being human.

For many men I've talked with, the anxiety is connected not to a wish to be idealized but to the fear of becoming like the stern, judgmental image of their own fathers. Many men seem to have difficulty imagining how to be a father in a way that is not authoritarian or overly controlling and instrumental when they are with wife and children.

Feeling as if the only role for a new father is to provide for his family, men like Mr. Baker may think it necessary for them to work harder now that they have a child. If the wife has worked, there is usually a drop in income as she goes on maternity leave or leaves her work. So fatherhood becomes defined by providing and breadwinning—as it was for our fathers—without much clarity as to what family participation characterizes Dad.

The man may wonder if he will become a father for whom the provider identity absorbs all. "Provider anxiety" is the term used to refer to the man's fear that he won't be able to support his family, given the increased financial responsibility. Yet provider anxiety may have less to do with money than with intimacy. Among many men the fear isn't only of not being able to earn enough money but is also fear of losing intimacy and family in the process of becoming the traditional father. In having a child one fears having less intimacy rather than more. That is the time we are told, and we believe, we must settle down, commit ourselves to a career, earn more, and provide well for the family. Ironically, that traditional husband's role may threaten to separate the new father more from intimacy than when he was childless. Just at the point when he yearns to stay home and participate in the new family, he feels it is time to go out into the world and do big things.

There is a reality behind that concern. Since we lack images of a truly participatory, emotionally involved father, many men will confront internal and social expectations to the effect that their main and primary task is to get out there and protect and provide for the family. There is nothing wrong with that message *per se*—it is basically true—but in the absence of other messages about what it means to be a father it feeds the alienation that an entire generation of men feel.

We become fathers not just to our children, not just in the eyes of the outside world, but in the eyes of our wives as well. When a wife becomes a mother, suddenly protective of the newborn, going through enormous role changes, she may also become concerned for her husband's role in the family. She may inadvertently or consciously put pressure on the husband to become more "fatherly." She needs to know she can depend on him, that he can take care of things. Just as men's yearnings for mother are stirred up by the changes a wife undergoes in becoming a mother, so too a wife's yearnings to be taken care of by a fatherly figure may be mobilized by seeing her husband become a father. She may want her husband to seem traditionally responsible and stable. And, too, she may unconsciously look down on his more "feminine" strivings to nurture and care for his child in nontraditional male ways.

Those pressures to become traditionally "fatherly" may create a profound sense of loss in some men, recreating feelings associated with earlier transitions out of the home and into adult life. A man may unconsciously feel as if he is being thrown out of Eden into the more difficult public world of work. If a man has experienced the task of growing up as a painful demand or an evil betrayal—e.g., school, college, or career as choices made by others—then the overtones of the transition to fatherhood may bring back those feelings of sadness, anger, or confusion. If the person is strongly ambivalent about career commitment (an ambivalence often present in quite overtly successful men), then the move toward career will feel doubly empty.

For some men there can be more rage and sadness in the stern face of fatherhood than they can bear; they have to distance themselves from their families and children, perhaps to "save" their kids from their own anger or to "save" themselves from their sadness and disappointment in their own fathers. Some men may act out, leaving or distancing their families in an angry, guilty rage, working harder to make up for their unexpressed feelings of failure and disappointment, or feeling "empty inside," repressing frightening or confused feelings.

The poet Reg Saner reflects on this generational legacy in his poem "Passing It On." The speaker recalls the dark love between himself and his father, whose anger made a child's world shake, and laments his father's sudden death. The wounded father lives as the speaker finds himself repeating this same angry pattern with his own young son, who looks at him with a wary, self-protective stare.[13]

A thirty-five-year-old high school teacher sits in my office crying about having started an affair with another woman while his wife was pregnant and then leaving his family six months after the birth of his son. Every time he talks of his child he cries, imagining how much the boy misses him and what it must be like not to have your father around. In fact, that man has partly identified with the child, replicating a situation where he had been emotionally deprived as a young boy, left to cope with a difficult mother by a psychologically unavailable father. He partly identifies with the parent—the frustrator—acting out his father's role as the unavailable one, and too identifies with the child, as if punishing himself and recreating his father's behavior all at once.

The ongoing relationship between a new father and his own father is particularly important. Psychologically, the process is often called "de-idealization," which means that we come to see our fathers more clearly, understanding their own struggles, gaining a new perspective from going through the kind of dilemmas they have experienced. When we de-idealize a father he becomes more real, a human figure with strengths and weaknesses rather than the godlike or devil-like creature of our imagination whom we both adore and rebel against. Becoming a father may foster the process of de-idealization in at least two ways: It helps the grown son to understand more of his father's behavior and may also help retrieve memories of his father as a caring, nurturant figure.

A man may find that he has identified with parts of his father he has been denying all along. That may not always be pleasant. "Whenever I discipline my son, I find myself yelling at him. I hear myself screaming 'No!' at him in the same voice I remember my father using. It drives me crazy to see myself doing that." We may unconsciously internalize patterns of behavior without necessarily wanting them.

On the other hand, in becoming fathers we gain a new perspective on our own fathers. The man comes to see that being a father is a constant struggle to hold onto family amid competing demands to be a success at work. From that the man may understand more of his own father's silent, hidden struggle, a view from the other side to which he was not privy as a child. In finding himself to be a good-enough father, the man may come to know that his own father was good-enough as well.

In the struggle to be present for my son Toby, I felt a new communality with my own father. Sitting in my office one day after rushing out of the house because of an early morning appointment, yearning to be still in our kitchen with my new baby and my wife, I wondered what it was like for my father to walk to his car every morning, beginning his long daily commute to the Bronx, leaving a cozy breakfast scene to make his way in the harsh public world of men. Did he feel the brief relief I did at getting back into the orderly, safe world of work? Did he too feel the sense of exile from a home within which he was struggling to find a place? Much of my father's behavior began to make sense to me.

Our fathers become grandfathers when we have a child, usually a beloved presence to the child, while the son faces the tough day-to-day challenges of being the father. There is an irony in this: While the grown son may now focus on his father, his father is often focused on the grandchild. They are once again out of synch with each other. Dad has moved into the grandfather role and may be different from the man he once was. He is no longer the father he once was, just as we are no longer a son in the way we used to be.

Yet seeing the love between a grandchild and grandfather can also help us recall the more nurturing parts of our fathers. And in seeing and remembering the caring sides of our fathers, we are literally healing the wounded father within our hearts, because we identify now with a fuller sense of masculinity. We let go of the angry resentment at what we did not get, which blocks our giving to our own children and to others.

A forty-three-year-old salesman told me of the new delight he felt at his father's visits now that he had children. "Before our kids were born, seeing my parents was a duty, a ritual I dreaded. Now when they're here I take such pleasure in seeing my father with our son and daughter. We all go on walks together, exploring." His father is a retired professor of animal husbandry at a Midwestern university. "He tells the kids all about the rooting behavior of pigs, tricks of taking care of animals, his experience on the university farm. I get such a kick out of it—its something we stopped doing as I got older at home." The father is identifying both with his children and with his own father—the one given to and the one who gives. Through his children the man now feels his father's love and is healed by it, a current flowing down through the generations and back again.

I am convinced that watching my father's care and love for his new grandson, his confident sense of authority as well as the depth of my son's response to him, has helped me recall those parts of my father in my own life. I began to recall memories that were wiped out by the tension of adolescence: the Saturdays I spent happily in his carpet store playing among the tall rolls of carpet, the wonderful summer trips spent driving across country, watching football games together in front of the TV or at Yankee Stadium. In that way I began to know again that my father had been there for me when I was young: He was a warm, nurturant presence before his business problems and my adolescence conspired to heat up the connection between us.

In watching our fathers "grandparent," in struggling ourselves with dilemmas similar to the ones they faced, and in feeling the love between grandparent and grandchild, we may retrieve the memories often lost in the transit to male adulthood.

The Flight into Work

An important way in which men become wounded fathers is by holding on too tightly to their careers. New fathers rarely report that becoming a father interferes with their career commitment in the same way their wives do.[14] Men will often talk about how the "structure of the workplace" inhibits their family commitment, citing the relative absence of paternity leave or social and practical difficulty of bringing their children to the office. No doubt those are real problems, but I have been equally impressed in my interviews with the numbers of new fathers for whom work becomes psychologically vitalized after the birth of a child and who make a strong separation between work and home.

Let's consider why work becomes so enticing for many men, using Mr. Abrams, the computer scientist, for illustration. He is telling me more about "the conflictive pressure" in his life. His wife wants him home more, yet he feels pulled toward work. His love for his work shines through as he says, "I find computers an intensely satisfying kind of work," and describes the orderly technical problems he can solve on his own at the office.

There is now even greater pressure to be at work, from a boss who routinely puts in sixty-hour weeks himself. "My boss is one year older than I am, and he looks ten years older." The example of his boss haunts him—a father figure whose love he wants: "I'm perfectly willing to do it for a short period of time, but I'm not will-ing to do it for a long period of time." Yet in truth he's ambivalent, because the work is really a joy. "The primary problem that creates is that my wife is dissatisfied. It doesn't really bother me, because I enjoy what I do." Note that he identifies the urge to be at home with his wife, but it is experienced as coming from her rather than an in-ternal prompting on his part. The need, the hunger for work seems too strong: He is still proving himself as an engineer; his identity is still dependent on showing a demanding father that he could indeed be as successful as the old man.

One might wonder why a man near midlife is still proving him-self at work, yet that is an increasing fact of life for men in profes-sional careers. The transition to fatherhood is strongly shaped by where the man is in his career cycle. Even though Mr. Abrams is almost forty years old, he is still in the establishing stage of his career. Like many men in technical careers—scientists, doctors, and some academics—the training and establishment phases of careers have been extended so far that many men at forty feel they are just getting off on their own at work, proving themselves. They are on the edge of success, and then they start families too and find a pull away from the career anchor in their lives.

Daniel Levinson notes that for many men work is a "hypermas-culine" world in which men can traditionally submerge them-selves, in a psychological attempt to give greater priority to mas-culinity as they understand it. Levinson points out that once established in that world, men during the midlife transition around age forty may be able to feel more comfortable exploring more feminine aspects of themselves and moderating their involve-ment in work.[15]

Levinson focuses, however, on rather traditional career paths. We can easily miss a dilemma for many new fathers in highly tech-nical and demanding careers: They may not feel that they've really proved their manhood enough to tolerate psychologically taking a fuller role in their families.

In tracing the career histories of men in the Adult Development Project, we found many had prolonged their advanced training so that by the late thirties they were still establishing themselves. Of the 370 men we studied 17 percent were still in the establishment stage of their careers and heavily centered on "making it" at work. Many of those men also postponed having children until their thirties. One such man, a physician who had completed a strenuous postdoctoral at a noted medical research center, told me that "after twenty-five years of school, it's time to go to work!" Almost forty years old, and he feels as if he's just getting out of school. A physician with a similar career path and a young child at home had just opened his first professional office. He spoke with impatience about his wife's postpartum depression and her wish that he take a day a week off to be with the kids, coming just at the time when he felt he was finally proving himself at work.

Among men in the Adult Development Project who now have children, almost 28 percent delayed parenting into their thirties. The problem is that such men may seem highly successful and advanced in their careers but may not feel so. Modulating their career commitments and spending more time at home may feel as if it is undermining the masculine identity they've worked so hard to achieve. For such men, work may affirm their masculinity, the family seeming a feminine or childlike world.

Mr. Abrams gave voice to the sense of affirmation he gets from work—in the eyes of others and by being able to master new tasks: "To actually write these computer programs that are going to get done, and have the things come out the way I felt they were going to, and have people say, 'Hey, that's pretty good!' "

For many new fathers home used to be a haven. Now it's been taken over by his young barbarians and needy wife. The office now is a haven, offering friendships and routines that are reassuring. Home may have changed, but work has not. Work feels better than ever. Mr. Abrams remembers longingly the time in his life "when I could be purely working, there was nobody else involved . . . I could really concentrate entirely on that one purpose in life. I found it immensely enjoyable." The new father may feel affirmed by the activities or relationships at work in ways that he does not feel affirmed at home.

So for men like Mr. Abrams work offers something vital: the picture of competent masculinity. His boss, his father-mentor, may work too hard, but he is safe and conventional: the image of the successful, overly driven older man that our society secretly worships even as it cautions against. At home, what picture of masculinity does he have to draw upon? There is the memory of his father, a source of irritation, since for the young Mr. Abrams (and for many other men) home was where strong men became weak. A successful English professor with a wide reputation, Mr. Abrams remembers his father at home: "He was like the fifth child, my mother was always babying him and coddling him. I hated to see it." The memory is painful, we may well surmise, because there is a part of Mr. Abrams that wishes to be babied, to regain the haven of family, a safe, relaxed, protective environment intruded upon by his young arrivals.

Clearly the flight into work of many new fathers has diverse sources. One is the increased pressure to provide for a new family. And, too, work becomes a way of holding onto masculine interests and preoccupations. Yet the flight into work may also stem from the father's need to distance himself from the needy and confusing feelings it stirs up within himself; work may be the place where the husband works out the aggression and anger he feels at his family for abandoning him and threatening to "feminize" him. Daniel Levinson sees the flight into work as an attempt to reduce what he calls the "strength of the little boy within him" by escaping the feminine overtones of the family.[16]

Let us consider what's involved in helping men create a fuller, more masculine place for themselves in the family during the transition to fatherhood.

Healing the (New) Wounded Father

Beware of making your wife the "family expert." Begin to think about yourself as a separate, nurturing presence in the home, and work together with your wife to create ways of feeling both competent and needed. Many new fathers I've talked to have spoken of how hard it is to take care of their kids when their wife is around, because the wife judges or criticizes or is just available to take over. So both Dad and the baby turn to Mom, who then feels trapped between the new baby and the old baby. It is important for men to spend time alone with their children rather than always together with their wives. That will help to head off our tendency to become passive and dependent around her.

The wife's attitude toward her husband's role is very important: Is she comfortable allowing him the opportunity to experiment with this new role?

The key element is for men to develop a sense of real-life competence as fathers. It is for men like Mr. Abrams, who value their instrumental, real-world competency and who need to develop a sense of skill and self-esteem as fathers, gaining some clarity and sense of mastery over the mysterious world of being a father, that parenting courses are particularly valuable.[17]

Remember that fatherhood begins in conditions of deprivation. Pay attention to your own neediness and to nurturing the marital relationship. Don't expect that no adjustments will be necessary, but rather take seriously the fact that you are in a new, often joyous, but also stressful life situation.

Do not forget that for all the good things that a child brings to a marriage, becoming a father can also complicate your relationship with your wife. Remember that the wife too is put back in touch with childlike fears and anxieties by the arrival of a child. She may fear being swamped by the motherhood role, feeling a sense of loss of valued adult competencies attached to her work life. She may feel suddenly needy and uncomfortably dependent psychologically or financially on her husband and have great difficulty acknowledging those feelings to her husband or herself. New parents have to develop new caretaking patterns between them that help each other to acknowledge and validate their feelings and that support the self-esteem of both partners.

A new baby brings with it many potential blocks to that caretaking between husband and wife. A husband may tend to blame the wife for any difficulties of childrearing that happen. If the baby is crying or upset and the husband feels anger at the baby, it may be directed at the wife. Rather than get angry at the baby, the husband will yell at the wife. "Well, after all, he is your kid."

And, too, couples can let the child express their feelings toward the spouse for them. Perhaps there is tension between husband and wife one night; one of them yells at the baby to stop crying or picks her up brusquely. The baby has a sobbing tantrum. Then husband and wife focus on her, comforting the baby in ways they won't do for each other. By the time the baby has calmed down, the couple forgets to focus on and listen to each other.

Pay attention to how the baby is affecting communication within the couple relationship. I soon learned that when my newborn cried or was uncomfortable, *I* felt ill at ease, impatient until we got him settled. Julie and I realized that our fights, our impatience with each other, the restless grumblings between us often began when Toby was crying or hollering about one thing or another. I was not used to being so viscerally attached to another human being.

Think about your father and your relationship as a son to both parents. Draw on the memories of their full participation with you. When do such memories stop? What caused your relationship with mother or father to change? What would you like to give your son or daughter that you did not get?

Mourn the losses involved in having a child and trying to be more present with your family. That sense of loss can be heard when men discuss a feeling of "sacrificing" their career involvement in order to be parents. If that sense of loss is not acknowledged and integrated within the man's value system and that of his spouse, it may spoil much of the joy that can be inherent in parenting and strain the marital relationship.

In the early years of parenting, taking time to be home with one's children may seem like a kind of death: the loss of the daydreams and possibilities of conquest that we associate with the real world. The treasured selves that are lost to fatherhood may bring our mortality and limitations to mind. Donald Hall expresses this sentiment in his poem "My Son, My Executioner:" "Sweet death, small son, our instrument/Of immortality/Your cries and hungers document/Our bodily decay."[18]

The gains that come from fathering are of a very different sort. We become aware of our limits as people, that we cannot do everything. Talking with men who do spend more time at home, sometimes making significant career sacrifices—turning down promotions or not writing that article for publication—I have been struck by how much courage it takes to let go of dreams, often at a time in one's life when parts of oneself and those around us press the new father to get out there and be a success for his family.

One of the most intensely debated questions at a recent Fatherhood Forum on Parenting and Men's Work Identities was: Can you be ambitious at work and successful as a father today? The consensus among the many men and women there was that really to be there for your children, not in a distracted way, it is necessary to give up some work attachments. That means accepting a very hard reality: This is what I can do, and this is what I can't. For many men it is the first time we put someone else so clearly above ourselves. Deciding to accept limitations on one's work activities in order to devote more time to parenting does not, however, eliminate all

potential problems. There are several traps for men who are trying to be home more with their children.

First of all, beware of overidentifying with your child and confusing your needs with his or hers. We may bring our own agendas
to the situation, inadvertently alienating ourselves from the very
child we think we are giving to. One man explained his dilemma
with embarrassment: "In my family my father was never home. He
was always at the store. He used to say, 'There'll always be enough
money in my house.' So he worked and worked, and I rarely saw
him. Now I seem to be going around saying to our children, 'In *my*
house there'll always be enough feelings.' " He chuckled, aware
that there are many ways for fathers to be lost at the store, unavailable for their kids. There are numbers of men with a real hunger
for intimacy who desperately want to be present for their children, feeling they did not get enough themselves as children and
not wanting to do the same to their families. If the husband is trying to satisfy his wish to nurture because he himself has not experienced proper nurturing, then he may not respect the child's need
for boundaries and separation and may smother the child emotionally. To punish his child for not accepting the attention and interest
he so relentlessly gives, the father may withdraw or become
critical and demanding, thus undermining the child's self-esteem.
In the guise of giving their children what they never got, some
fathers may become, subtly and inadvertantly, distant, angry, or
secretly vulnerable like their own fathers.

In some marriages the husband's attempt to provide better care
is really a competitive struggle with the wife, expressing the man's
rage at how little he feels he got as a child from his mother. Such
men are often trying to get even with their own mothers—with
women in general—proving to all mothers that they are incompetent or unnecessary. Once again, the child is a surrogate for
oneself: He's going to have what we didn't get, but along with that
is the silent message to the wife-mother that she can't do a good
enough job. Watching this silent family drama, the child may grow
up believing he must choose between his mother and his father.
Once again the father becomes a disguised version of his own
father.

The psychological residue of their own experience as children
and the social influences today encouraging men to take a more
participatory role as fathers leave some men so intensely commit-

ted to "being there for our children" that any inability or restriction on them creates anger and resentment not necessarily in the best interests of the child. At one public conference on parenting a speaker was suggesting that the father's role becomes really important in the second or third year of the child's life, when he functions as the "ambassador" to the outside world, leading away from the intensity of the mother–infant bond. The speaker said that the comings and goings of father play a healthy role in the child's separation-individuation struggle: The child sees mother as the stable center, while father begins to demarcate the notion of moving away from mother. The heat that topic can generate became apparent when one member of the audience angrily commented during the discussion period: "Here I try to be more present for my daughter and I don't know how. Now you're telling me I shouldn't be. I don't think you should be allowed to say such things at a conference such as this."

Yet if men are going to take a greater role in the family, we need to remember that the mother plays a vital role in the infant's life, and it is not yet at all clear that the father can replace mother or that some of the distance of the father, the way he beckons to a larger world beyond mother, is all bad. Perhaps comparison and contrast between the parents are what matters: If father is more present, then mother may be able to become the ambassador to the real world. But we don't know for certain that such role-switching really works, and we do know that the stability and integrity of the mother–infant bond plays a large role in the infant's first impressions as to the trustworthiness of the world itself. Distance indeed may be the curse of fatherhood—not the alienated and wounded distance many of our fathers experienced, but some distance nonetheless from the closeness of that first mother–infant bond, which we must accept.

Fatherhood in today's world encompasses many different tasks: taking care of the wife who has become a mother, holding one's infant and experiencing his or her centrality over our own, accepting that we are growing older, feeling our fatherhood as part of the lineage of fathers through history. Seeing our children struggle to come to terms with their fathers, with us, we must accept the reality of frustration and loneliness in life. And each of us, as fathers, must help a son or daughter find the healthy, healing side of masculinity, reconciling ourselves to that search in our own lives.

7

Healing the Wounded Father

The blond hair of my client glistened in the sun shining through my office window. Rod's childhood nickname was "Sunny," a name he didn't like; he wasn't sure whether or not the other kids were making fun of him when they gave him the label. Today, though, his rage was focused on his father.

"My father always steamrollered over everyone, me included. I know there was a shy, caring side to my father—I know it was there, I could sense it. But he never showed it to me. Whenever he expressed his softer side he acted like such an idiot. You know, getting drunk, all maudlin. I needed him and he wasn't there."

Rod wants to press his rage home. He has concrete evidence of his father's failure from the horse's mouth: "A couple of years ago, back when I was about twenty-five, we were at a family party in Texas. Maybe it was Thanksgiving, a holiday. He came up to me and said, 'Rod I've always been better as a father than as a friend to you. I want you to know that I didn't think I could be both your friend and your father when you were young.'"

Rod looked at me as if to say, "You see?"

"What did you reply when he told you that?" I asked.

"I said, 'Dad, that's okay,' and we pretty much stopped talking about it."

I wondered aloud to Rod: "What would have happened if you had said, 'Dad, you're right'?"

"No, no. He wouldn't have known what to say." Rod thought a moment. "Hmmn. That's interesting. I think I didn't want to hear it, what he said. He was reaching out to me, but I turned away from him. What he said makes me sad for all I've missed from him, makes me sad for him. Maybe I don't want to forgive him. I didn't even think of being friends with him now.

"When I said, 'That's okay,' I was angry, not forgiving. I mean, it isn't okay, is it?"

Rod clearly wasn't comfortable with his own anger at his father. Despite his pain and anger Rod, like many men, seemed more comfortable being alienated from the father of his childhood than making real peace with the father of his adulthood. Martin Acker, a psychologist at the University of Oregon, asked each of the men in a seminar on men's issues to write a letter to his father. There was no expectation that the letters would be sent, and none were, yet Acker noted the underlying fear of their own anger in the sons' letters. The deepest fear seemed to be, in Acker's words, that if I told you "how I felt as a child in relation to you . . . I am afraid that you would not be able to take it."[1] For many men, the fear that their fathers do not have the emotional strength to tolerate openness with them blocks their deepest yearnings to talk things through.

Communication between son and father may also be blocked by the son's fear of his father's anger at him. He may fear that in approaching his father he will provoke the rage that might, finally, destroy the son.

What does it mean for sons to heal the wounded father, our internal image of father as wounded or angry, which lies at the core of our own sense of masculinity? Healing the wounded father means "detoxifying" that image so that it is no longer dominated by the resentment, sorrow, and sense of loss or absence that restrict our own identities as men.

There are several avenues by which the process of healing takes place. They include recognizing our fathers' actual wounds, the way they have been wounded by their lives, the complex crosscurrents within our families that led to disconnection, and by exploring and testing out richer, more satisfying male identities as fathers, husbands, and co-workers in our everyday lives.

We are speaking here of a process of grieving. Sadness is involved. Many men have learned to act as if they don't need intimacy, and recontacting their hunger for real intimacy with father can be very uncomfortable. Men learn to drive others away when needy, to act as if they can get along without others. I've been impressed by how many men cry when they come to see what they have not received from their fathers. In trying to understand our fathers, we confront the depths of our neediness and that of our fathers.

Unatoned Sins: Our Fathers and Ourselves

One way of healing the wounded father is to plunge into your father's history. A man needs to find ways of empathizing with his father's pain. The women's movement has provided many daughters with a way of understanding and forgiving their mothers, but we have little corresponding sense of our fathers. We have to understand our fathers' struggle and see the broken connection between fathers and sons as part of the unfinished business of manhood.

The poet Robert Bly writes of his father that "I began to think of him not as someone who had deprived me of love or attention or companionship, but as someone who himself had been deprived, by his mother or by the culture. This process is still going on. Every time I see my father I have different and complicated feelings about how much of the deprivation I felt with him came willfully and how much came against his will—how much he was aware of and unaware of. I've begun to see him more as a man in a complicated situation.[2]

A University Professor, fifty years old, remembered his father as someone who "worked as a labor organizer as well as a mineworker during my childhood. He wasn't around much, I felt his absence a lot. For years I couldn't understand why he was so unavailable to me. Used to go drinking and carousing. I couldn't forgive him for it. He died about eight years ago, and I was talking to my mother recently. She told me that he lost his job when I was fifteen—got fired for his union work. I never knew that, but I can understand what a blow that must have been for him. He supported us with part-time jobs for years, and my mother said he was always ashamed of that."

Then he revealed the connection of his father's plight to himself:

"I've had my tenure battles, lost a few jobs myself, and feel I can understand better why he withdrew from the family, how hard it must have been for him to be there for us when he felt so humiliated in his worklife. I wouldn't want to do the same thing, but I can see how caught he was in the trap of only feeling good about himself in terms of how well he supported his family. Now that I know that family secret about his lost mineworking job I feel I can forgive my father." It is striking how many family secrets about father have to do with a work setback that cripples, temporarily or permanently, the father's relationship with his family.

Let's face it. Our fathers couldn't win, particularly fathers of minority families: Catholics, Jews, blacks. The postwar world of the late 1940s and 1950s contained a tremendously seductive trap for them. Here they had fought a war and won, a war that seemed right, "the good war" that had defeated fascism, one in which our fathers were unambiguously identified with America. All the seeming "rewards" of that righteous victory seemed due them, and forthcoming: the GI bill, upward mobility, a home in the suburbs, and working hard to take advantage of the financial rewards that seemed just at their fingertips. Don't drop the ball now! What was a few years, a decade of giving your all to work, even if that meant not being home much? After all, many of them imagined, the kids would still be there, and how much it'll all mean to them—the good life. A house, two cars, their college education. Have you noticed how many older men lament how quickly their kids grew up? Almost while their backs were turned. As Senator Paul Tsongas observed, talking of his decision to resign from the Senate and return to Massachusetts: "No man on his deathbed ever lamented that he spent too much time with his family."

No, it was work that dominated in peculiar, unexpected ways. Many of our fathers had to commute to work, a very different way of life from what they knew when they were growing up. Instead of having the family close by, just down the street from Dad's store or office, as it was for them growing up, now they left the family in the morning and didn't come back for eight or nine hours; the family was something remote from their daily lives. One result was the undercurrent of anger and exile within our fathers discussed in Chapter 1.

Many moved into new suburban towns dominated by the success ethic, where achievement was defined in terms of public, career activity. The dominant message was that everything was just dandy, even as the lives of our fathers were changing in ways hard for them to comprehend. Much of the family texture they had known as children was gone, and work and financial success became the marks of how well they were doing. Many fathers lived with a mixed message from their own parents: In order to be successful, they had to go forth into America and become good professionals and consumers, yet in doing so they had to give up many of the values and ideals that their parents personified. To live up for their parents, they had to kill them, a task that must have caused grief for many fathers, even though they whistled while they worked.

By the time Don Larsen pitched his phenomenal World Series perfect game in 1956, many of our fathers had become parents, and how many saw in their sons an ambivalent future? Here was their heritage *really* Americanized, as we went to nice suburban schools, and left our ethnic and immigrant ways behind. To be true to their sons they had to encourage this—we were becoming part of the "perfect" America—but to be true to their hearts many must have wanted to oppose their sons too. Fathers both encouraged and undercut their sons' dreams at the same time. Then the Beatles, long hair, and flower power began to undercut openly all the efforts our fathers had made during the 1950s when love was measured by days at the office or hours in the store. They heard that what they did wasn't enough. Why, it was hardly anything at all, a message that most fathers at some level probably agreed with, but were enraged to hear from those ungrateful messengers, their sons.

The film *Heroes and Strangers* is about two young adults' search for reunion with their fathers.[3] Tony, one of the filmmakers, is in his late twenties. His father-hunger leads him home to talk to his elderly father, the man he remembers as the stranger in the house, the parent who made the home uncomfortable by his presence, the disciplinarian. After bombarding his father, a retired railroad employee, with questions, Tony finds that it helps to stop asking too many questions of his father; he begins to listen to what his father likes to talk about and finds how much he can learn from opening himself up to his father in that way. Walking along those very railroad tracks that dominated his father's life, Tony hears things never before told him by either parent, secrets hidden from him when young—that his father, for example, worked three jobs most of the years his family was young, often away from home more than sixteen hours a day. Tony leaves his father with a new appreciation of the pressures of being responsible for a family, of having to provide, of measuring success as a parent by how much money and status one has earned.

When he starts listening, he discovers his father's love for the teletype and his fascination with mechanical objects; he hears his father confess that he "still dreams of overlooking train orders that came through." After all, he finds his father is willing to talk, if he is willing to listen.

At the end of *Heroes and Strangers*, both Tony and Lorna, the other young adult whose visit home forms the emotional core of the movie, find some resolution, even if incomplete. One says, "something happened between me and my father—not what I expected, not exactly what I wanted," but the implication is that for both the visit home, the listening, was enough, satisfying. At the end each is able to describe what a good father is and both feel their fathers were, after all, just that. Being reassured that they were loved, even if it was hard to see, satisfies them. Each feels proud to be the father's offspring, a valuable gift for both parent and child.

In this way both Tony and Lorna are healing the wounded father within them; one has the impression Tony will be a more complete father and husband, Lorna a more complete wife and mother, for having explored their own fathers' lives.

The process of healing is not necessarily dominated by talk about "feelings" between father and son or rehashing each disappointment or miscommunication. Working things out with father need not be a long psychological process. For many fathers and children healing involves an unspoken recognition of their love for each other, of their caring and shared history. One man told of merely becoming more interested in his father's fascination with horse racing and gambling at the track. "When I began to understand what pressures he had been under working at a high-power corporate job and raising a family with three sons in it, I could see how much of a release gambling was for him." This man made a more crucial discovery as well: "I realized that just because he gambled didn't mean that I had to do it too; that made it easier to accept my father for who he is."

In learning about their fathers, sons can come to see them as separate people, different from them. That can help the separation-individuation process, as the son realizes that he is responsible for his own identity as a man, that he is not chained to his father's attitudes and values. So the process of exploration may lead to an acceptance of father, even if not a deep connection with him. A physician, married with several children, said that "one of the most important things for me as I learned more about my father over the years was that his visits to our home for Easter no longer left me feeling angry and impatient and on edge. I could be with my father without feeling as if someone was constantly scratching their fingernails on a blackboard."

For many men the process of exploring their fathers' lives, empathizing with their pain, gets blocked. They seem uninterested or afraid to approach their fathers. Many in fact keep the connection broken and will not accept a reconciliation. It's striking in therapy to ask bitter patients: Would you take love from your father now, if he were to give it? A startling number will reply, as Rod did, "No!" At a workshop on "Healing the Wounded Father," an anguished trial lawyer told of driving up to his family home on a Sunday visit and driving away without stopping if his mother's car was not parked in the garage. "It's too embarrassing to be alone with my father, we don't know what to say to each other." That man, who can hold his own in the battle of the courtroom, didn't want to be left alone with his father!

So healing the wounded father presents the son with inner feelings so uncomfortable that he wants to turn away. The twin tasks of identity and separation-individuation progress in tandem. As we explore the outer world (what actually happened in our father's lives), we are reacquainted with material from the inner world (our feelings and fantasies about father).[4] Those unfinished feelings often block men, as they fear being swamped by their shame, their guilt, and their yearning for father, if they get too close to him.

The man may be put back in touch with his anger at what he

didn't get and his wish to be taken care of by a perfect father who will have all the answers for him. It is certainly easier to be angry with a parent, to blame one's father for not giving enough and thus lament the fact that you can't get on with your life. Many men harbor a profound wish for a perfect father who really will save them from the risks and anxieties of making a marriage work, raising children, and dealing with success and failure in the world of work—an Odysseus brought down from the clouds by the gods rather than Ol' Dad, who let you down and leaves you to deal with life on your own. Healing the wounded father means accepting some of our aloneness, giving up the wish that Dad will take care of you, will set you on your feet so you'll never fear slipping. There is grief in that loss of the fantasied all-powerful father we wish we had. Accepting that loss means tolerating the wish for such a father and seeing that it is really a childhood dream. Our fathers harbored such a yearning too; it doesn't make one less of a man to admit to it. So one man could finally write of his father, "Dad, we share the same bewilderment, the same mystery in the face of what is."[5] Seeing our fathers as human, accepting their frailties and lapses, allows us to accept our own frailties and imperfections in this world.

A second uncomfortable feeling involves our bodies and our yearning for "holding" from father. When men recontact their wish for father, they often experience a visceral wish to be held by or to hold their own fathers; that can be very disturbing for a man, bringing up homosexual panic. I am convinced that many men yearn for physical contact with their fathers. We don't feel that connection very much: direct physical holding, comforting, the warmth of our father's bodies, their ability to hold us, and ours to comfort and hold them. That physical yearning may reflect the bond or "ontological link" between father and son that the sociologist Thomas Cottle notes from his interviews with fathers and sons.[6]

When I realized how much of my life I had spent distancing my father, feeling angry at and scared of him, the feeling led directly to a wish to hold him that shocked and scared me. "This whole year," I wrote at one point in my journal, "I see now I have been wrestling with you, Dad, having it out on a dusty plain, locked together, exhausted. I want to take your grief into mine, bury your head on my chest weeping while I cry on yours."

Such yearnings, which men probably feel as children for their fathers, can feel disgusting and repulsive, particularly for men who have repressed or renounced their hunger to be held and comforted. But when we imagine holding and caring for our fathers and letting them do so for us, we are freeing our own ability to hold and care for others. We heal our own connection to our bodies. So Robert Bly can merge imagery of the father's body and the son's in his stunning prose poem, "Finding the Father":

> This body offers to carry us for nothing—as the ocean carries logs—so on some days the body wails with its great energy, it smashes up the boulders, lifting small crabs, that flow around the sides. Someone knocks on the door, we do not have time to dress. He wants us to come with him through the blowing and rainy streets, to the dark house. We will go there, the body says, and there find the father whom we have never met, who wandered in a snowstorm the night we were born, who then lost his memory, and has lived since longing for his child, whom he saw only once . . . while he worked as a shoemaker, as a cattle herder in Australia, as a restaurant cook who painted at night. When you light the lamp you will see him. He sits there behind the door . . . the eyebrows so heavy, the forehead so light . . . lonely in his whole body, waiting for you.[7]

In order for us to be able to "hold" others as men, we have to imagine ourselves being held by our fathers, perhaps the first male we wanted to hold and be held by.

A third set of uncomfortable feelings involved in healing the wounded father involves our fear of our fathers and our guilt at our betrayal of them. "After all, I did choose my mother," a man at a workshop on fathers admitted, laughing nervously. Many men as children or adolescents did enter into an alliance with mother to exclude father. It was an ambivalent alliance in that many sons also wanted contact with father, and it was usually an unconscious alliance in that the son wasn't aware of his preference to be with mother. Nonetheless, many men did feel more comfortable having Dad on the outside of the family, not having to deal with him. We carry around a wounded father within who is constructed out of our imagining of what he felt at our betrayal.

To think about father, to talk to him honestly, means to be plunged back into a shadowy, scary world of family cross-currents and divided loyalties, of a father who will accuse us, who never forgets our unnamed sins.

Bruce Springsteen's song "My Father's House" is about a man who runs desperately at twilight through the meadows he used to play in as a child, crossing the highway in front of his childhood home, in search of the father who is no longer there. At the screen door he finds his father gone and his way blocked by a woman (his mother?) who knows nothing. The refrain:

My father's house shines hard and bright,
It stand like a beacon calling me in the night.
Shining and calling so cold and alone
Shining across this dark highway
Where our sins lie unatoned . . .[8]

The silent male struggle with unatoned sins toward the father prevents many men from coming to terms with him. It's too terrifying to bring into the open. The following memories of how much my mother meant to me throughout my childhood and how distanced I was from my father led me to picture a frightening scene of accusation between me and him.

Father's Room and Mother's Room

When I was a little boy and my parents went out at night, my mother would always bring back a present for me. I'd be still awake, reading, when they got home from the movies, or a dinner or a dance. Once it was a treat off the table at some banquet. It was a flower inside a shell. When you put the shell, all closed up, into water, it slowly opened, and a long flower came out. I remember it was late at night, I was in bed with the light on, and she came in wearing her long evening dress, carrying this present. We watched the beautiful flower open up in the light refracted through a glass of water. In my memory, my mother looks beautiful too, all radiant and bright in her dinner dress. Her perfume fills the room. The room seems bathed in light. I am maybe seven or eight.

In most of my childhood memories my mother appears as the source of light, of energy, of optimism. She represents those terribly important gifts. When I got home from school on a cold winter day, my mother and I would sit and talk, the table lamp in her room shedding its glow around us. (Much, much later, when beginning the required therapy for a psychologist, I asked for a late afternoon hour because I liked the comfort of my therapist's desk lamp casting away the chill dark of the Boston winter afternoon as it scattered light across the room. He didn't have such a time available, and that become our first lesson in separating reality from fantasy.) The light in my mother's room cast away the gloom for me. I felt safe near her.

This was an adolescent gloom, which I think of as having gripped my entire family during my teenage years.

I have one very clear memory about that gloom. We were coming home from a winter vacation in the Catskills. A glorious week away, my brother and I from school, my father from his store, and my mother away from the house. We had a grand time skiing, wonderful meals, long walks, free time together. My father was relaxed; both my parents seemed to enjoy themselves. Then on Sunday night we drove back to our house in the suburbs.

Gloom descended at once. It was torture to think of the next day. Sunday evening TV started: "Maverick," "Gunsmoke," "77 Sunset Strip." None of those palliatives seemed to be doing any good. We all acted as if in a state of shock. I wandered into the kitchen, where my mother had spent an inordinate amount of time cleaning up. I found her in the pantry. I walked over, and, seeing me, she started to cry. Both of us knew the reason. Vacation, a brief week of light and companionship, was over. In the TV room my father sat in his usual chair. He had disappeared again behind his mask.

I didn't know what to make of that mask. He just seemed down—not really there. Depressed. It's not only that my mother had the light, she had the feelings and showed them. My father was a mystery.

He was my father, a bigger version of me. That message I got. I realized, to my sadness, that my mother could be nothing like me as I would be as an adult. I assumed it would be my father. Before I even heard the word depression, I learned to mime it.

During this year, though, something has changed in my feeling for my father. Perhaps it's the birth of my son, seeing his joyful tender love for his grandchild and the strong confident way he holds, talks to, and plays with him. It's a tenderness he and I rarely showed each other. Perhaps it is seeing how much my father is willing to talk to me, his recognition of "how hard things were with us all in adolescence. I wish I had been home more, I was so preoccupied with that store—your generation is doing it better." That long walk we took down Commonwealth Avenue before Toby was born when he wanted to talk about what it was like to be a father. The goodwill and humanity he revealed by talking about the "remarkable capacity to show affection, to be nurturant in men of your generation—we couldn't do it as easily. You know I was working in the Air Force the day you were born." Perhaps it is those talks, perhaps it is watching him with Toby, or perhaps it is just seeing his goodwill and optimism these days that leads me to remember the wonderful parts of my father I forgot, or perhaps he forgot as well. We both became blinded.

To regain my father I have to understand how important my mother was to me and my brother. At some level she seemed the center of the family, holding it together. And at that level we were, without knowing it, terrified of losing her, symbolized by our fanaticism about her smoking. And my father—who knows?—maybe around the time of the kosher rebellion, when I ordered the veal parmigiana and committed myself on her side, he must have feared the marriage would come apart. My mother was going to work, eating shrimp, signaling her resentment in a hundred ways. What was his sense of failure and guilt, particularly since her going to work coincided with financial pressure because of business difficulties he experienced? My father must have been very scared then of losing the wife he loved. And we, her sons, were afraid she would die. The centrality of mothers in the family seems very oppressive and too powerful when looked at from this perspective!

I have a strange memory about that intoxication with my mother that dates back to when I was very young. My parents were going out, and instead of giving everyone the difficult time I usually did at bedtime, this evening I was good, turned off the TV, washed, got into my pajamas, and hopped into bed. My mother, on her way downstairs to leave, came in and complimented me on being such a good boy. I looked up at her, filled with a combination of longing and rage that I just barely comprehend, even now, though the memory is strong, and said:

"That's okay, Mom, you're going to die soon and I wanted to make your last days as good as possible."

What a bizarre thing to say! My mother recoiled with a look of *shock, even repulsion, on her face. I, too, was shocked at what had come out of my mouth. For the longest time the memory filled me with shame. I don't remember what my mother replied. Most likely she chalked it up to a demonic version of "kids say the damndest things." It was never mentioned again; the whole incident was tucked away and forgotten.*

I think I was expressing my terror that my mother would leave us and also the depth of my need for her. For young children death means "leaving." And here she was doing a small leaving, leaving our safe home in the night, transforming it into a frightening place until she returned. My comment now seems a stone I hurled, welding together my need and my rage at her for going ("you're going to die" so let's get the worst over with) with my love acting out the good boy (". . . make your last days as good as possible"). It also may have been some kind of child's magic to prevent the tragedy. Was I deathly afraid of losing the one person in my life who nurtured my feelings and helped me feel really alive? Yet perhaps even then I recognized she was too important. Maybe my words also had some nastiness in them—a boy wishing to get that smothering female presence away from him.

Where was my father in that memory? I didn't seem angry that he was leaving.

Recognizing the pressures on my father during my teens is a shocker. His sadness seems understandable, poignant, yet all these years I've thought of him as angry. I never thought of him as intensely sad in those days. His sadness was one of those family secrets no one was allowed to talk about. Yet family secrets of that kind you sense as a kid; I wanted to protect him even as he enraged and frightened me.

The TV room in our house was his room, the place where he spent most weekday evenings; it was his after-hours office. He sat there for hours, with a bowl of fruit or other food beside him. He retired there after dinner like a Victorian husband retiring to the smoking room for a cigar. Often we joined him, and to be with Dad meant to be with the TV. We'd talk and the TV would be on. It's not that he particularly wanted to be alone, but we rarely had contact without the accompaniment of the TV, the commercials eternally in the background, and the favorite heroes: Sid Caesar with his amazing manic humor; elegant, tough Richard Boone in "Have Gun, Will Travel," or just plain tough James Arness of "Gun-

smoke," Ephraim Zimbalist, Jr., of "77 Sunset Strip," or my favorite, James Garner as Brett Maverick, the cocky, cool, smart, and fancy riverboat gambler.

There were men of action in my father's den, strong, silent men. But they were on the screen, not in the chairs or on the couch. What a heavy burden our fathers lived with in the 1950s and 1960s, how oppressive those mythic TV figures were, presenting to their own children images that degraded them. What fertile ground for resentment in children whose fathers didn't measure up to the TV ideals! Perhaps "naming your father," accepting him as your own, means saying goodbye to James Garner and accepting the real struggles of our real fathers. It's time to turn off the TV.

A vast longing fills me, even as I write this. Those were the fathers I wanted, men who might give me courage, a powerful strain of masculinity that would reassure me of my own. A man like Maverick or Boone, who would stand behind me when I had to deal with the toughs in Tuckahoe High School and make mincemeat out of the kids in the playround. With his wits and his fists. Those were the ersatz men I compared to my father, and found him wanting. What a torture to turn off the TV and say goodbye. They were real and they weren't. My father, my brother, my mother, and I were being ripped off by that innocent, evil TV screen. Christ, it was on for me as much as for my father, wasn't it? And when it was off, there was just my father.

When I talked with my father, I might want to ask him a question but was afraid to interrupt the show, or even the commercial. If I did get through, the questions I asked were never anything like the ones I felt I could ask my mother. I'd ask about objects, or facts. "Dad, could a car engine really explode?" Then there was the time when I had the big revelation about atoms and the universe. Atoms and solar systems were described as so alike, then if I banged my ruler against my desk, was I destroying whole worlds? I even asked him to come upstairs and talk about it. Up the stairs to my room he did come, during a break in whatever TV show was on. But he seemed puzzled by what I was asking; a few minutes of disconnected talk followed, and then back to TV. Another chance missed.

Come to think of it, I was always asking my father about violence: battles, wars, destroying devices, explosions. The talk *was always indirect, through things connected with male aggression. Never personal questions about the things that were really bothering me.*

It was my mother I asked, "How come I feel so shy in school?" or "I get so angry at my brother sometimes. Why?" And we'd discuss it, she'd talk about herself, growing up, her feelings then, too.

This went on upstairs in her bedroom with the door shut, while my father, and usually my brother, were downstairs at the TV. Long receptions held by my mother in her small salon; I'd be in a chair next to the end table with the warm light on, while she'd be sitting on top of her bed, usually sewing or something. Our talk ranged everywhere, from my plans for the future to what to do about a teenager's self-conscious fear of stuttering.

My father's TV room and my mother's bedroom: The distance between them seems enormous even now, though one was almost directly above the other in our two-story house. How embarrassed I feel today about sitting up there so many evenings, separated from my father and brother. I think of my father in that TV room, and I know I rejected him, even as I felt he was rejecting me.

Adolescence. The word rings in my head. That's when the shit hit the fan. I was a teenager, and it was time to cut the nonsense and become a man. Before age twelve or so, I was a happy kid. When I became a teenager, all sorts of things not only hit me, they hit my family like a tidal wave.

There was a business failure—a major event. When the carpet stores were expanded, problems arose, ending in a huge financial loss. It took years—almost all my teens—for my father to get out of that. He paid back every penny he owed, and to his honor kept his business alive until it became healthy again. He could have declared bankruptcy, but he chose the difficult and courageous route. Yet what a trauma it must have been for him!

There is a particular pressure point in the lives of most fathers and sons, a point where unpredictable life cycle idiosyncrasies put each unavoidably at odds with the other. When a son's adolescence coincides with the father's business problems, setbacks that profoundly shake his self-esteem, the pressure must rise exponentially. During adolescence the son truly emerges as a separate being struggling with sexuality and aggression. If there are special failures or vulnerabilities with which the father himself is struggling with, their relationship undergoes tremendous strain.

There was, too, the revolutionary change in the family's eating habits, the Kosher Rebellion. My parents loved each other and worked hard to keep their marriage together. They have succeeded in growing closer, not more distant, through all shocks and changes. That's no small accomplishment—I'll be happy if Julie and I can do as well. It's taken me twenty years to see that. Strange how memories of your father can be dominated by a single, sharp time in his and your life; we forget or ignore the parent as he or she was before and after that time. Is not the loving and confident man of today also my father?

The dominant image of my father was as he appeared in the 1950s, true or false as it may be, nursing his wounds, feeling he had failed as a man and as a husband. Having dragged himself into the courtroom of American success, he then judged himself wanting. At the same time he had allowed his Jewish heritage to be betrayed.

And there I was, good old Sam, running full tilt into puberty, into manhood.

I feel it was at that point my mother said to my father, without words, "He's yours," meaning he should take me over, be the role model. And my father and I kept staring at each other, not knowing how to do that dance.

It all seems to be summarized in one scene from that TV room. I remember walking in with a homework assignment: "Dad, we have a debate in history class tomorrow about whether England should have signed the Munich accords and delayed World War II for a year. What do you think?"

He is sitting alone on the couch in his room, looking overweight and angry. But he gives me his attention, turning his gaze away from the screen to me. His eyes are full of love but also speak to me of mourning and preoccupation.

I couldn't care less about his answer, I just want to make contact with him. What I really want to say (and of course don't) is: "Why is this house so sad? Mom is upstairs working on a film dubbing project and doesn't seem so happy; you're down here and you don't seem so happy. I'm in my room doing homework and don't feel happy at all. How come nobody's happy? Is this what life is all about?"

I want and I don't want to talk to my father. Embarassment, fear, and love fight it out silently along every neural pathway from my brain to my suddenly dry mouth.

"The Munich accord allowed England to develop radar, a key to the Battle of Britain," he answered.

But I can hear another, a silent fantasy dialogue. And see again before me (or imagine?) a look of accusation on his face.

"You've stolen my wife from me. Why is she upstairs all the time, and not down here with me? You she talks to, not me. You think you're such a smart-ass, so good with words, boy. Time to grow up. You're just a woman's boy. You can't do the hard work. Every day I go to the store, even though I hate it. I don't sit around and talk, have a good time. I do what I'm supposed to do. While you sit around and flirt with my wife. You rotten kid, putting me to shame. It's time for you to be a man!"

And how did I look at him? What was I wanting to say?

"What is ailing you, Dad? What is it? Why is your job so painful? Why can't you do something about it? Or at least talk about it? Is it because you're a man? Is that what it means to be a man? Mother talks, she takes charge of things, she's optimistic, exciting. Smart. Is that what it means to be a woman?

My head reels even as I write this, caught up at age thirty-seven in feelings I knew at age twelve. Except now I can say what they are. To be a man: to be boring and narrow, doing your duty, having a pain you can't talk about, giving up everything but working hard and hating it. I wouldn't accept that then. How angry and trapped I felt!

"But yes!" my high school teachers threw back at me. *"That's exactly what a man must be. Powerful, narrow, doing things. Looking and acting important even if hollow at the core. Strength and cockiness."*

Those subjects I had such trouble with were the real male ones: algebra, geometry, chemistry. Christ, our algebra teacher was the football coach! I can see his flattop haircut still. And the chemistry teacher, making rules, deriving formulas, doing experiments—he even looked like my father. How could he not? In the 1950s all adult males looked alike.

None of that was apparent to me in high school or in college courses. Instead I got caught up in halfway rejection of the prevalent version of maleness, but since my desire to hold onto what seemed feminine felt "shameful," I felt forced to swallow an identity I didn't want but couldn't or wouldn't reject. That split started with the split between my mother's room and my father's room at home and my complicated relationship with my father.

I didn't actually fail those subjects in high school as much as reject them, refuse to get good grades. That was a rebellion against the conveyor belt of adolescence that I had stepped onto and couldn't get off, since it was leading me to that great god Manhood, a merciless and unrelenting god. Stripping me of feelings, and converting girls who had been friends into sex objects I must score with; transforming closeness and enjoyment into aggression.

But I got on that conveyor belt of my own accord. I wanted to score, get good grades, be an athlete, go out and do, conquer.

Also, I didn't want to.

Ah, the heart turned against itself, not atypical of adolescence. You want to do two things at once and so use a classic strategy for an intolerable situation: You do what's demanded of you and reject it at the same time. Most kids are pretty good at that contortion. I rebelled but didn't quite; I tried to be a real man but always held myself back, on the periphery. Become a scientist, but grouse about the scientific method; freeze up at work during the week, but let it out on weekends. Get involved but hang back, care but don't care.

There truly is a terror in each of us at looking at who we are; perhaps it's easier to blame someone else or the world for "not letting us be what we want," as if we didn't feel ambivalent ourselves. I see no more imaginary accusations from my father; none from me to him. We each do the best we can. There are such pressures on a man to live up, to perform. He had his struggles with his mother and father, and with his sons. And he did it! He did fine. Ah, Dad, we truly do "share the same bewilderment."

The Wounded Father in Our Hearts

Healing a wounded father may not come in actual dialogue with him. There are at times real limits on the degree of rapprochement a man can achieve with his father. Fathers as they age may not see the same importance the son does in "processing things." They may want to feel that everything is "okay," that they can turn things over to the younger, stronger generation—not to open up the past and get into "all that" again.

By the time many men try to work it out with their fathers, having aged into their thirties or forties, they don't get to work it out because the roles are almost reversed; father may be ill, less productive, less energetic. The separation and rapprochement, coming at the end of the father's life cycle, may in such cases be short-circuited. As one forty-year-old man said, ruefully recounting his failed attempt to make peace with his father after a visit home, "age seventy is not the best time for a father to learn new psychological defenses." What's left to many men, then, is to "make it up" to father in some way, to show father that they are a good son, and thus perpetuate the acting-out tradition.[9]

While many men have fathers who are alive and accessible, many do not. A man may not know where his father is, or a parent may have died before there can be any reconciliation. The unavailability of fathers when their grown sons search for reunion is likely to become an increasing problem, given the high divorce rate. A recent survey of father–child contact after parental divorce found that by early adolescence 50 percent of the children had no contact with their fathers, while 30 percent had only sporadic contact with him; only 20 percent of the children saw their fathers once a week or more.[10] We may be facing a psychological time bomb within the younger generations of men and women now coming of age.

Healing the wounded father becomes more complex when a father is dead, emotionally inaccessible, or physically unavailable. In such cases one is deprived of the actual emotional healing that comes from reaching common ground with one's father, hearing and seeing a new bond forged between the generations. And the son is deprived too of feeling that he has been able to give to his father, helping to heal his father's emotional wounds.

Steve is a thirty-nine-year-old musician who spoke of the death of his father fifteen years earlier from emphysema, and the importance of a single, final act of forgiveness between them. Coming from a wealthy upper-class family in the South, he told of how "we had fought throughout my adolescence about who I dated, and which women were 'proper' for a person of my class and background. This was all during the 1960s, and his attitudes made me furious. So of course I started living with a woman completely unacceptable to him; she was never invited to the house." Then, unexpectedly, Steve's father was hospitalized for his chronic emphysema. The son had to rush home from Atlanta to find his father on a respirator, close to death. "I walked in the room, and he smiled at me. He couldn't talk because of the tubes in his throat, but he wrote me a note. It said 'I want to meet Anne, I want everything to be . . ." And then he made a sign with his hands that meant 'A-OK . . . when I go.' I cried so when he did that, and we hugged. I said I wanted everything that way too. He died later that day, before he could meet her. But I can hardly tell you what those last words meant to me. It freed me from the guilt and anger I felt, it allowed me to realize how much he meant to me." Steve stopped and then added: "It meant I don't have to remember him being angry and disappointed in me. I think often of that final sign he made: let's leave everything A-OK."

Steve provides clear expression of what it means to heal the wounded father. The inner image of his father was no longer an angry, critical, and disappointed one, but rather more accepting and forgiving. That means Steve is freed of thinking of himself as one who disappointed his father and finds that fathers can forgive and accept—they are not merely stern, judgmental figures. After learning that lesson, the son may then have less need to be an authoritarian, unyielding figure in his own relationships.

When a father dies before the son can heal the relationship, the grieving process is likely to continue longer after the death, as the son tries to come to terms with his father and his feelings about him without a sure sense of how to do so. One man told me a year after the sudden death of his father that "a day doesn't go by when I don't think about my father at some point. But my thoughts of him are fleeting, as if I don't want to stay too long with them, like I'm scared to look too closely."

However, it is possible still to engage an absent father in a dialogue of emotional growth. The son may write imaginary dialogues between himself and his father and other family members, or write unmailed letters to a dead or absent father. Such exercises may temper the wounded image of father a man carries in his heart. They allow the son to examine the anger and disappointment in the father–son relationship, often giving way to greater acceptance and understanding. Through imaginary dialogues we can remember the abandonment and betrayal we felt, and it may hurt less; we are no longer prisoners of memories we can't retrieve.

Several men with dead fathers talked of finding letters, journals, or diaries their fathers kept and reading them with a hunger for information about the man's feeling and experiences.

Whether father is available or not, it is important to remember that reconciliation or friendship with father and healing the wounded father are different. It is certainly possible to heal oneself without reconciliation with father. And it is conversely possible to achieve a surface friendship with father without healing oneself. That is because the essential elements in healing are the internal image of father and the sense of masculinity that the son carries in his heart. The son needs to be able to understand the always poignant reasons why the past was the way it was, thus freeing him from his sense of having been betrayed by father or having been a betrayer of him, and he needs to explore satisfying ways to be male that reflect his own identity. We can recognize that we are our father's son without feeling that we have to accept and love everything about him or all that happened between us.

Ultimately it is the internal image of our fathers that all men must heal. All sons need to heal the wounded fathers within their own hearts, on their own. The process involves exploring not just the past but also the present and future—ways of being male that reflect a richer, fuller sense of self than the narrow images that dominated the past. In truth that is the task of all men today: to explore the masculine nurturer and caretaker within, to test out and evolve a strong manly sense of oneself as a father, in relation to a wife, children, and peers.

The search to identify what it means to be a male nurturer, to be a father who cares and protects in a fuller, more engaged way than just by imitating a John Wayne tough guy/soldier or a businessman/breadwinner, is the serious quest that underlies the at times seemingly comic male self-explorations of our times. How to be strong and caring? Those are themes that men are struggling with.

Sitting at lunch with a former Harvard administrator who has just turned forty, I hear about his recent week at a men's retreat north of San Francisco. Of all the activities of those days, one incident stands out for him.

"One of the exercises we did was based on those American Indian initiation ceremonies where the brave has to run a gauntlet composed of all the men of the tribe."

The entire group of fifty men lined up in a gauntlet, and each person ran down it, *holding a doll, an infant.*

"The doll was to give us a purpose, we were to shelter it from the blows as we ran."

Enfolding the vulnerable with male strength.

Another image: As I sit at a playground with my young son on a pleasant spring Sunday, we are surrounded by other parents and children. It being a weekend, there are many fathers with their kids. Suddenly across the playground I see a familiar scene. An older boy, about seven, goes up to a younger one and punches him on the shoulder. The blow is not particularly savage, and the littler kid seems more shocked than hurt. The older boy seems quite angry and upset; he's clearly working something out. One could easily imagine that boy getting a good spanking from his father. I wonder what I'd do if he comes near *my* boy. As I watch though, the boy's father comes over and gently picks him up. The boy writhes and protests, crying in his father's arms, while the man carries him over to a nearby bench. Despite his son's fighting, the father does this forcefully yet also gently. He sits and rocks the boy in his lap, and then I hear him whispering, almost singing, in his son's ear:

"I'm not going to let you go until you say, 'I am a gentle boy and I do not hit other children.' " As they sit there, the boy sheltered in his arms, the father repeats the refrain: "I am a gentle boy and I do not hit other children." Finally the boy seems soothed, sings along with his father, and runs off to play by himself.

Sheltering with male strength. Is this the old identity or a new one? The underlying wish seems to be to find a way to be a strong male without also being destructive.

Becoming a parent helps. As we have seen, the transition to fatherhood has the potential for creating a vastly changed perspective on one's self and one's father. Yet not all men are parents, and there are other ways to heal the wounded father in our hearts. Creative solutions such as the arts, music, crafts, which allow the exploration of the self, may be very helpful.

One man in a childless marriage, who felt his father left him emotionally at age five, remembered as an adult how much he and his father both loved music. He plays the piano as a hobby today, but recently he realized how much hidden love lay secretly in their shared love of the instrument. "My involvement in music seemed to express a repressed part in himself. . . . He especially liked to walk around in the backyard in the summer listening to the sounds of my piano practicing coming through the back windows." This man had completely forgotten for twenty years the pleasure his father took in the son's talent; he spoke now of imagining his father listening happily at the window when he plays the piano, transforming his image of father as a demanding, withdrawn presence into a satisfied, supportive one.

At bottom, healing the wounded father is a process of untangling the myths and fantasies sons learn growing up about self, mother, and father, which we act out every day with bosses, wives, and children. It means constructing a satisfying sense of manhood both from our opportunities in a time of changing sex-roles and by "diving into the wreck" of the past and retrieving a firm, sturdy appreciation of the heroism and failure in our fathers' lives. Wallace Stevens reminds us of "the son who bears upon his back/The father that he loves, and bears him from/The ruins of the past, out of nothing left."[11] Every man needs to identify the good in his father, to feel how we are like them, as well as the ways we are different from them. From that, I believe, comes a fuller, trustworthy sense of masculinity, a way of caring and nurturing, of being strong without being destructive. That way still reflects masculine musculature, our history and our bodies, and our active participation in the future. It is a way of sheltering those we love without infantilizing them, of holding them and transmitting the sure, quiet knowledge that men as well as women are lifegiving forces on earth.

Notes and References

Introduction

1. A variety of questionnaires and personality inventories were administered to a representative sample of 25 percent of the Harvard classes of 1964 and 1965 throughout their college years. Beginning in 1978 we sent a detailed questionnaire to the 510 men who participated in the college research. It was returned by 370 men, or over 70 percent of the original group. The questionnaire obtained a broad picture of these men's life experiences since leaving college, and their current life situation. Fifty men from this group were randomly selected to be interviewed, subject to the constraint that most of them lived in the Northeast and all were currently active in professional careers. These men were interviewed twice within a week on an annual basis over two years, with a third-year interview scheduled in selected cases of special interest. Each interview session lasted two or three hours, and followed a semistructured life history format I have developed as a research method. The technique allows the subject to construct a picture of his own life history and obtains for each subject detailed information on the work, parenting, and

marital parts of present life as well as the key developmental experiences of the person from childhood, through adolescence and college, into young adulthood and at midlife. Subsequently, twenty-five of the wives of these men were similarly interviewed as part of a doctoral dissertation at the Harvard Graduate School of Education.

See S. Osherson and D. Dill, "Varying Work and Family Choices: Their Impact on Men's Work Satisfaction," *Journal of Marriage and the Family*, May 1983; S. Osherson, "Work–Family Dilemmas of Professional Careers," final report to the National Institute of Education, NIE-G-77-0049, 1982; and D. Hulsizer, "Marriage and Adult Development: Views from Midlife," unpublished doctoral dissertation, Harvard Graduate School of Education, 1983.

2. See S. Osherson, *Holding on or Letting Go: Men and Career Change at Midlife* (New York: The Free Press, 1980).

3. D. Ullian, "Why Boys Will Be Boys: A Structural Perspective," *American Journal of Orthopsychiatry*, 1981: 493–501; J. Lever, "Sex Differences in the Games Children Play," *Social Problems*, 23 (1976): 478–487; G. W. Goethals, "Male Object Loss: A Special Case of Bereavement, Anxiety, and Fear," *Psychotherapy*, Spring 1985, 22 (1): 119–127; E. Pitcher and L. S. Schultz, *Boys and Girls At Play: The Development of Sex Roles* (New York: Praeger, 1983); I. Bretherton, *Symbolic Play* (New York: Academic Press, 1984); Z. Luria, S. Freidman, and M. D. Rose, *Human Sexuality* (New York: Wiley, 1986).

4. Peter Davison, "Rites of Passage: 1946," in P. Davison, *Half-Remembered: A Personal History* (New York: Harper and Row, 1973).

5. The historical vicissitudes of the father–son relationship is a neglected aspect of our cultural history. Family historians are beginning to explore our father history and have pointed to evidence of periods of positive relationship and closeness as well as ones of more distance and alienation. De Tocqueville, for example, praised the intimacy and affection of the father–son relationship he observed during his travels in America during the 1830s. Joseph Pleck reviews the historical literature on changing images of the father–son relationship in his paper "The Father Wound," The Center for Research on Women, Wellesley College, Wellesley, MA 02181. I am indebted to him for drawing my attention to several of the references discussed in this section.

6. S. Hite, *The Hite Report on Male Sexuality* (New York: Knopf, 1981), p. 17.

7. J. Arcana, *Every Mother's Son: The Role of Mothers in the Making of Men* (Garden City, N.Y.: Doubleday, 1983); p. 143.

8. J. Sternbach, "The Masculinization Process," unpublished paper, RFD Box 607, Vineyard Haven, MA 02568.

9. S. Cath, A. Gurwitz, and J. M. Ross, (eds.), *Father and Child: Clinical and Developmental Considerations* (Boston: Little, Brown, 1982).

10. Donald Bell begins his book *Being a Man* with a chapter on "fathers and sons," essentially beginning his own self-portrait by talking about his father. D. Bell, *Being a Man: the Paradox of Masculinity*, (Brattleboro, Vt.: Greene, 1982).

11. J. Pleck, "The Father Wound."

12. E. Erikson, *Childhood and Society* (New York: Norton, 1963).

13. N. Chodorow, *The Reproduction of Mothering* (Berkeley: University of California Press, 1978); D. Dinnerstein, *The Mermaid and the Minotaur: Sexual Arrangements and the Human Malaise* (New York: Harper and Row, 1976); L. Rubin, *Intimate Strangers*, (New York: Harper and Row, 1983); G. W. Goethals, "Symbiosis and the Life Cycle," *British Journal of Medical Psychology*, 46, 1973: 91–96; G. W. Goethals, "Male Object Loss: A Special Case of Bereavement, Anxiety, and Fear."

14. J. Pleck, *Working Wives, Working Husbands* (Beverly Hills, Calif.: Sage, 1985), and J. Pleck, "Husbands' Paid Work and Family Roles: Current Research Issues," in H. Lopata and J. Pleck, (eds.), *Research in the Interweave of Social Roles*, Vol. 3, Greenwich, Conn.: JAI Press, 1983.

15. G. Vaillant and C. C. McArthur, Natural History of Male Psychologic Health. I. The Adult Life Cycle from 18–50. *Seminars in Psychiatry*, 4 (4), 1972: 422.

Chapter 1

1. Z. Rubin, "Fathers and Sons: The Search for Reunion," *Psychology Today*, June 1982, pp. 23 ff.

2. S. Bliss, review of *Brother Songs: A Male Anthology of Poetry*, edited by J. Perlman, *WIN*, November 15, 1980.

3. R. Shelton, "Letter to a Dead Father," *You Can't Have Everything* (Pittsburgh: University of Pittsburgh Press, 1975).

4. D. Thomas, "Do not go gentle into that good night," in D. Thomas, *Collected Poems* (New York: New Directions, 1957).

5. F. Rebelsky and C. Hanks, "Father's Verbal Interaction with Infants in the First Three Months of Life," *Child Development*, 42 (1971): 63–68, and F. A. Pedersen and K. S. Robson, "Father Participation in In-

fancy," *American Journal of Orthopsychiatry*, *39* (1969): 466–72. These findings as to the low quantity of contact between fathers and children are often understood in emphasizing the quality of father's time at home rather than the literal amount. Yet it is precisely this limited role of the father that may lead to the kind of fantasy constructions I am describing as "the wounded father." See R. Atkins, "Discovering Daddy: The Mother's Role," in S. Cath, A. Gurwitz, and J. M. Ross, eds.; *Father and Child: Clinical and Developmental Considerations* (Boston: Little, Brown, 1982).

6. J. Carroll, review of *Good Morning, Merry Sunshine*, by B. Greene, *New York Times Book Review*, June 10, 1984.

7. Rubin, "Fathers and Sons," p. 28.

8. M. Komarovsky, *Dilemmas of Masculinity* (New York: Norton, 1976).

9. Quoted in Ken Auletta, "Profiles," *The New Yorker*, April 9, 1984, p. 51. Emphasis added.

10. M. Goldstein, "Fathering: A Neglected Activity," *American Journal of Psychiatry*, *37*, 4 (Winter 1977): 325–36.

11. M. Farrell and S. Rosenberg, *Men at Midlife* (Boston: Auburn House, 1981), p. 125.

12. W. Stevens, "Aesthetique du mal," in W. Stevens, *The Palm at the End of the Mind: Selected Poems and a Play* (New York: Vintage, 1972).

13. From his detailed interviews with men in their thirties, Yale's Dr. Rick Ochberg, a psychologist, notes how the imagery of work and careers for many men reveals "a preoccupation with movement and advancement," which offers one solution to separation conflicts with their fathers. The symbolism of movement that work provides "is connected to the son's renouncing . . . the unconditional love of early childhood, in favor of the father's highly conditional respect for achievement." Throughout men's lives work provides an illusion of movement away from relationship problems. See R. Ochberg, "Middle-Aged Men and the Meaning of Work," unpublished doctoral dissertation, University of Michigan, Ann Arbor, 1983, p. 5.

14. J. M. Ross, "In Search of Fathering: A Review," In Cath, Gurwitz, and Ross, eds., *Father and Child*.

15. D. Hall, "My Son, My Executioner," *The Alligator Bride* (New York: Harper and Row, 1969).

16. P. Wright and T. Keple, "Friends and Parents of a Sample of High School Juniors: An Exploratory Study of Relationship Intensity and Interpersonal Rewards," *Journal of Marriage and the Family*, *43*, No. 3 (August 1981): 559–70.

17. M. Norman, "For Us, the War Is Over," *New York Times Magazine*, March 31, 1985, p. 68.

18. Robert Bly discusses this theme in his paper "The Vietnam War and the Erosion of Male Confidence," *The Utne Reader*, October–November 1984, pp. 74–81. See also J. Fallows, "What Did You Do in the Class War, Daddy?" *The Washington Monthly*, October 1975, pp. 5–19.

19. Homer, *The Odyssey*, trans. R. Fitzgerald (New York: Anchor, 1963), pp. 295–96.

20. K. Thompson, "What Men Really Want: An Interview with Robert Bly," *New Age*, May 1982, p. 50.

Chapter 2

1. G. Vaillant, *Adaptation to Life* (Boston: Little, Brown, 1977), p. 219.

2. D. Levinson *et al. The Seasons of a Man's Life* (New York: Knopf, 1978), pp. 99–100.

3. Vaillant, *Adaptation to Life*, p. 218. Emphasis added.

4. *Ibid.*, p. 219.

Chapter 3

1. L. Rubin, *Women of a Certain Age: The Midlife Search for Self* (New York: Harper & Row, 1979).

2. This classic pattern is obviously not the only way to arrange work and parenting. Among the most striking findings of the Adult Development Project was the remarkable diversity of ways of timing and arranging work and family choices among a group of highly educated professional men in structured careers. In contrast to early starters in single-career marriages, like Mr. Henderson, 10 percent of the sample married soon after college and began families with wives who from the beginning had careers of their own. These are early starters in dual-career marriages. Twenty-five percent of the sample were currently married but had delayed parenting into their thirties, while another 20 percent of the men were in childless marriages at thirty-eight. See S. Osherson and D. Dill, "Varying Work and Family Choices: Their Impact on Men's Work Satisfaction," *Journal of Marriage and the Family*, May 1983, pp. 339–46.

Clearly the sociologist Bernice Neugarten is correct when she informs us that the "social clock" in our society no longer ticks as clearly as it once did—there is no *single* dominant or normative way of timing and arranging work and family. As we'll see in later chapters, the tasks and challenges for men at midlife in these different patterns to some extent vary; to become a father for the first time at age thirty-five is a very different experience from saying goodbye to your teenage son at the same age, even if men from those different situations attend the same college reunion.

3. G. Baruch, R. Barnett, and C. Rivers, "A New Start for Women at Midlife," *New York Times Magazine*, December 7, 1980, p. 198.

4. Rubin, *Women of a Certain Age*; M. F. Lowenthal, *et al. Four Stages of Life* (San Francisco: Jossey-Bass, 1975); and S. Osherson, *Holding On or Letting Go: Men and Career Change at Midlife* (New York: The Free Press, 1980).

5. D. Heath, "Some Possible Effects of Occupation on the Maturing of Professional Men," *Journal of Vocational Behavior, 11* (1977): 263–81.

6. G. Lish, "A Protecting Father," *New York Times Magazine*, July 15, 1984, p. 50.

7. P. Wright and T. Keple, "Friends and Parents of a Sample of High School Juniors: An Exploratory Study of Relationship Intensity and Interpersonal Rewards," *Journal of Marriage and the Family, 43*, No. 3 (August 1981): 559–70.

8. F. Porter, "The Loved Son," in K. Moffett, *Fairfield Porter*, Boston: Museum of Fine Arts, 1983.

9. D. Levinson *et al., The Seasons of a Man's Life* (New York: Knopf, 1978), p. 200. See also D. Guttman, "Individual Adaptation in the Midlife Years: Developmental Issues in the Masculine Mid-life Crisis," *Journal of Geriatric Psychiatry, 9* (1976): 41–59.

10. M. Farrell and S. Rosenberg, *Men at Midlife* (Boston: Auburn House, 1981).

11. Ibid, p. 125.

12. *Ibid*, p. 124.

13. E. Jacques, "Death and the Midlife Crisis," *International Journal of Psychiatry, 46* (1965): 502–14. In this classic paper Jacques is particularly concerned with the person's increasing awareness of mortality at midlife and the sense of fragmentation that may result as the adult struggles with an infantile residue of love and rage. Jacques reminds us that the infant's struggle with life and death occurs in "the setting of his survival being dependent on his external objects," particularly his mother, and his chaotic feelings toward them. Jacques comments that "a person who reaches mid-life either without having success-

fully established himself in marital and occupational life, or having established himself by means of *manic activity* and *denial* with consequent emotional impoverishment, is badly prepared for meeting the demands of mid-life age, and getting enjoyment of his maturity" (pp. 507, 511; emphasis added). I have been impressed at how often a wife's going to work as well as the launching of children, provokes imagery of death and fragmentation for men, as if the rearranging family becomes a metaphor for mother's body being destroyed.

14. See D. Ullian, "Why Boys Will Be Boys: A Structual Perspective," *American Journal of Orthopsychiatry, 51* (1981): 493–501, and K. Toomey, "Johnny, I Hardly Knew Ye: Toward a Revision of the Theory of Male Psychosexual Development," *American Journal of Orthopsychiatry, 47* (1977): 184–95.

15. Men often respond to neediness by becoming instrumental, because that's how we learn to get taken care of. Yet the struggle of men to be taken care of as boys is so mixed in with aggression and punishment that the response of many men to becoming needy is to get violent, physically or psychologically, as if at an unconscious level the man sees his need as evidence of something terribly wrong with himself or his wife and children. That may explain why many men act out, becoming destructive of self or other when family life gets frustrating.

16. M. Farrell and S. Rosenberg, *Men at Midlife,* p. 142.

Chapter 4

1. B. Menning, "The Emotional Needs of the Infertile Couple," *Fertility–Sterility, 34* (1980): 313–17, and H. Simons, "Infertility as an Emerging Social Concern," unpublished doctoral qualifying thesis, Heller Graduate School of Social Welfare, Brandeis University, Waltham, Mass., 1980.

2. A. Shostak, quoted in J. Wolinsky, "Men Often Phantom Figures in Emotional Abortion Drama," *APA Monitor,* May 1984.

3. T. MacNab, "Infertility and Men: A Study of Change and Adaptive Choices in the Lives of Involuntarily Childless Men," unpublished doctoral dissertation, Fielding Institute, Berkeley, Calif., 1984, p. 64.

4. *Ibid.,* p. 79.

5. *Ibid.*

6. When I refer to the fetus as "a baby," I wish to convey the deep emotional attachment of parents to the pregnancy. Using "fetus" may

diminish the reality of this attachment, just as "baby" may be said to overstate the facts of fetal development.

7. *Ibid.*, p. 134.

8. "Understanding Infertility," *Population Bulletin*, Vol. 39, No. 5, December 1984.

9. H. Pizer and C. O. Palinski, *Coping with a Miscarriage* (New York: New American Library, 1980).

10. MacNab, "Infertility and Men," p. 138.

11. *Ibid.*, p. 139.

12. M. D. Schecter, "About Adoptive Parents," in E. J. Anthony and T. E. Benedek, eds., *Parenthood: Its Psychology and Psychopathology* (Boston: Little, Brown, 1970), p. 359.

13. "When Parents Lose a Child," *The Keene Sentinel*, August 1, 1983.

14. MacNab, "Infertility and Men," p. 137.

15. *Ibid.*, pp. 100–101.

16. Shostak, quoted in Wolinsky, "Men Often Phantom Figures."

17. Pizer and Palinski, *Coping with a Miscarriage*, pp. 119–21.

18. MacNab, "Infertility and Men," p. 97.

19. A. B. Shostak, and G. McLouth, *Men and Abortion: Lessons, Losses, and Loves* (New York: Praeger, 1984).

20. MacNab, "Infertility and Men," p. 97.

21. B. Bettelheim, *The uses of Enchantment* (New York: Knopf, 1975), p. 6.

Chapter 5

1. "Opinions about motherhood: a Gallup/Levi's maternity wear national poll," San Francisco: Levi Strauss and Co., September 1983.

2. A. D. Beck, M. D. Young, B. Robson, and D. Mandel, "Factors Which Influence Fathers' Involvement with Their Infants," Symposium at Annual Meeting of the American Orthopsychiatric Association, Toronto, April 1984, and F. K. Grossman, and W. S. Pollack, "Good-enough Fathering: A Longitudinal Focus on Fathers Within a Father System," paper presented at Annual Meeting, National Council on Family Relations, San Francisco, 1984.

3. A. J. Stewart, M. Sokol, J. Healy, N. Chester, and D. Weinstock-Savoy, "Adaptation to Life Changes in Children and Adults: Cross-Sectional Studies," *Journal of Personality and Social Psychology, 42*, No. 6 (1982): 1278.

4. J. Updike, *Couples* (New York: Knopf, 1968), and J. Didion, *The White Album* (New York: Simon & Schuster, 1979).

5. E. Jacobson, "Development of the Wish for a Child in Boys," *The Psychoanalytic Study of the Child,* 5 (1950): 144.

6. S. Osherson *et al.* 1984, "Expecting A Child: The Therapist's Experience," Boston: Simmons School of Social Work, p. 70.

7. J. Maynard, *Babylove* (New York: Avon, 1982), pp. 154–55.

8. S. Bittman and S. Rosenberg-Zalk, *Expectant Fathers* (New York: Hawthorne, 1978), and W. H. Trethowan, and M. F. Conlon, "The Couvade Syndrome," *British Journal of Psychiatry,* 111 (January 1965): 57–66.

9. Bittman and Rosenberg-Zalk, *Expectant Fathers.*

10. C. Gilligan, *In a Different Voice: Psychological Theory and Women's Development* (Cambridge: Harvard University Press, 1982).

11. S. Feldman, S. Nash, and B. Aschenbrenner, "Antecedents of Fathering," *Child Development,* 54: 1628–36.

Chapter 6

1. S. Elledge, *E. B. White: A Biography* (New York: Norton, 1984), p. 144.

2. D. Levinson *et al., The Seasons of a Man's Life* (New York: Knopf, 1978).

3. L. J. Kaplan, *Oneness and Separateness: From Infant to Individual* (New York: Simon & Schuster, 1978), p. 67.

4. *Ibid.* Note the equation of nurturing in early childhood with "mothering"; there is no mention of fathering in this context.

5. R. Bly, "For My Son Noah, Ten Years Old," in J. Perlman, ed., *Brother Songs: A Male Anthology of Poetry* (Minneapolis: Holy Cow! Press, 1979).

6. A. J. Stewart, M. Sokol, J. Healy, N. Chester, and D. Weinstock-Savoy, "Adaptation to Life Changes in Children and Adults: Cross-Sectional Studies," *Journal of Personality and Social Psychology,* 42, No. 6 (1982): 1278, and M. Mahoney, "Intimacy and Social Support: The Meanings of Relationship for Employed and Unemployed Mothers," unpublished paper, School of Social Sciences, Hampshire College, Northampton, Mass.

7. Since home has associations to mother for both men and women, when home becomes a confusing place it may feel as if mother has turned on them—no longer nurturing but now demanding. Men may

experience this mother–home relationship differently, depending on their childhood experiences. Some may experience the changed home and wife-mother as a kind of inner sadness: mother telling them to grow up, the little boy can't hang around Mommy's skirts any more. These men may turn more to work to fill themselves up emotionally and psychologically, often fueled by a typical male fantasy that if he produces more, does a better job at work, his wife will take better care of him. Other men, with greater early mother difficulties, may experience wife and family as doing something harmful to them: mother turning on them, abandoning them, possibly leaving them to die or killing them. Those intolerable, frightening fantasies may lead to bizarre, out-of-control behavior such as wife or child abuse, or leaving the family. Some men may leave their family or flee into work as a way of protecting the family from their own rage at the sense of loss they feel.

8. F. K. Grossman, "Separate and Together: Men's Autonomy and Affiliation in the Transition to Parenthood," unpublished paper, Department of Psychology, Boston University, Boston, Mass., 1984, and P. Daniels and K. Weingarten, *Sooner or Later: The Timing of Parenthood in Adult Life* (New York: Norton, 1982).

9. M. Greenberg and N. Morris, "Engrossment: The Newborn's Impact upon the Father," in S. Cath, A. Gurwitz, and J. M. Ross, eds., *Father and Child: Clinical and Developmental Considerations* (Boston: Little, Brown, 1982).

10. G. J. Craig, *Human Development* (Englewood Cliffs, N.J.: Prentice-Hall, 1983).

11. D. H. Heath, "What Meaning and Effects Does Fatherhood Have for the Maturing of Professional Men?" *Merrill-Palmer Quarterly*, Vol. 24, No. 4, 1978; *idem.*, "Competent Fathers: Their Personalities and Marriages," *Human Development*, 19 (1976): 26–39; and M. Gerzon, *A Choice of Heroes: The Changing Faces of American Manhood* (Boston: Houghton-Mifflin, 1982).

12. M. Goldstein, "Fathering: A Neglected Activity," *American Journal of Psychology*, 37, No. 4 (Winter 1977): 325–26.

13. R. Saner, "Passing It On," in R. Saner, *Climbing Into the Roots* (New York: Harper and Row, 1976).

14. Stewart *et al.* "Adaptation to Life Changes," and Daniels and Weingarten, *Sooner or Later*.

15. Levinson *et al.*, *Seasons of a Man's Life*.

16. *Ibid.*, p. 236.

17. The Fatherhood Project at Boston University, for example, offers fathers courses and workshops—using videotapes and written exercises—to teach men the emotional skills of parenting.

18. D. Hall, "My Son, My Executioner," *The Alligator Bride* (New York: Harper and Row, 1969).

Chapter 7

1. M. Acker, "With Natural Piety: Letters of Adult Men to Their Fathers," unpublished paper, University of Oregon, Division of Counseling and Educational Psychology, Eugene, Oregon, 1982, p. 2.

2. K. Thompson, "What Men Really Want: An Interview with Robert Bly," *New Age*, May 1982, p. 51.

3. *Heroes and Strangers: A Film About Men, Emotions, and the Family*, 1984, New Day Films, c/o Lorna Rasmussen, 412 W. Fairmount Ave., State College, Pa. 16801.

4. S. Osherson, *Holding On or Letting Go: Men and Career Change at Midlife* (New York: The Free Press, 1980).

5. S. Bodian, "To my Father on His Seventieth Birthday," *The Men's Journal*, August 1984, p. 9.

6. T. J. Cottle, *Like Father, Like Son: Portraits of Intimacy and Strain* (Norwood, N.J.: Ablex, 1981).

7. R. Bly, "Finding the Father," in R. Bly, *This Body Is Made from Camphor and Gopherwood* (New York: Harper and Row, 1977).

8. B. Springsteen, "My Father's House," record album *Nebraska*, Columbia Records, New York, 1982.

9. This is not an exclusive problem of sons, of course. A woman in her mid-thirties related how robbed she felt when trying to work things out with a father who was no longer the same person she had fought so bitterly with as an adolescent. "At age twenty-three I went home to do battle with my father and I won. He flipped just like that, a beaten man. . . . What a weird win/lose situation." Her words remind us that many women too grow up with a wounded image of father, feeling abandoned or rejected by the father in whom their sense of masculinity is rooted. Linda Leonard explores the "father–daughter wound" in her book *The Wounded Woman* and notes how often career and intimacy problems of adult women are linked to a damaged relationship with their fathers, resulting from the father's idealized place in the family. Leonard sees a central task of a woman's

adult development to be one of redeeming the internal image of her father: "to understand her father's failed promise and how his fatherhood has affected her life." See L. Leonard, *The Wounded Woman* (Boulder, Colo.: Shambala, 1983), p. xix.

In my clinical practice I often encounter women whose self-esteem is crippled by a feeling of emotional rejection or betrayal by their fathers. Often the great rage of such women at men is rooted in the narcissistic wound they have suffered in a household that secretly worshiped father, while mother—their crucial figure for identification—seemed emotionally "dead." What contrasts to the father–son relationship is that often the daughter will retain some avenue for communication and reconciliation with father, which the son is denied by virtue of the male tendency to strive for a false appearance of separation and "independence." Without denying the pain many daughters feel, we can acknowledge that the competitiveness and intensity of the same-sex bond between father and son may add a special complexity to men's task of healing the wounded father.

10. F. F. Furstenberg, J. L. Peterson, C. Nord, and N. Zill, "Life Course of Children of Divorce: Marital Disruption in Parental Contact," *American Sociological Review, 48* (1983: 656–68).

11. W. Stevens, "Recitation After Dinner," In *Opus Posthumous: Poems, Plays, Prose*, ed. S. F. Morse (New York: Vintage, 1982), p. 87.

Index

Goal - $50,000 year

20 hrs./wk - clinical work @ 50⁰⁰/hr.

5 - Kids
5 - teenagers
8 - families : couples
2 - indiv. adult
___
20

5 hrs - professional growth
1 - therapy
2 - supervision
2 - case conf. /class

5 hrs - teaching /supervision

5 hrs - community /political work (free)

—